DATE DUE

ULSTER PRESBYTERIANISM
The Historical Perspective

Every earthly kingdom depends, under providence, for its origin, support and continuance, upon *mere opinion* . . .
Henry Cooke

For Walter Firpo,
poet and painter.

Peter Brooke

ULSTER PRESBYTERIANISM

The Historical Perspective 1610-1970

GILL AND MACMILLAN
ST. MARTIN'S PRESS
NEW YORK

Published in Ireland by
Gill and Macmillan Ltd
Goldenbridge
Dublin 8
with associated companies in
Auckland, Dallas, Delhi, Hong Kong,
Johannesburg, Lagos, London, Manzini,
Melbourne, Nairobi, New York, Singapore,
Tokyo, Washington

British Library Cataloguing in Publication Data
Brooke, Peter
  Ulster presbyterianism: the historical perspective.
  1. Presbyterian Church in Ireland — Northern Ireland — History 2. Northern
  Ireland — Church history
  I. Title
  285'.2416   BX 9061.N6

ISBN 0-7171-1465-1

Published in the United States of America by
St. Martin's Press, Inc.,
175 Fifth Avenue,
New York, NY 10010
ISBN 0-312-01271-3

Library of Congress Cataloging in Publication Data
Brooke, Peter
  Ulster presbyterianism
  Bibliography: P.
  Includes index.
  1. Presbyterian Church — Ulster (Northern Ireland
  and Ireland) — History. 2. Presbyterian Church in
  Ireland — History. 3. Ulster (Northern Ireland and
  Ireland) — Church History. 4. Ulster (Northern
  Ireland and Ireland) — Politics and Government.
  I. Title
  BX 9061.U47B76   1987   285'.2416   87-16705
  ISBN 0-312-01271-3

Print origination in Ireland by Galaxy Reproductions Ltd, Dublin
Printed in Great Britain by
The Camelot Press, Southampton

Contents

Introduction:
An Irish Intellectual Tradition

The aim of this book is to draw out the main characteristics of an intellectual tradition — the tradition of Ulster Presbyterianism. 'Tradition' is a much-abused word, especially in Ireland. Richard Kearney, in his introduction to *The Irish Mind: Exploring Intellectual Traditions*, talks about 'our "discontinuous" tradition', but this is a contradiction in terms. Tradition is what is handed on from generation to generation. Continuity is basic to it. Until the eighteenth century Gaelic Ireland was a highly traditional society, though its tradition was repetitive and conservative, with little capacity for development. ⌐In the nineteenth century there was a comprehensive break with the Gaelic past. A new, Roman Catholic and English-speaking society developed, which is perhaps the least traditional society in the British Isles.⌐

The 'discontinuous' tradition celebrated by Richard Kearney is an attempt to find common characteristics in widely diverse phenomena — in effect, to invent a tradition. Such an exercise can only be justified on the basis of a theory of racial types, or, if Celts and Anglo-Normans are to be equally regarded as 'Irish', an even more tenuous theory of the mysterious influence of the Irish soil. This kind of thinking is not necessary in English history, where there is a clear continuity of political tradition embodied in institutions — the crown and parliament. The other principal institutional embodiment of national, as opposed to local, tradition is the church. The Roman Catholic Church in Ireland, however, was virtually reconstructed in the nineteenth century on the basis of strict Ultramontanism. As the popular saying has it, it took its religion from Rome. It did not have the strong independent national intellectual traditions which characterised the Roman Catholic Church in Spain, France, Germany or Poland. The man who argued most cogently for ⌐the development of an Irish national Catholicism equivalent to French Gallicanism,⌐ the seventeenth-century Franciscan Peter Walsh, is today almost entirely forgotten.

⌐The Ulster Presbyterians, by contrast, belong to a strong, independent intellectual tradition, rooted in an impressive institutional continuity,⌐ achieved without the help of and often in opposition to the state, and dating back to the seventeenth century. It is part of my argument that the church ceases to be the intellectual centre of Presbyterian Ulster in the nineteenth century, about the time the Roman Catholic Church becomes the intellectual centre of Catholic Ireland. But of course the Presbyterian intellectual tradition continues, albeit at a much lower level of importance, to the present day.

This intellectual tradition was capable of great development. In the seventeenth century it stood, in almost impossible circumstances, for the ideal of the church as a kingdom or polity separate from the state, with authority in matters of faith and morals.⌐In the eighteenth century it functioned as the organising centre of a distinct, quasi-national society.⌐At the end of the eighteenth century there seemed a real possibility that this society would provide the nucleus of an all-Ireland national democratic culture. In the nineteenth century it became a private worshipping society in the essentially secular national culture of the British Isles. Throughout the process it conducted within itself a wide-ranging intellectual debate on politics and religion, in which every opinion between Calvinism and freethinking latitudinarianism, or between republicanism and constitutional conservatism, was energetically canvassed. While Anglicanism and Roman Catholicism in Ireland can each boast many more prominent national leaders, neither can lay claim to the continual, popularly based intellectual vigour which is embodied in the controversial literature of the Ulster Presbyterians.

In order to understand this tradition, I have had to compare and contrast it with the other traditions that surrounded and

influenced it, chiefly with Scottish and English Presbyterianism. It is a serious mistake to try to understand the Ulster
tradition without relating it to the wider British culture of
which it was a part. I stress a 'British' rather than an 'Irish'
context, not from any political prejudice, but simply as a
matter of historical fact. In the late eighteenth century some
Presbyterians flirted with the idea of national separatism. But
this was the result of an attachment to American and French
democratic ideals that were widespread in the rest of the
British Isles. In so far as a distinctively non-British Irish culture developed, the Ulster Presbyterians had little to do with it.

Similarly, I stress the term 'Ulster' Presbyterianism rather
than 'Irish' Presbyterianism. A small Presbyterian interest did
develop in the south of Ireland in the form of the Southern
Association or, as it later became, the Synod of Munster, but
it was quite independent of the Ulster development. Some
congregations in Dublin were attached to the main Presbyterian body, the Synod of Ulster, and acquired a particular
importance through their proximity to the seat of government; but as a social force to be reckoned with, Presbyterianism in Ireland was an Ulster phenomenon, and since Irish
nationalism has so far failed to subsume the different religious
traditions into a common national identity, the geographical
distinction remains politically and socially important.

It is indeed part of the argument of this book that religion
is a crucial element in the formation of national identity.
This may seem so obvious that it barely needs to be said, but
we still hear complaints that there is a conflict in Ireland
between 'Protestants' and 'Catholics' from people who would
see nothing untoward in conflicts between 'French' and
'Germans'. The quotation from Henry Cooke which I have
used as a motto for this book is an apt reminder that being
French or German or Irish or British is as much a matter of
'mere opinion' as being Protestant and Catholic, and the
history of religion is largely the history of the process by
which such 'mere opinions' are formed.

I am principally concerned with the Presbyterians at a
time (from the mid-seventeenth to the mid-nineteenth centuries) when they almost constituted a nation in their own
right – when their church courts (sessions, presbyteries and

synods) were the real political centres of their lives, much more so than the shadowy governments in Dublin or in London. I argue that as a virtual nation within the nation they were, for most of this time, a unique phenomenon in the British Isles. We may perhaps compare them with the Roman Catholic Church in Ireland in the late nineteenth century when it had established its authority while the British administration was still in place; but even the Roman Catholics had less of the characteristics of a self-reliant nation than the Ulster Presbyterians. While the Presbyterians were responsible only to themselves, the Roman Catholics had their centre outside Ireland, in Rome.

Since the Presbyterian Church is no longer the intellectual and moral centre of a self-directing community, my story has a pleasing aesthetic shape to it. It has a beginning, a middle and an end. But this does not mean that it has no modern relevance. The island of Ireland is divided by two national communities. Much more needs to be said about the role of the Church of Ireland in this development, but no one could doubt that the Presbyterian tradition, with its long experience of self-definition and self-organisation, has had a crucial part to play. I have heard it said of the people of Berlin that they have never had a government with which they could identify or feel at ease. With the exception of the Northern Ireland government of 1920-72 (which, however, was only a subordinate government), the same may be said of the Ulster Presbyterians. They are used to looking after themselves in spite of governments that have been ill-disposed towards them.

I end this book by proposing that the differences between Protestant and Catholic in Northern Ireland would be less virulent if both were allowed to take part in the politics of the state in which they live – the United Kingdom state. They are excluded from United Kingdom politics by the refusal of the major Westminster political parties to take members or contest elections in Northern Ireland. The end of the story should have shown the dissolution of local political and religious allegiances into the party politics of the state as a whole. But this development was aborted by the imposition of a devolved government on Northern Ireland in 1920 and by the policy of the major British political parties to boycott the area. When I started writing this book it was on the assumption that the resolution of this problem would be inevitable though regrettably slow. Before I finished, the determination of the British political establishment to keep Northern Ireland out of their political system had taken the extraordinary form of the Anglo-Irish Agreement of November 1985, endorsed by an overwhelming majority of M.P.s, only one of whom, John Hume, belongs to a political party that submits itself to the electorate in Northern Ireland.

I am not a Presbyterian and have no particular interest in the well-being or otherwise of the Presbyterian Church in Ireland. I had, however, hoped from the start that⌐my book would help people realise what a truly remarkable and in many respects delightful people the Ulster Presbyterians are.⌐ Now I must hope in addition that it will help some of those who belong to that tradition to recover the skill they have shown in the past in defying despotic government and flourishing in spite of it.

Peter Brooke
Belfast
September 1986

Note on Terminology

Presbyterianism is a system of church government under which all ministers are considered to be equal in status and the affairs of the church are decided by a majority vote among them. Each congregation is governed by its ministers meeting with the *elders*, elected from among the congregation, in a *session*. Ministers begin their careers as *licentiates* who are entered on *trial* by congregations who are in need of a minister (*vacant* congregations) until one of them gives him a *call*. In the Roman Catholic use of the term, a *presbytery* is a priest's house, but in the Presbyterian use it refers to a regular meeting of the ministers of a particular locality. A larger area which includes several presbyteries is governed by a *synod*, and a larger area still by a *General Assembly*.

1

Clearing the Ground

1. *The Reformed Tradition in Europe*

The Ulster Presbyterians are part of, and have developed through, the Christian tradition, and the starting-point for trying to understand them must therefore be Christianity in general — the two-thousand-year-old tradition that started as a Jewish sect, became the state religion of the Roman Empire, provided the basic values through which the tribes which invaded the Roman Empire settled down and developed, and eventually provided, in competition with Marxism, an idealistic impetus for the spread of the values of Western Europe and America throughout the world.

What are the ideas of Christianity that distinguish it from the other major world religions?

The principal idea unique to Christianity is the idea of salvation — that mankind is in a fallen state from which it cannot escape by its own efforts. Human beings are condemned by the justice of God and require to be saved by a force external to themselves. That force is identified with the founder of the Christian religion; and because, for his work to be effective, there can be no question of his will conflicting with that of the just God, or his power being less, he is identified with that God through the doctrine of the Trinity.

That idea is common to both Roman Catholics and Protestants, and to all the other branches of the Christian tradition. In contrast, it is not found as a central, universally held belief in Islam, Judaism, Hinduism or Buddhism, or in the state philosophies of China or Japan.

In the Christian tradition an important part of the work of salvation is membership of a church, but the nature of the church is one of the great points of disagreement among Christians. Is it simply a congregation under the leadership of an individual pastor, or should it be a vast, international, centralised organisation embracing all Christians? What should be its relations with the civil power in any political society? How independent should it be of the civil power? Should it be superior? Should it be subordinate? These issues are very largely the substance of the present book.

Within Christianity, the Ulster Presbyterians belong to the Protestant tradition. Within the Protestant tradition, they belong to the Reformed tradition.

The Reformation of the sixteenth century, in so far as it was supported by civil governments, can be divided into two main streams — the Lutheran and the Reformed, the Lutheran originating in Saxony, in the Holy Roman Empire, and the Reformed in some of the German-speaking Swiss city-states, notably Zurich and Berne. Initially the chief difference between them was the degree of the rejection of Roman Catholic practice. Both claimed to return to the source of Christianity in the Bible, and to reject the accumulated theological and ritualist tradition which, they argued, overlay Biblical simplicity. Luther rejected those parts of Roman Catholic practice and belief which he thought were incompatible with Biblical teaching — purgatory, indulgences, intercession of saints, clerical celibacy, the power of the priesthood to absolve from sin, papal supremacy. Zwingli, chief spokesman in the early development of the Reformed tradition, went further. He rejected those parts of Roman Catholic practice and belief not specifically enjoined in the Bible. Everything necessary for the work of salvation, he argued, was in the Bible, and anything added to this was dangerous. Thus Luther did not object to the use of statuary and paintings in church so long as it was clear that they were not being used directly as objects of or aids to worship. Zwingli banned all religious imagery from the church. The spirit was to be understood as immaterial and invisible.

The Reformation followed hard on and interacted with the movement known as the Renaissance. In painting, the

Renaissance is known chiefly for the development of one-point perspective. It was for the first time clearly understood how an illusion of three-dimensional space could be created on a two-dimensional flat surface. Previous to this, religious painting had been obviously emblematic and symbolic: its beauty had been the beauty of the movement of form and colour. Now it became a matter of illusionistic trickery: its beauty was the borrowed beauty of the natural world. Spiritual realities were represented through the appearances of the material world. The Renaissance was a great period of scientific advance when the modes of reasoning necessary to understanding the laws of the material world were stated. The Reformation marked an impulse to separate the material and spiritual worlds in rejecting the attempt to give spiritual realities a material form, whether through illusionist imagery or through the veneration of material objects such as relics. This tendency of the Reformation was more marked in the Reformed tradition than in the Lutheran and led to a sharp quarrel between them over the doctrine of the Lord's Supper. Luther insisted that the words 'This is my body and blood' were to be taken literally, while Zwingli argued that the bread and wine should be taken as commemorative symbols of Christ's body and blood.[2]

With the publication in 1536 of his *Institution of the Christian Religion*, the Frenchman John Calvin began to emerge as the leading spokesman for the Reformed tradition. He did not, however, simply continue Zwingli's work. In one respect, full of importance for the future, he sharply contradicted it. This was in the question of the relations that ought to exist between the church and the civil power.

The Reformation in Saxony and Zurich had been the work of governments. A large part of the appeal of Reformation ideas to civil rulers was the independence it gave them from entanglement with the great international power structure of the Roman Catholic Church. This aspiration was not unique to Protestant rulers. A Roman Catholic reformation had been conducted in Spain at the end of the fifteenth century by the civil power independent of and in some respects in opposition to Rome. A struggle for control of the national church had also been taking place between the pope and the King of

France. There was nothing in this that was either new or incompatible with long-standing traditions within Roman Catholicism, going back to the endless quarrels between the pope and the Holy Roman Emperor.

Protestantism, however, in its first manifestation with Luther and Zwingli, seemed to cut the Gordian knot and proclaim that the organised church should be co-terminous with the civil political unit and subordinate to the civil government. Luther argued fiercely against the idea that there was a special authority granted to the clergy. The 'power of the keys' had been given to the disciples, he argued, as representatives of all Christians, including the laity. All Christians had all the powers of the clergy, who only existed as a separate caste as a matter of organisational convenience. Thus the lay rulers in society could – and, where possible, should – exercise authority in the church. They had as much right to determine the organisation of the church as any churchman, though it was not unreasonable of them to delegate this responsibility to specialists. The actual form of the church – whether it was ruled by bishops or presbyters – was a matter of indifference and could be altered to suit local convenience or traditions. Luther himself encouraged a diversity among the churches who asked for his advice. We shall see Luther's theories of church/state relations emerge later in English ecclesiastical history, under the title of 'Erastianism'.[3]

Calvin, on the other hand, insisted, in contradiction to Zwingli, that the 'power of the keys' was given to the disciples as representatives of the clergy, and that the clergy had a real, divinely ordained authority in the church independent of that of the civil power and, in religious matters, superior to it. Calvin established a headquarters in the French-speaking town of Geneva, and his career there was marked by recurrent quarrels with the civil authorities over whether the final right of appeal in questions of excommunication lay with the church authorities or with the lay authorities. Calvin also argued, perhaps more in line with Zwingli, that the constitution of a true church could be found in the Bible and that it was the duty of the church to try to conform as closely as possible to the Biblical model.

nised by the presence of
iefly preaching the Gospel
Wherever those functions
be said to exist, even if it
ses, superfluous traditions,
rue church was recognised
h in time and in space as
centre in Rome: there is
there could be many true
e to imitate the one scrip-
e was no scriptural justifi-
ter' to exercise authority
'bishop' in the Bible was
er' and did not imply any
ters governed the church
ers'. The elders could not
gether with the minister,
story, which exercised dis-
had the power of excom-
st faith or morals. Ideally,
loss of civil and political
eal was never reduced to
time), the civil ruler in the
ch discipline, of no more
he church. Like any other
ome authority through be-
coming an elder, but it was an authority that had to be exercised collectively with his fellow-elders; no authority in church
matters was inherent in him by virtue of his position as a
secular ruler.[4]

It is hardly suprising that, while Lutheran churches were
usually established by civil rulers, Calvinist churches were
usually established in opposition to them.

Calvin's ideas of church government were worked out in
relation to the small city-state of Geneva, where the distinction between the church as an individual congregation
and the church as a collection of congregations was not clearcut. The whole church, including its outlying regions, was
governed as a single unit and treated as a single congregation
even though there were several ministers. The system would

require modification when it became a matter of organising the church over a larger territory. The first people to face this problem were the French Reformed Church, who devised a Calvinist discipline to cover congregations scattered over the whole of France in 1559. The first, and almost the only, fully national church in the Calvinist tradition, supported by the civil power to the exclusion of all other churches, was the Church of Scotland, which adopted its First Book of Discipline in 1560.

2. *Calvinism in Scotland*

The first establishment of the Protestant Church of Scotland was not the result either of a popular uprising or of a governmental decision. It was the result of a *coup d'état* by a group of Protestant nobles unhappy at the increasing tendency of their queen-regent, Mary of Guise, to tie Scottish policy more closely to France, where her daughter, Queen Mary of Scotland, had just become queen as the wife of Francis II. The identification of Protestantism with a policy of alliance with England rather than France had already been established in an abortive attempt at a coup in the 1540s. The English alliance was especially popular among southern lords who suffered most through the recurrent wars with England. John Knox had emerged as the leading theorist for the Protestant rebels in the 1540s, and he returned to Scotland in 1555, after a period as a French galley slave and having been actively involved in the reformation of the Church of England under Edward VI and having worked closely with Calvin in Geneva.

Knox was the first architect of the Church of Scotland, but his base in 1560 was so narrow that the final strength of Scottish Protestantism sometimes seems little short of miraculous. The *coup d'état* of Knox's allies, the 'Assured Lords', was only successful through the intervention of Elizabeth of England, who herself had only just succeeded to the throne after her Catholic half-sister, Mary Tudor.

The Church of Scotland was established by a parliament whose own authority was very doubtful. It was acting in defiance of Mary of France, whom it acknowledged as its rightful sovereign. With the death of her husband, Francis II, in 1560, Mary lost her position as Queen of France and returned to Scotland to rule in person, as a Roman Catholic member of the Guise family, the main advocates of the suppression of Protestantism in France.

The Protestant Church of England had been established by royal command, first by Henry VIII, then, after a brief Roman Catholic restoration, by Elizabeth. The existing church, which had been Catholic, was made Protestant, complete with all its personnel, its church buildings and its legal rights, including its legal entitlement to the support of its clergy through tithes. Knox, by contrast, insisted on establishing the Church of Scotland as an entirely new church, independent of the existing structure. The Scottish parliament passed legislation which forbade the officers of the existing church from performing any spiritual functions. But this legislation left it in being, complete with all its legal rights, as a vast property-owning corporation which, on paper at least, held about half the wealth of Scotland. Knox in the First Book of Discipline claimed this wealth for the new reformed church, but the claim was difficult to enforce, especially under a Catholic monarch and a nobility for whom the old church was a bottomless source of easily acquired wealth. Between 1560 and 1567 Knox was engaged in a power struggle with the queen, and for the next five years Scotland was plunged in a civil war after parliament had forced Mary to abdicate because of her marriage to the Earl of Bothwell. It was not until Mary's defeat became certain in 1572, shortly before Knox's death, that the problem of the church's wealth could be seriously addressed.

In 1560 there was only a small handful of trained Protestant ministers in Scotland. The personnel of the new church had to be largely supplied from the old one, and neither their understanding of nor their commitment to the new doctrines could be fully relied upon. The First Book of Discipline therefore put the committed Protestants into a position of authority, in contradiction to the egalitarianism of the Genevan discipline. The legal rights of the old church were tied up with its hierarchical structure. Its wealth was divided into smaller benefices for priests and larger benefices for bishops. An arrangement had been worked out for the smaller benefices, but in 1572 it was proposed to transfer the larger benefices as their incumbents died. This meant transferring bishoprics to the new church — the legal rights inhering not in the church as such but in its bishoprics from which they were legally inseparable. This was initially acceptable to the church, and was endorsed by Knox just before he died. But to the then regent, Morton, as later to the king, James VI, Mary's son (still in 1572 a six-year-old child), the bishops were a means by which the church could be harmonised with his own secular authority after the manner of the Lutheran churches or of the Church of England. The introduction of bishops and the attempt to give them formal authority in the church produced a Presbyterian reaction which climaxed in 1580-81 when the General Assembly voted to abolish bishops and adopted the Second Book of Discipline as its ideal programme for church organisation and church/state relations.

The main point here is that the Church of Scotland was not from the start unambiguously Presbyterian. The extent to which the hierarchy outlined in Knox's First Book of Discipline was a product of principle or expediency is still a matter of passionate dispute, although it seems to me that the example of France shows clearly that an equality of ministers even in churches organised over wide territories was the Reformed ideal, and Knox on every other issue adhered to the Reformed rather than to the Lutheran tradition. Still, the supporters of hierarchy could claim some support from the First Book of Discipline. A large part of Scotland was still Roman Catholic, principally the Highlands, which were largely outside the scope of the royal authority, though like pre-Reformation Ireland their relations with the international Roman Catholic Church were as arbitrary as their relations with the king. In the twenty years between the First and Second Books of Discipline it is hardly to be expected that even the Lowlands could have been wholly committed to Protestant ideas. Despite the Second Book of Discipline's insistence on the independence of the church from the secular power, the Reformation had been the work of laymen, who could support the church's independence while they were themselves in conflict with the queen, but who were hardly likely to take the same attitude once a government was established with which they could be satisfied. A large part of their own political idealism was bound up in the idea of an alliance, and even eventually a union, with England which would be greatly facilitated if there could be a harmony in ideas of church government. The Church of England was an episcopal church which recognised the sovereign as its supreme governor. This was a largely successful formula for a truly national church able to incorporate wide differences in religious belief and practice. By taking the high ground and insisting on a Calvinist purity, the Scottish Presbyterians, without the enthusiastic support of the civil power, were condemning themselves, despite their formal legal establishment, to becoming a sect.[5]

3. *Absolutism in Ireland*

The Plantation of Ulster took place under the auspices of James I of England, James VI of Scotland; and it took place at a time when James had succeeded, after a long and bitter struggle with the Presbyterians, in turning the Church of Scotland into an episcopal church. Bishops, appointed by him, were incorporated into the church structure and had positions of authority, albeit less than their English counterparts, over it. James's chief source of anxiety was not the principle of equality of ministers as such, but the doctrine, clearly set out in the Second Book of Discipline, of the Two Kingdoms – the Earthly Kingdom and the Heavenly Kingdom – by which all church matters were part of the Heavenly Kingdom, whose only king was Christ. The earthly king had a duty to support the church, but not authority over it. In matters of faith and morals he was to be subject to the church, whose ministers, acting corporately, had a power delegated to them by Christ.[6]

James was an advocate of the idea of absolute monarchy, the leading political idea of the seventeenth century, which had been formalised in France in the sixteenth century by the legal theorist Jean Bodin. Bodin had written in the midst of the French wars of religion when, over a period of fifty years, France was torn apart by a series of conflicts between the Catholic and Calvinist churches. Bodin belonged to the *politiques*, a group who believed that the religious conflict should be subsumed under the authority of the king. Both Catholics and Calvinists had argued for theories of limited monarchy, under which the subject had the right to rebel against tyranny. The Calvinist François Hotman had argued for a right of rebellion in the wake of the St Bartholomew's Day massacre, authorised by the then regent, Catherine de' Medici, in 1572 (an event that did much to weaken the cause of Mary Stuart in Scotland). The Catholic League, organised round the Guise family, had argued for a right of rebellion when the king, Henry III, threw in his lot with the Protestants, whose leader, Henry of Navarre, later Henry IV, was the next heir to the throne. Bodin, by contrast, argued that the king was the source of all law and that there were no circumstances under which he could lawfully be resisted by his subjects. He was still subject to divine and natural law, and if he broke these, he was guilty of tyranny, but for that he could only be punished by God or, conceivably, by his peers — his fellow-monarchs in other countries. The only redress for a subject ordered by a tyrant to act against his conscience was to leave the country. Both Bodin and James (the latter in his *Basilicon Doron*, in which he outlines his own theories of kingship) admit that if a king behaves tyranically, he runs the risk that his subjects will rebel, and though they will be in the wrong, they may well get away with it. But there is no authority in the society, either the church or parliament, with the right to exercise any form of legal jurisdiction over the king. Bodin, extending his theory of authority to the family, argues that a father has a legal right to kill his child. He also expounds the theory that property is inalienable, and therefore the king has no right to take the property of a subject without his permission, though the subject has no means of redress if the king does it (the theory of the divine right of kings does not assume that the king is always in the right). The king should have enough property of his own for the normal purposes of government, and the function of parliament is to offer advice (which the king may refuse but should, as a point of good government, accept as far as possible) and to provide free-will gifts in the event of exceptional exigencies such as war.[7]

This absolutist theory provided a basis for national unity at a time when great lords or chieftains, notionally subject to the king, exercised almost unlimited sovereignty over their own territories, which they could use as a base for attacks against the king. The French wars of religion were a case in point. So were the Scottish wars in which James as a child came to his throne. The Scottish Highlands were still a law unto themselves. So, until the end of the sixteenth century, was Ireland and especially Ulster.

An analysis of Ireland on the basis of absolutist legal theory was made in 1612 in *A Discovery of the True Causes Why Ireland Was Never Entirely Subdued* by Sir John Davies, who, as Attorney-General in Ireland, had been responsible for much of the legal work attending the plantation. The *Discovery* is a history and analysis of the failure of Irish society to develop a national unity on the basis of its own traditions, and of the failure of the Normans to impose national unity on it. National unity is identified with royal authority. (Republican systems of government at the time were only possible in small societies such as the Italian and Swiss city-states. The United Provinces is the exception that proves the rule. It was a loose alliance of small states which could only act in a united, national manner under the hegemony of the House of Orange. During the war against Spain William the Silent maintained the legal fiction that he was acting as the representative of the Spanish king, Philip II, against the usurpation of his lieutenant, the Duke of Alva. After William's assassination the Provinces tried desperately to persuade Elizabeth to become their monarch.)[8]

Davies argued that Ireland could not develop until a unified, centralised system of law was established throughout the whole country to which everyone, even the greatest of the nobility, would be subject. In order for this to be achieved, Ireland had to be divided into counties, administered by sheriffs, who would be responsible only to the king and who would have authority over everyone living in the county. A start had been made after the Norman invasion by King John, who reduced Munster and Leinster to counties, but his successors had lost their grip on their own barons in Ireland, and the area of royal authority had been reduced to the Pale. Ireland had become, or had returned to being, a confused mass of independent lordships engaged in continual warfare with each other, and with each lord ruling as sovereign over his own territory. The process of reducing them to the status of subjects equal before the law had been resumed in the sixteenth century when the Munster and Leinster counties had been re-established and new counties created in Ulster and Connaught.

Davies was outlining a programme he believed had largely been implemented. It was the programme of the Normans in England, the initial programme of the invasion of Ireland, and the long-standing programme of the Kings of Scotland once they came under Norman influence in the twelfth century. The aim was to form the existing Irish aristocracy into a 'commonwealth' by breaking their independence. It was not intended to replace them with a new aristocracy. The 'mere Irish' (meaning the Gaels — the Irish who could trace back their ancestry in Ireland to before the Norman invasion) were to be brought under the law from which the Old English, descendants of the Normans, had tried to exclude them. Davies subsequently boasted that the Irish parliament of 1613 was the first parliament in which the whole island, including the 'mere Irish', was represented.[9]

The exception to this principle of incorporating the existing aristocracy was Ulster, large areas of which had been simply abandoned by the native aristocracy, leaving the followers who had fought for them over the previous fifty years without the legal rights they would have enjoyed as their dependants and tenants. Ulster was the most backward and intractable part of Ireland. It was the equivalent of the Highlands and Islands of Scotland which James in his *Basilicon Doron* said could be subjected only by brute force. The Highlands and Islands were dominated by the MacDonald clan, whose territory included north-east Antrim. Unlike the O'Neills and O'Donnells, Randal MacDonnell, Earl of Antrim, was able to adapt to the new system of centrally administered law, to subject himself to the commonwealth, and thus retain his territories and even, while establishing a centre of

Catholic missionary activity in Scotland, contribute to the work of the plantation.[10]

Davies could not have envisaged that in the middle of the seventeenth century a Puritan revolution in England and Scotland would force the Irish Catholic aristocracy to unite in war in which their defeat resulted in their replacement throughout the whole island by a new Protestant ascendancy. Nevertheless, the fact that they could unite, that the Confederation of Kilkenny took the form of a representative parliament, and that they clearly wished to be loyal to the king testifies, like the later unity of the Irish Catholics under James II and his parliament, to the essential correctness of his analysis. They had become a commonwealth.

2

The Birth of
Ulster Presbyterianism

1. *A Ferment in the Church of Ireland*

The planters who came to Ulster from Scotland were leaving the care of the Church of Scotland to come under the care of the Church of Ireland. They were leaving the care of a Protestant church which was popular in large areas of lowland Scotland, which had already transformed the character of the areas where it was influential, which exercised a close supervision over the morals of its members, which had developed in opposition to the civil power, and which had a strongly established intellectual and moral independence, even despite the introduction of episcopacy. The Church of Ireland, on the other hand, was the merest creature of government policy. It had no popular base outside the area surrounding Dublin. James Ussher, Archbishop of Armagh, had claimed for it an impressive historical tradition, but this existed on paper rather than in any intellectual independence on the part of its members or clergy. Throughout most of Ireland it was virtually non-functional. It was especially non-existent in Ulster, most of which had until recently been outside the law. It had to be created as part of the plantation.

The Church of Ireland, run by a hierarchy appointed by and responsible to the king, was an instrument of the absolutist policy of creating an Irish commonwealth. The church was not just a place in which to worship God on a Sunday. In the days before newspapers, mass-based political parties or television it was a major means of communication between the government and people. It was an important centre for social organisation at local level. It was a means by which moral and political values were inculcated and cultivated. It ensured in an age when contacts between even neighbouring localities were few that a common identity and world-view was shared over wide territories. That religion was not of itself sufficient to create a national culture, all other things not being equal, is shown by the Irish Catholic Church, which had had a theoretically unified national hierarchy since shortly before the Norman invasion in the twelfth century but which failed to establish a united Irish nation. But the church was still an important part of the process of establishing a common culture, which is why dissent was so worrying. That Presbyterianism should have developed in the most solidly Protestant part of Ireland was, to say the least, a misfortune for the Church of Ireland.

It was not an inevitable result of the plantation of a Scottish population. As we have seen, the Scottish church at the time of the plantation was episcopal. Its Episcopalianism was 'low'. Bishops responsible to the king were regarded as a permissible, or, for the more enthusiastic Episcopalians, desirable part of the constitution of the church, in opposition to the Presbyterians, for whom they were impermissible. They were not regarded as indispensable. But at the same time the Church of England, together with its appendage, the Church of Ireland, was also 'low' in this period, compared with what it was shortly to become. Under Elizabeth there had been a substantial Presbyterian movement within it, whose best-known spokesmen were Thomas Cartwright and Walter Travers. They had been suppressed in the 1580s more thoroughly and speedily than the Scottish Presbyterians, but the arguments used against them by Richard Hooker in his classic defence of Anglicanism, the *Laws of Ecclesiastical Polity*, had been based on the expediency of bishops, not their absolute necessity. Hooker argued that they were a normal part of the constitution of the church, but he did not argue that the non-episcopal churches of the continent were not true churches. Bishop Bancroft, who had attempted to put the case for the intrinsic divinely ordained power of bishops, had been silenced on the subject. Elizabeth was as strongly opposed to the independent power of bishops as she was to the independent power of presbyters.[11]

The Churches of England and Ireland also encouraged a Calvinist theology familiar to the Church of Scotland. Salvation was confined only to those predestined to be saved. It was wholly a work of grace and had nothing to do with the merits of the saved individual. Thus despite remaining differences, mainly on the means by which the morals of the society were to be regulated, and on the degree of ritual to be permitted, the prospects for harmony between the churches appeared to be good, and James was continuing his work of trying to bring the Church of Scotland closer to the Church of England, notably through the Articles of Perth of 1615, which required, among other things, kneeling at communion. The point was that James could not be head of two churches one of which regarded the practices of the other as incompatible with the constitution of a true church (William III was to be the first British monarch to achieve this feat without too many difficulties of conscience). At the same time James supported the rigid Calvinists in the United Provinces at the Synod of Dort, which was attended by two Church of England bishops.

The new church being established in Ulster included Scottish bishops, notably Andrew Knox, appointed Bishop of Raphoe (Donegal) while he was still Bishop of the Isles in Scotland. Knox was James's agent in trying to apply to the Isles, in opposition to Randal MacDonnell's relatives, a policy similar to that which was applied with more success in Ulster, the policy he had outlined in the *Basilicon Doron* — outright warfare combined with the plantation of Lowlanders accustomed to the rule of law. Bishop Knox was to have a role to play in the introduction of Ulster Presbyterianism.[12]

Within the Church of Scotland a small hard core of opposition continued against the royal supremacy, against the bishops, and especially against the Articles of Perth. Some of the Presbyterian ministers came over to Ulster to join the fledgeling Church of Ireland, which was anxious to acquire an energetic and capable clergy for its population newly settled in still largely hostile territory. The Scottish bishops of the Church of Ireland, Andrew Knox and Robert Echlin, Bishop of Down and Connor, were willing to allow such ministers to be ordained in an ambiguous manner which could be interpreted either as episcopal or Presbyterian. Other ministers had already been ordained within the Church of Scotland. Some were invited over by James Hamilton, Lord Clandeboye, the remarkable scholar-adventurer who controlled much of Co. Down. They included Josias Welch, whose father, John Welch, married to one of John Knox's daughters, had been prominent in the Presbyterian opposition to James VI. They also included two men who were to be prominent in the Scottish Presbyterian resurgence of the 1630s and 1640s, Robert Blair and John Livingstone.

Blair is especially important in the history of Ulster Presbyterianism. He was the leading figure in the remarkable religious movement of the 1620s known as the Sixmilewater Revival, the first manifestation of the existence of a distinct religious community among the Ulster Scots, with principles of its own that were not those of the Church of Ireland.

The Sixmilewater Revival was part of a wider 'revival' taking place at the same time in Scotland in the form of the Stewarton and Kirk o' Shotts revivals. Both Blair and Livingstone have left accounts of the Ulster revival and are anxious to stress that it was mainly a development of a new religious earnestness among a population that had been previously irreligious and profane — that had come to Ulster in search of quick wealth or to escape from debt or bad reputations at home. When the revivalist movement was suppressed both in Scotland and in Ulster in the 1630s, most stress was laid on the 'physical manifestations' that had accompanied it, and Blair was accused of preaching that 'physical manifestations' — fainting, shaking, hysteria, etc. — were necessary to salvation, a charge he strongly denied. Livingstone ridicules the idea, saying that some members of one congregation began to breathe heavily during sermons, but it was found that they could be induced to breathe heavily on other occasions as well, and they did not, on examination, show any signs of being especially devout.

The Sixmilewater Revival has been seen as a precursor of the 1859 Revival, but it is separated from it by over two hundred years, during which time outbreaks of enthusiasm are not at all typical of the Ulster or even of the Scottish Presbyterian tradition, despite the proximity of enthusiastic

Methodism in England. The 1859 Revival was a short outburst which, whatever smaller revivals might have followed, only lasted a year, whereas the Sixmilewater/Stewarton/Kirk o' Shotts 'revival' took place over a period of at least six years, from around 1624 to 1631. It seems that it was in fact a process of intense theological training, concentrated in south Antrim, when the basic doctrines of Calvinism were hammered into a population that was eager to receive them. The task was performed by a group of about six ministers acting in close co-operation with each other, without reference to their bishop. We may be sure that the Book of Common Prayer was not an important part of their devotional practice and that kneeling at communion was not encouraged. Indeed, Robert Blair quarrelled on this subject with his patron, Hamilton, who, possibly with an eye on the law of the land, insisted on kneeling but eventually had to give in, though he would only sit if he could be served in his own pew (where presumably he could not be seen breaking the law). The revival was started by the eccentric James Glendinning, who was persuaded by Blair to move from the fashionable and populous Carrickfergus, where he was much admired, to the obscure Oldstone, an assumption of authority on Blair's part which was quite unjustified under the Church of Ireland's constitution. Blair exchanged pulpits with another revivalist minister, Robert Cunningham, again without reference to the bishop. And he complains of the interference of the bishop in his exercising discipline over his own congregation, where he established Presbyterian-style deacons and elders. Glendinning himself, according to his fellow-workers, was mentally deranged. According to Blair, he believed that people who turned in their sleep at night were showing that they had doubts about Christianity, and that anyone who followed a strange practice of groaning out prayers while lying face down on the earth would be saved. Blair, again without reference to the bishop, seems to have persuaded him to quit his ministry.

The revivalist ministers — Blair, John Ridge, Cunningham, James Hamilton (Clandeboye's nephew), Livingstone (who, however, arrived only shortly before the movement was suppressed) — could not establish an open Presbyterian system, and we do not know if they were arguing the full Presbyterian case for the independence of the church from the civil power, though Blair had been expelled from Glasgow University for advocating it and, together with his friend David Dickson and other ministers associated with the Scottish revival, was soon to reassert it in the Covenanting movement. They were, however, behaving independently of the existing church structure and were acting on their own authority as presbyters — an authority which they believed was possessed by every minister and which was equivalent to the authority of a bishop.

They were pioneers of what was known in Scotland as the 'privy kirk' — the group of dissenters from the Established Church who insisted on exercising their rights as ministers, often in a very unorthodox and un-Presbyterian manner, becoming itinerants in times of persecution, preaching to enormous crowds in the open air in political, religious and sometimes military opposition to the authorities. Under such circumstances the emphasis was on individual feeling rather than on Presbyterian discipline which was impossible to maintain. We shall see that despite the pioneering role played by Ulster in the development of the 'privy kirk' in the 1620s and 1630s, it did not have such an important part to play subsequently, since in the 1670s and 1680s the Ulster Presbyterians, unlike their Scottish counterparts, managed to maintain an almost fully functioning Presbyterian church.

But that is to anticipate. We must return to the 1620s and 1630s to look at the developments which upset the possibility of harmony between the Anglican and Scottish churches, put an end to the marginal Ulster/Scottish revival, and set the stage for the Covenant.[13]

2. *The Birth of High Church Anglicanism*

I said earlier that the Reformation, in so far as it was supported by governments, could be divided into two main streams — the Lutheran and the Reformed. At first sight, the Church of England seems to be a large exception. But in so far as the Church of England was Protestant it belonged to the Reformed tradition. Whatever did not belong to the Reformed tradition was inherited from the pre-Reformation church.

The Church of England was the pre-Reformation church, taken over and reformed by monarchs who continued to have Catholic sympathies or were aware of the need to incorporate a population that still had Catholic sympathies and to engage in diplomacy with the Catholic powers of Europe. The monarchs, it should be remembered, were a distinct caste which saw itself as above national society and which could not, according to the arguments of Bodin, be judged by it. Their peers were their fellow-monarchs, and it was only among their peers that they could marry — marriages that were fraught with political consequences. Most members of the European monarchical caste were still Roman Catholic. All the English Protestant monarchs until William III had Catholic sympathies. Henry, Elizabeth (if we accept Froude's view) and Charles I wanted to keep open the option of a return to Catholicism. Charles II and James II both attempted it.[14]

The Church of England maintained the machinery of the pre-Reformation church, shorn of its religious orders, of the power of its priests to absolve from sin, and of much of its ritual. By this means the loyalty of a large part of the population, who might otherwise have remained Roman Catholic, was secured. The intelligentsia, who were well represented among the bishops, tended towards a Reformed theology, and this was reflected in the Calvinism of the Thirty-Nine Articles. When the church deviated from Calvinism to positions that might seem closer to Lutheranism, it did so in terms of disputes which were occurring in the Reformed tradition. Its theory of church/state relations, which resembled Luther's, was called 'Erastianism'; the theory of the operations of grace which developed during the seventeenth century and which also resembled Luther's was called 'Arminianism'. Both Thomas Erastus and Jacobus Arminius belonged to the Reformed tradition.

Thomas Erastus had come to the fore in 1568 in a dispute in Heidelberg in the lower Palatinate where the Elector, Frederick III, was proposing to introduce a Reformed discipline. Erastus was opposing the view that the church could impose its discipline on the king, but he went further, and argued that it had no right to refuse communion to anyone who seriously wished it. In particular, the church could not on its own authority refuse communion on grounds of immorality. Since society could not function with two governments, it must be the responsibility of the secular government to exercise discipline, both in moral and ecclesiastical matters.[15]

Erastus did not publish his theses, but they were published in England in 1589 after his death as part of the campaign waged by Elizabeth in 1589-90 against the English Presbyterians. Under the Erastian system the ministrations of the church become a right that can be demanded of the minister under all but the most extraordinary circumstances, rather than a privilege to be conferred on those who have deserved it. The role given by the Reformed tradition to the minister and elders as governors of their congregation is completely undermined.

Jacobus Arminius (Jacob Hermans) was a professor of theology at Leyden University in Holland. Leyden University had been founded in 1575 by William of Orange (William the Silent), leader of the Netherlands revolt against Spain, to celebrate the raising of the siege of Leyden, a major turning-point in the war. Calvinists played a leading part in the revolt, and William himself had joined the Reformed Church in 1573. Leyden University was conceived of as a centre for Calvinist orthodoxy. However, the Reformed Church was still a minority in the United Provinces, which still, even after their final separation from Spain, had a large Catholic population. The victory of the anti-Spanish Calvinists was followed by an attempt to turn the Provinces as a whole into a Reformed state on Genevan lines. This was resisted both by the Catholics and by a moderate party among the Protestants known, after their Genevan counterparts, as the Libertines. A theology was developed for the Libertines by Dirck Volckertzoon Coornhert, who argued that theological truth was essentially unknowable and who therefore opposed any attempt to codify it into a creed and impose it as a condition of membership of a church. I mention Coornhert because we shall see his ideas flourishing among the Ulster Presbyterians of the eighteenth century. They appealed especially to the governors of the various states and councils which made up the loose federation of the United Provinces, since it enabled them to reconcile the widely differing religious views of their subjects. Under this liberal theology the only religious views that required to be suppressed were those that were felt strongly.

Arminius could be said to have succeeded Coornhert as the theologian of the Dutch political establishment. From the moment of his appointment in 1603 he was engaged in a fierce dispute with his fellow professor of theology, the Calvinist Gomarus (Francis Gomar). Arminius died in 1609, but in 1610 his followers, led by Simon Episcopius, presented a document known as the Remonstrance to the Dutch government, outlining their principles and craving toleration. Their argument was opposed to the Calvinist doctrine of predestination by which men were damned for sins they were infallibly bound to commit. The Arminians argued that God, being omniscient, certainly had foreknowledge of who would be saved and who would not, but this was foreknowledge of decisions freely made by the individual. Christ died for all men, and saving grace was available to all men, though men could not attain to saving faith by their own unaided efforts. They required the help of the Holy Spirit. They had, however, the freedom and ability to resist this saving grace and were therefore, if they did so, freely responsible for their own damnation.[16]

The effect of Arminianism was to encourage an emphasis on morality rather than doctrine, and individual responsibility rather than membership of a religious community. This seems to be why it was favoured by governments. Good citizenship had a role to play in the work of salvation, which was a concern of the individual rather than of the church, which was not seen as the Kingdom of Christ independent of the state. The emphasis on morality rather than on doctrine also enabled people with differing doctrinal views to worship together and reduced the occasions for division. The Calvinist theology of the Church of England had not been taken to heart by the great majority of its members, and the church barely attempted to exercise Calvinist discipline. In the early seventeenth century the more relaxed Arminian theology became increasingly popular.

The Church of England therefore had a theory of church/

state relations which was uncongenial to the Scottish Presbyterians but which had to some extent been adopted by the Church of Scotland; and it was developing a theology of grace directly opposed to that of the Calvinists and probably most of the Church of Scotland as well. In addition it had a constitution and ritual, parts of which had been grudgingly adopted by the Church of Scotland. In this area too, early seventeenth-century Anglicanism was developing in a way not calculated to promote harmony between the two churches.

We have seen that one of the principal characteristics of the Church of England was its continuity with the pre-Reformation church. In the disputes with the Presbyterians the Anglican apologists had argued that this was one of its great virtues, facilitating its development as a national church. Throughout the seventeenth century the bishops of the Church of England increasingly turned to the view that this institutional continuity was an essential mark of a true church. Calvin had declared that a true church could be recognised by its true doctrine, the administration of the sacraments, and the exercise of discipline. But doctrine was of its own nature contentious and divisive, while discipline was dangerous to the state. It established a government separate from and independent of the national government. Instead, the Anglican theologians argued, the authority of a true church resides in the bishops. Episcopacy was more than just a desirable or normal part of church government: it was essential, and the authority of the bishops derived from their institutional continuity going back to the days of the Apostles.

The argument was fraught with danger. If the bishops had an authority over the church conferred by means of the apostolic succession, they would have as much justification for asserting their independence from the civil order as the Presbyterians. Why should the authority of the Apostles always follow an appointment made by the king? Froude sees this as an essential, debilitating absurdity at the heart of Anglicanism. Elizabeth had suppressed the full development of the doctrine in the person of Bishop Bancroft. James I warned his son Charles against patronising Laud, and at the end of the seventeenth century a group of bishops did in fact assert a Presbyterian-style independence from the civil power when the schismatical Non-Juring Church of England was briefly established in the wake of the Williamite Revolution.[17]

With the bishops appointed by the king, however, and eagerly committed to Erastianism and absolute monarchy, such dangers seemed remote. The merit of the High Church programme was that it enhanced the authority of the king's agents in the church and brought the Church of England more into harmony with Roman Catholic thinking. The argument was a renewal of the arguments used by the conciliar movement in the Roman Catholic Church at the time of the Great Schism in the late fourteenth and early fifteenth centuries, when there were two, and later (as a result of the conciliar movement's own efforts) three popes. It attempted to resolve the problem by arguing that authority in the church lay with the bishops, who had delegated that authority to the pope. A council of the bishops of the whole church (an ecumenical council) therefore had an authority independent of, and greater than, that of the pope.[18]

With the triumph of the papal party at the Council of Trent, this thinking fell into disfavour in the Roman Catholic Church. In Protestantism the superintendents of the Lutheran churches did not claim continuity from Catholic bishops, nor did Elizabeth's bishops, nor, naturally enough, the bishops of the Church of Scotland. The Anglo-Catholics were therefore reviving the doctrine of the continuity of the church through bishops almost as a new idea, though one with very respectable antecedents. It was, however, to become central, not just to Anglo-Catholicism but also to the Gallican church of Louis XIV, as defined in the Gallican articles of 1682. Ironically enough, one of the pioneers of the new thinking was none other than James Ussher, the Archbishop of Armagh, who was also to be greatly admired by Presbyterians for his attempt in the 1640s to work out a compromise between episcopacy and Presbyterian discipline.[19]

Erastianism, Arminianism and the Anglo-Catholic theory of episcopal continuity provided the Church of England with what it had rather lacked previous to the 1620s — a character and authority of its own. The continental Reformation, for all its dependence on civil governments, had been the work of great individual churchmen with a coherent vision of what the church ought to be. The Church of England had developed in an *ad hoc* improvised manner. Archbishop Laud in the 1630s was to the Church of England what Knox had been to the Church of Scotland. He gave it its character and, with the support of the king, methodically set about reorganising it throughout the whole of England, and attempted to bring the Churches of Ireland and Scotland into harmony with it. The fledgeling Presbyterianism in Ulster was suppressed by Laud's friend and ally, John Bramhall, who came to Ireland as chaplain of Lord Deputy Wentworth and became Bishop of Derry. Blair and Livingstone, however, together with their allies of the 'privy kirk' in Scotland, were soon to have their revenge.

3. *A Scottish Calvinist Revolution*

The fate of the Covenanting movement bears some resemblance to that of the Dutch Presbyterian movement which we have seen triumphing at the Synod of Dort in 1618. On both occasions the convinced Presbyterians came to power in alliance with secular powers who were acting from very different political motives. In both cases the defeat of the common enemy resulted in quarrels between the allies and the failure of the Presbyterians to secure their ascendancy. Nowhere in the world did Presbyterianism ever achieve its ambition to realise a Presbyterian state — a state in which a Presbyterian church had full control over the religious life of the nation independently of the government. It could only fight for such an end in alliance with a secular military force which would then suppress the church's ambitions once victory had been achieved. The Scottish Covenanters overthrew episcopacy in alliance with Scottish military forces, who then defied the church in pledging themselves through the pact known as the Engagement to support Charles I against the English Parliamentarian army. After the defeat of the Engagers at Preston the church took power in Scotland with the aid of Cromwell, but opposed the execution of the king, was forced back into an alliance with the remnants of the Engagers, and was finally defeated by Cromwell at the Battles of Dunbar and Worcester, after which it existed as a tolerated church closely supervised by the Cromwellian military government until it was wiped away after the Restoration.

The Covenanting alliance formed between the Presbyterians and a substantial section of the Scottish nobility in 1638 was almost an alliance of opposites. The common enemy was the bishops and the policy of harmonising the episcopal Churches of Scotland and England through the introduction of a Scottish Prayer Book. Despite its enforced acceptance of bishops and of James's Articles of Perth, the Church of Scotland had still retained a distinct character given to it by its early reformers acting largely independent of or in opposition to the secular powers, and an important part of this character was a fierce anti-Catholicism and opposition to all forms of ritual, including the use of liturgy — of set prayers and responses. The worship of God, in the Reformed ideal, was to come from the heart. It was to be 'spiritual' — that is to say, a product of real feeling. Prayers therefore should ideally be extempore. Singing from the heart was encouraged and obviously required specified words, but these should come solely from the inspired Word of God — the Psalms, or metrical paraphrases of passages from the Bible. In areas of the Lowlands, and most notably in the Lowlands area closest to the north of Ireland where the 'privy kirk' had been active, this ideal ran deep, and Laud's innovations were a standing affront to it.

Nevertheless, this religious instinct would not of itself have been strong enough to bring about a war with England were it not for the alliance with the nobility argued for by the militant Presbyterian Samuel Rutherford, exiled in 1636 by the High Commission Court of the Church of Scotland to Aberdeen, a stronghold of Scottish Episcopalianism. This alliance was put into effect by the remarkable political skill of the Presbyterian lawyer Archibald Johnston of Warriston. I do not wish to suggest that the nobility were not sincerely inspired by the very able preaching of the Presbyterians and did not genuinely believe on the strength of it that they were doing God's work. But their principal complaint was that Charles was using the bishops as reliable agents of government in Scotland, responsible to himself alone, and ignoring the old Scottish nobility that had been so troublesome to his ancestors. As part of this process, Charles and Laud were trying to return to the church the property that had been alienated to the secular nobility during the sixteenth century. This had also been a demand of the First Book of Discipline and was an important part of the Presbyterians' programme, though of course they did not envisage the property being put at the disposal of bishops. Similar legislation was passed during the brief period that the Presbyterians exercised sovereign power in Scotland after the Battle of Preston.[20]

The organised Presbyterian Church in Ulster was established by the Scottish Covenanters during the civil war conditions of the 1640s. Their concern for Ulster was doubtless stimulated by Blair and Livingstone, both of whom were leaders of the Scottish movement. Robert Baillie, one of the Scottish commissioners conducting negotiations between the Scots and the English parliament, noted that the extremist wing of the Scottish Presbyterian movement (and he himself looked quite extreme to the English) had been strengthened by ministers exiled from Ulster in the 1630s.[21]

It should be made clear that there were two Covenants: the National Covenant of 1638, by which the signatories, representing a large part of the military power in Scotland at the time, opposed Laud's innovations; and the Solemn League and Covenant of 1643, whereby the English parliament, in return for Scottish assistance against Charles I, agreed to harmonise the Churches of England and Scotland on a Presbyterian basis.

The National Covenant was based on the 'King's Covenant' or 'Negative Confession' which James VI had signed in 1580 as a comprehensive repudiation of Roman Catholicism and all its works. Calvinism, and especially Scottish Calvinism, can only be understood if its deep emotional and intellectual revulsion against Roman Catholicism (and therefore against the continuing lively Anglo-Catholic tradition within the Church of England) is taken into account. Calvinism, for all its claims to be a revival of primitive Christianity, was a new, revolutionary sensibility which aimed to re-make the world, transforming men's images of themselves and of their relations with God. Its hatred of Catholicism was like the hatred of the communist movement in its vigorous heyday for capitalism. The Negative Confession, as incorporated in the National Covenant, is an elemental expression of it, and it will be useful to quote it at length, especially since it expresses so well a sensibility that is fundamental not just to Scottish but also to a large part of English culture. The great merit of British culture is its ability to absorb a variety of often violently conflicting sensibilities, but this has developed over a long period of time, and Catholicism was perhaps the element it has found most difficult to digest. At least until the middle of the nineteenth century anti-Catholicism could easily be seen as the single most salient defining characteristic of British national culture; and it finds vigorous expression in the text of the National Covenant:

> Therefore we abhor and detest all contrary religion [to the Scots Confession of 1560] and doctrine; but chiefly all kind of papistry in general and particular heads, even as they are now damned and confuted by the Word of God and the Kirk of Scotland. But in especial, we detest and refuse the usurped authority of the Roman Antichrist upon the Scriptures of God, upon the Kirk, the civil magistrate, and consciences of men; all his tyrannous laws made upon indifferent things against our Christian liberty; his erroneous doctrine against the sufficiency of the written word, the perfection of the law, the office of Christ, and his blessed evangel; his corrupted doctrine concerning original sin, our natural inability and rebellion to God's law, our justification by faith only, our imperfect sanctification and obedience to the law; the nature, number and use of the holy sacraments; his five bastard sacraments, with all his rites, ceremonies and false doctrine added to the ministration of the true sacraments without the Word of God; his cruel judgment against infants departing without the sacrament; his absolute necessity of baptism; his blasphemous opinion of transubstantiation or real presence of Christ's body in the elements, and receiving of the same by the wicked, or bodies of men; his dispensations with solemn oaths, perjuries and degrees of marriage forbidden in the world; his cruelty against the innocent divorced; his devilish mass; his blasphemous priesthood; his profane sacrifice for sins of the dead and the quick; his canonisation

of men; calling upon angels or saints departed; worshipping of imagery, relics and crosses; dedicating of kirks, altars, days; vows to creatures; his purgatory, prayers for the dead; praying or speaking in a strange language; with his processions and blasphemous litany, and multitude of advocates or mediators, his manifold orders, auricular confession; his desperate and uncertain repentance; his general and doubtsome faith; his satisfactions of men for their sins; his justification by works, OPUS OPERATUM, works of supererogation, merits, pardons, peregrinations, and stations, his holy water, baptising of bells, conjuring of spirits, crossings, sayings, anointing, conjuring, hallowing of God's good creatures, with the superstitious opinion joined therewith; his wordly monarchy and wicked hierarchy; his three solemn vows with all his shavelings of sundry sorts, his erroneous and bloody decrees made at Trent, with all the subscribers or approvers of that cruel and bloody band, conjured against the kirk of God.[22]

4. *The First Presbytery in Ulster*

The first formal presbytery in Ulster was established at Carrickfergus on Friday 10 June 1642 by the Scots army that came over to quell the Irish rebellion that began in 1641. The rebellion had two main parts. It began as a straightforward rising of the Ulster Gaels against the plantation. In 1642 the southern Catholic gentry, alarmed at the upsurge of anti-Catholic militant Puritanism in England and Scotland, formed the Confederation of Kilkenny to defend their religion. I have already suggested that this was a remarkable development, quite unlike the Elizabethan rebellions in that it was a national movement, led by a body which had some claim to being a representative parliament. It also generated what had previously been unknown in Ireland, a political literature. The fact that there were quarrels and divisions among the Confederates is not at all surprising. What is surprising is the amount of unity they achieved.

The Confederates' policy was to support the king on condition that he gave substantial safeguards for the free practice of the Catholic religion in Ireland. Their main problem was that the pope took an interest in their affairs and sent over an agent, Archbishop Rinuccini, who insisted on an impossibilist programme of establishing a Catholic state. Rinuccini was supported by the Ulster Gaels, now led by the Spanish-trained Owen Roe O'Neill, who devoted himself to preventing the signing of a treaty between the Confederation and the king's forces in Ireland, led by the Duke of Ormond, a Protestant member of the Catholic Butler family. The Protestants, then and subsequently, declined to draw a distinction between the Ulster Gaels and the Confederation, since it was the massacre in Ulster that provided the justification for the expropriation of the Catholic gentry in the south which was the basis for the Cromwellian land settlement of the 1650s and largely continued (under Ormond) after the Restoration.[23]

The Scots army had been organised just before the English civil war broke out. It was a Scottish army, raised by the king and paid for by the English parliament. Notionally it was under the supreme command of Ormond as the king's representative in Dublin. Ireland was acknowledged to be an English dependency, not a Scottish one. Nevertheless, the Solemn League and Covenant — the treaty between the Scots Presbyterians and the English parliament — was introduced in Ulster by Scottish ministers, and with it the presbytery took, or at least claimed the right to take, control over the religious life of the whole area controlled by the army. They suppressed the rebellious 'Presbytery of the Route', formed largely by ministers who had been and were again to become Episcopalians. They suspended Church of Ireland ministers whom they judged to be 'scandalous' — one of the scandals being resistance to the authority of the presbytery. In all this, according to Patrick Adair, the presbytery claimed to be acting on the basis of a request made to the Scottish church by the English parliament and on the recommendation of the Assembly of Divines meeting at Westminster to reorganise the Church of England. This was confirmed by the arrival of commissioners from the English parliament in 1645, but Adair is anxious to make it plain that the presbytery, though glad of the comissioners' support, did not regard itself as acting on the basis of an authorisation of the civil power;

it was acting on the basis of the authority of the church, of Christ's Kingdom. The prelatic English and Irish churches were in suspension, and the Westminster Assembly was not a valid church court. The Church of Scotland was the only valid, functioning church authority in Great Britain. The presbytery was, in the eyes of its members, the only valid, functioning church authority in Ireland.[24]

This 'arrogance' (as I have described it elsewhere in a spirit of admiration) can also be seen in the *Necessary Representation of the Present Evils and Eminent Dangers to Religion*, published by the presbytery in 1649 in opposition to the execution of the king. Patrick Adair, reminiscing about it forty years later, is himself impressed by the courage, or foolhardiness, of the 'few young men concerned with an inconsiderable people in two or three counties in the north of Ireland', and though it was thoroughly in accord with the Scottish policy of the time, he says that the Scottish leaders advised them against it. It was a savage attack on the policy of the English army which, under Cromwell's leadership, had just purged the parliament of its Presbyterian majority and executed the king. This was a disastrous reversal for the Church of Scotland, putting an end to hopes of establishing Presbyterianism throughout the British Isles — a hope that had seemed very credible only a year previously. The king was an essential part of this policy, even if he himself was less than enthusiastic about it, since it was he, and only he, who united the three kingdoms. He was, in any case, King of Scotland as well as King of England, and the Scots were naturally aggrieved that he had been executed, not only without their consent, but against their very strong representations. And the ascendancy of Cromwell and the army, the party which had performed the deed, signalled the end of hopes for establishing Presbyterianism in England, since they were for the most part what the Presbyterians called 'sectaries', who upheld what are known as 'Independent' principles of church government. To understand this we must go back to the earlier history of the Church of England.[25]

5. *An English Calvinist Revolution*

The Church of Scotland, even when it accepted rule by bishops, was a Calvinist church. Calvinism, however, even when it had the support of bishops, had developed as a sect or faction, albeit a dynamic one, within the Church of England. The role of the national church played a greater part in Scots Calvinist thinking; English Calvinist thinking had a stronger individualist bias. Cromwell believed that he, as an individual, aware of himself as one of the elect, was supported by God in his political struggles. The Scots felt most confident that they were supported by God when they were doing work sanctioned by and in support of the church. In England a 'proud Puritan' was most likely to be a layman. In Scotland the term was most likely to be used to refer to a minister.

In Scotland in the 1570s Genevan-style Presbyterianism, identified with the person of Andrew Melville, had triumphed in the General Assembly, which had adopted the Second Book of Discipline but had been prevented from implementing it fully by the secular power. In England Melville's equivalent in the same period, Thomas Cartwright, had had very little success with the Church of England, and the Presbyterian discipline he devised had been used only briefly by a small minority who had been quickly suppressed. Cartwright had shared the Scottish emphasis on the importance of a national church and had continually insisted that he was a minister of the Church of England. His views, however, were attacked in the early 1580s by Robert Browne in his *Treatise of Reformation without Tarrying for Any*. Browne argued that the elect should not wait for the approval of the civil powers before they could enjoy the ministrations of a pure church. They should establish such a pure church on their own initiative. Browne's book was published in Holland, where it was suppressed at the request of the English government. Browne himself then went to Scotland in 1583, and his ideas attracted some attention there. His main influence, however, was in England, though the separatists were still a very marginal element in the early seventeenth century, still mainly based in the Netherlands. They achieved an importance beyond their numbers, partly because they represented an extreme point of view which was continually referred to in the controversies of the period, but more especially because it was an English separatist congregation from the Netherlands which in 1620 pioneered the plantation of Massachussets, with a settlement at New Plymouth. Throughout the 1620s and to an even greater degree under the increasing pressure from Laud in the 1630s there was a continual flow of English Puritan emigrants to New England, where the separatist idea could be freely developed. Naturally enough, the experiment created a great deal of interest, and it had a profound influence on Calvinist thinking in the English civil war.

Among the Calvinists who remained members of the Church of England after the defeat of the Presbyterian movement, the idea developed of the 'gathered church'. A Calvinist minister, functioning as a minister of the Church of England, usually professing the Church of England to be a true church, and serving all the people of his parish, would gather a congregation of 'true professors' who would meet separately as a pure church of the elect. The mainstream Presbyterian tradition regarded the church as a means of organising and disciplining the whole society and therefore did not try to judge who were the elect or who were the reprobate, except by external profession and decent conduct. But in this English 'gathered church' tradition a substantial literature developed, aiming to identify the visible signs of election. In order to join the gathered church, the professor had to give evidence of his conversion, and a psychological process of conversion, from a serious interest in religion through a conviction of sin to an assurance of grace, was worked out by a number of writers, most notably by the Cambridge theologian William Perkins. Edmund Morgan, in his book on the development of this idea of 'visible saints', argues that such a vigorous trying of spirits was not typical of the original separatists and of the first settlers in New England, for whom adherence to a confession of faith was sufficient, as it was for the mainstream Presbyterians. The idea was first introduced to New England by John Winthrop, who had refused to separate from the Church of England. He arrived in New England in 1630 and was soon followed by a wave of like-minded non-separatists, who adopted the Congregationalist mode in New

England, where there was no established church, and gave American Puritanism its distinctive emphasis on the experience of the new birth. To anticipate a little, the easily available classic of the literature of the conversion process is John Bunyan's *Grace Abounding to the Chief of Sinners*, written after the Restoration, while the more theological and methodical defence of an intensely emotional religious life, represented by Perkins, is developed in the *Treatise concerning Religious Affections* of the American Jonathan Edwards in the early eighteenth century. What we have been describing is the origins of modern 'born again' Christianity.[26]

I have emphasised this as an English rather than a Scottish tradition. Similar developments did occur among the Scots 'privy kirk' in times when the reform of the whole church seemed hopeless, in the 1620s and in the 1670s, and they contributed, as we have seen, to the Sixmilewater/Stewarton/ Kirk o' Shotts revival. It is, however, with Edwards that revivalism among large bodies of people begins to fit more easily into the conversionary literature. The process of conversion described by Perkins is a long, slow, solitary and painful process, even if an awakening under powerful preaching has a part to play. We have still not reached the stage at which a conviction of sin can be happily telescoped with assurance of salvation into one or a few days of excitement in the midst of a large crowd. And although there are many exceptions to the rule, the generalisation holds good that an emphasis on an individually experienced conversion remains typical of English Calvinism, while an emphasis on a true church co-terminous with the nation and defined not by individual experiences but by intellectual assent to the propositions of a confession of faith remains typical of Scottish Presbyterianism.

Nevertheless, this difference did not dominate the debates of the Westminster Assembly and did not come to the fore until the English army asserted itself as a force to be reckoned with, independent of the English parliament, in 1648. The English Parliamentarians who supported the Assembly had found the activities of high-handed bishops intolerable, and they took it for granted that the alternative to a church ruled by bishops was Presbyterianism — a national church ruled by assemblies of ministers meeting as equals. The issue on which the Westminster Assembly came to grief in its relations with parliament was the same issue on which Calvin and his successor Theodore Beza had come to grief in their relations with the secular authorities in Geneva — the issue which had been raised by Thomas Erastus in Heidelberg — the issue of the right of the secular power to act as the final court of appeal in questions of excommunication. The doctrine that the secular power should have supreme authority over the church proved to be firmly established in English political culture, and the Presbyterian parliament proved to be as thoroughly 'Erastian' in its outlook as the king.

In 1641 the Long Parliament abolished the Court of High Commission, the highest of the ecclesiastical courts, and abolished all the temporal powers of the bishops, depriving the lower ecclesiastical courts of all their functions except that of bringing in tithes. Parliament finally passed the act which abolished episcopacy altogether in January 1643, after the outbreak of the civil war. This left parliament itself, in the areas under its control, as the sole authority in ecclesiastical affairs in England. The Westminster Assembly first met in July 1643, as parliament was being forced to appeal to the Scots for aid against the king. The treaty between parliament and the Scots — the Solemn League and Covenant — was made in September 1643, and thereafter the Westminster Assembly sat under the close supervision of Scottish commissioners urging them to reform the Church of England according to a Scottish model.

Within the Assembly, however, was a small group of ministers who supported the American model. They were the 'Independents', and one of the first references to them came in a debate in parliament when Sir Edward Dering, mover of the Root and Branch Bill against episcopacy, talked of 'a certain newborn, unseen, ignorant, dangerous, desperate way of Independency'. The principal difference between Independents and Presbyterians was that the Independents recognised no church other than the individual congregation, which they claimed had the right freely to order its affairs without reference to any other assembly. They therefore opposed the Presbyterian pattern of classical, provincial, national and ecumenical synods placed in a hierarchy above the individual congregation. The Independents were a small minority of about ten or eleven ministers in an assembly which, if it were fully attended, would include just over one hundred (the usual attendance, according to the Scottish commissioner Robert Baillie, was just over sixty). But they had a great advantage over the Presbyterians in that their system of congregational autonomy under parliament corresponded to what existed on the ground after prelacy had been abolished and before presbytery was established. It also provided a means by which the great variety of religious views which had been unleashed after the removal of Laud's discipline, and which were especially represented in the New Model Army, could be accommodated; and it appealed to that body of opinion which had been a driving force in the Long Parliament and which was reluctant to see the clergy as a body entitled to exercise any form of corporate jurisdiction over the country. That had been the grounds for opposition to the ecclesiastical courts of the bishops, and it was to be the grounds for the long debate on excommunication which took place in 1645 and 1646, resulting in June 1646 in the establishment of a standing committee of parliament to whom, in defiance of the rights claimed for the church by the Scots, disputes over excommunication could be referred.[27]

Another factor strengthening the hands of the Independents was simply resentment against being expected to adopt a Scottish model. Progress towards legislating for a full Presbyterian system depended on the English reliance on Scottish help, and it waned dramatically with the emergence of the New Model Army. The drift of sympathy to Independency can be seen in the work of the poet John Milton and the preacher John Owen, both of whom were writing in favour of Presbyterianism in the early 1640s but were converted to Independency by the end of the decade.[28]

The Westminster Assembly drew up a Presbyterian system which was approved by parliament and became, together with the Westminster Confession of Faith, a basic document of Scottish Presbyterianism. The legislation of the Long Parliament approving a Presbyterian system was not repealed

after Pride's Purge, nor was legislation introduced to enable
Independency to be formally established. But it was only in
London and Lancashire that a Presbyterian system was
actually established in reality over any considerable area, and
in the absence of organised Presbyterianism elsewhere, Independency prevailed, if only because nothing else was possible.
In these circumstances, the work of supervising ministers
and ensuring that they performed their duties was entrusted
to commissioners ('triers' and 'ejecters') appointed by parliament. The rule of the saints in England was rule by the
laity.

6. *Presbyterianism under Cromwell*

With the *Necessary Representation* of 1649 the Ulster
Presbyterians enter British literary history, since, together
with the treaty eventually signed between Ormond and the
Irish Catholic Confederation, it was replied to by John
Milton. Why should Milton have taken such trouble to reply
to a body on whose obscurity and insignificance he dwells at
some length? The execution of the king split the forces
opposed to the king in two. The anti-prelatic Parliamentarians
who had initiated the civil war, the whole of Scotland and
the one section of opinion in Ireland who had supported
parliament were now ranged against Cromwell and the army.
The Belfast Presbytery was expressing the views of the great
majority of those in the British Isles who had previously
opposed the king but not to the extent of doing away with
the monarchy, which was still seen as the guarantor of the
unity of the commonwealth. To advance these views in
Ireland, however, was to run the risk of entering into an
alliance with the Royalist forces which were putting themselves at the disposal of the Catholic Confederates, tarred
as they were with the 1641 massacre; and this, of course, is
a major theme of Milton's pamphlet. Charles I and his son
had the choice of an alliance with Irish (and Scottish) Catholicism or with Scottish (and Irish and English) Presbyterianism.
It was a difficult choice, and both wavered between the two.
At the time of the *Necessary Representation* Ulster was
controlled by the Parliamentarian forces. The Belfast Presby-

tery helped to organise a revolt among the locally controlled armies which resulted in the main Parliamentarian forces being bottled up in Derry. But the treaty with the Confederates made their position untenable, for the reasons Milton outlines; and in the same year the presbytery, now in Bangor, called on the Presbyterians to disassociate themselves from the Royalists. The two documents — the *Necessary Representation* and the Bangor Declaration — were to become centrepieces of the debate in the early eighteenth century on 'Presbyterian loyalty', which we shall be looking at later.[29]

Cromwell finally defeated both the Scots and the Irish, and a military government was imposed throughout the British Isles. The Confederates were deprived of their property and political rights, and a new Protestant landowning class was imposed on the south of Ireland. The effects were less dramatic in the north, where a Protestant landowning class, together with a largely Protestant population, was already in place. The new government, however, introduced an 'Engagement', an oath which ministers were required to sign, renouncing Charles II (who had finally thrown in his lot with the Scottish Covenanters and been proclaimed king in Scotland, only to be defeated at the Battles of Dunbar and Worcester). Most of the Presbyterian ministers refused to sign and were forced to flee to Scotland, leaving only six or seven of their number, conducting services in private houses and hunted by the army.[30]

The Interregnum of 1649-60 was a period of ecclesiastical anarchy in which the first preference of the military government was for the 'Independent' system of church organisation by which each congregation had the right to order its own affairs independently of any other congregation. The Anglican, Presbyterian and Roman Catholic systems all saw the church as a body which, even if it was completely subject to the civil power, was still a distinct administrative unit, covering the whole nation, with its own discipline which individual congregations were expected to observe. Not only did the new government oppose this in principle, but among the Independents there was a strongly established view that the true church should consist only of those who were visibly saved and who could prove to the congregation that they had good reason for believing themselves to be among the elect. This was especially the view of the Baptists, for whom only adults who could show that they possessed grace could be baptised.

In Scotland Presbyterianism was too strongly established to be interfered with, and the Ulster ministers who went to Scotland seem to have had no difficulty in being placed in congregations. In England a functioning parish system was already in existence, for the most part supplied with ministers who, deprived of the upper levels of their church organisation, became *de facto* Independents. But the Church of Ireland had not managed to establish such a parish system. Over wide areas of the country the new administration was faced with what one of them referred to as 'a white paper'. Nor was the population, either Catholic or Protestant, in any way predisposed towards Independent or Baptist ideas — and in the early 1650s the Baptists were a very strong element in the army in Ireland. In Ireland the saints were ruling over a country in which there was virtually no provision for the ministrations of any sort of Christian religion, since Roman Catholicism was being rooted out with a ferocity that was never seen before or since.[31]

Ulster was, of course, the most promising ground for those who shared a basic Calvinist theology — but the Ulster Calvinists had delcared that the new government was a usurping tyranny. They would submit to it because they had no option, but they would not acknowledge its legality and would support a restoration of the monarchy the moment it became possible. Ulster shared this attitude with Scotland, and its proximity to Scotland rendered it very dangerous in the eyes of the Dublin administration — hence the proposal for transplanting the Ulster Presbyterian population to Tipperary.

There was also a small Presbyterian population in the south, mainly grouped round Cork. This had more of an English character. It was a faction within Anglicanism, and its leading spokesman, Dr Edward Worth, was to become a bishop after the Restoration. Worth had his counterparts in Ulster. We have already mentioned the Presbytery of the Route, which refused to acknowledge the authority of the presbytery established by the Scots in the 1640s. Its leading spokesman was Thomas Vesey, who conformed after the Restoration and whose son, a future bishop, published the collected works of Bramhall, the great Anglican opponent of Presbyterianism. Worth's Presbyterianism took the form of arguing for informal 'associations' of ministers to enable them to co-operate in the work of reorganising parishes and evangelising the country. Such associations were also being formed in England and are largely associated with the name of Richard Baxter, later a leading advocate for attempting to reconcile Presbyterian and episcopal principles — devising a form of episcopal government which would administer a close Presbyterian-style moral discipline. By the mid-1650s the principle of association was beginning to gain favour with the administrations both in England and Ireland. The elements of the old order — an absolute sovereign, an advisory parliament, a national church — were gathering together again.

As part of this policy, the Presbyterians began to be tolerated. Adair describes a debate in which he participated with some Independent ministers in 1652, in which the main point of difference was that the Independents would only allow the elect into the church, while the Presbyterians allowed everyone except the openly scandalous. It is clear that the Presbyterian system was more suitable to the church's role as a means of social organisation. After the debate the persecution began to loosen up. The proposal to transport the Ulster Presbyterians to Tipperary was made in 1653 and seems to have been a device to enable the re-establishment of a Presbyterian church, safely removed from Scotland. However unfair it might have been to the residents of Tipperary, considerable efforts were put into making it attractive to the Presbyterians. Presbyterian meetings were resumed in 1654. The government began to pay ministers salaries in 1655, though this was objected to on the grounds that they felt they had a legal right to tithes rather than to government stipends. They were given the right to tithes in 1657, and by the end of the decade there were at least seventy Presbyterian ministers in the province, divided into five 'meetings' which, Adair insists, did not have the full rights of presbyteries. They could not send prospective ministers to be tried by congregations, or ordain without the permission of the whole body (though whether or not presbyteries have the right to ordain without the permission of the whole church or synod has continued to be a matter of controversy in Presbyterian thinking to the present day).[32]

This, then, is the period in which the organised Presbyterian Church was established in Ulster, and this was in general the structure with which the ministers withstood ejection from their parishes after the Restoration. The ministers came from Scotland, and the great majority had not been in Ireland during the turbulent 1640s. They came at a particular moment in the history of the Church of Scotland, when it was split into two great parties; and it will be useful to finish with a comment on this which will give us some idea of what sort of people the founders of the Presbyterian Church in Ulster were.

We have seen that, after the execution of his father, Charles was finally forced, very reluctantly, to throw in his lot with the Scottish Presbyterians and was proclaimed king in Scotland in 1650. As the price of his acceptance, he had to sign the Covenants and solemnly renounce his father's errors. The Presbyterians wanted a 'Covenanted King', a king who could be guaranteed to establish Presbyterianism throughout the British Isles. The Stuarts, however, were poor material for this ambition. They had been at war with Scottish Presbyterianism since the Reformation, and though, as King of Scotland, Charles might be under the continual supervision of the church, as King of England he would be out of their reach. How could his conversion to the Covenant, as bitter and reluctant as it obviously was, be genuine?

This issue split the church into two parties, called Remonstrants and Resolutioners. The Remonstrants had doubts about Charles's sincerity and resolved to withhold their support from him until he had proved that his professed adherence to the Covenant was genuine; the Resolutioners condemned their decision and declared that Charles's action in signing the Covenants was sufficient to justify their support of him. The Remonstrants proving to be in a minority, they withdrew and formed a separate synod, known as the Protestors' Synod. The division, however, was not quite that simple. The Resolutioner Synod had around 750 ministers, as against the Protestors' 113. According to Ian Cowan's study of the Covenanters, however, only 600 of the Resolutioners had actually subscribed the Resolution. The rest included many who opposed it but who regarded the establishment of a separate synod by the Protestors as an act of schism. Throughout the 1650s there was a party in both camps anxious to heal the breach, and these included Robert Blair in the Resolutioner Synod and John Livingstone in the Protestors' Synod.[33]

When the Ulster Presbytery was formed again, one of its first actions was to devise the 'Act of Bangor' to prevent the dispute from being imported into Ireland. As one of the means for achieving this, ministers from Scotland were only accepted if they could produce testimonials from 'worthy ministers' on both sides of the division. Since the division was very fierce, we may assume that these ministers belonged to the moderate party that was seeking accommodation. This 'moderate party' in church affairs, however, was an intractable party in its attitude to state affairs. The great majority of those in the Resolutioner Synod who had actually supported the Resolution conformed after the Restoration. We shall see that conformity was made more difficult in Ireland than in Scotland, but it is still impressive that hardly any of the Ulster ministers conformed. During the Interregnum an extreme wing of the Protestors entered into an alliance with the Cromwellians, securing a statute which, if it had been implemented, would have given a committee sympathetic to them the un-Presbyterian right to nominate and depose ministers throughout the whole of Scotland. We can assume that the centre party which formed the Ulster Presbyterian interest was made up mainly of members of the Resolutioner Synod who had opposed the Resolution, together with members of the Protestors' Synod who opposed the accommodation with the Cromwellian regime. They were principled enough to resist very strong political pressure on both sides, yet flexible enough to agree to sink their differences in the Act of Bangor. It was a combination that was to serve them well in the difficult years following the Restoration.[34]

3

A Church without
Patrons

---

1. *The Restoration*

If the world was turned upside down during the Interregnum,
it still retained its basic shape and sprang back again with
remarkable speed at the Restoration. The Cromwellians had
failed to establish new authoritative forms of government.
They had even failed to establish new political principles
which could survive as a credible dissenting opposition. The
'Whig' principle of a limited monarchy — a sovereignty
divided between parliament and the king — was based on the
experience of the Long Parliament of the 1640s. The tradition
which had been suppressed in Pride's Purge was revived to
undertake the work of the Restoration, triumphed with the
Glorious Revolution, and was finally ratified with the
Hanoverian succession. This political tradition was associated
with English Presbyterianism, but English Presbyterianism, as
we have seen, was somewhat different from Scottish Presbyterianism.

Scottish Presbyterianism also held to the idea of divided
sovereignty, but it saw sovereignty as divided between the
king and the church. Gilbert Burnet, the Scottish Episcopalian
who played a prominent role in the Glorious Revolution,
describes in his *History of His Own Time* how the King of
Scotland came to control the Scottish parliament. The
business of the parliament was determined by the 'Lords of
the Articles' who were largely controlled by the king, through
his power over the bishops. The king chose eight members,
and the rest were chosen as follows: 'The nobility came to
choose eight bishops, and the bishops to choose eight noble-

men: and these sixteen choose the eight barons (so the representatives for the shires are called), and the eight burgesses. By this means our king did upon the matter choose all the Lords of the Articles. So entirely had they got the liberties of that parliament into their hands.' (p. 210) The power the nobility exercised over the king was largely extra-parliamentary, violent, and considerably less effective if the king was out of their reach in London. The royalist ideal would undoubtedly have been a Scottish parliament and an English church.

The Long Parliament, in its debates on the recommendations of the Westminster divines, had rejected the Scottish Presbyterian ideal of a church independent of and in some respects sovereign over the civil government. The English Presbyterians broadly accepted the Long Parliament's view, and there was to be no substantial English equivalent of the Scottish Covenanting movement based on the Second Book of Discipline's ideal of the Two Kingdoms. English Presbyterianism was a movement which at first concentrated on the need for a closer moral supervision exercised by ministers over their parishes. Its representative figure was Richard Baxter, who rejected the term 'Presbyterian' and called himself a 'moderate Episcopalian'. His moderate Episcopalianism manifested itself in a call for a great increase in the number of bishops presiding as permanent moderators, over much smaller dioceses. His great objection to Episcopalian discipline as practised in the Anglican Church was that the bishop's authority was too remote: the bishops' courts, presiding over very large dioceses, could not possibly exercise a close scrutiny over the moral life of individual parishioners, and the parish minister was not given any disciplinary authority distinct from the bishops' courts. Baxter believed that his tighter discipline could be incorporated into the Church of England under the supervision of the king, and this was the substance of his demands at the Savoy Conference, held after the Restoration to organise the re-establishment of the church. A delegation of Ulster Presbyterians had arrived in London in 1661 to present a loyal address to the king and were persuaded by, among others, the London Presbyterian ministers to remove references to the renewal of the Covenant and to the suppression of prelacy.[35]

At the time of the Restoration the Presbyterians were, superficially, very strong. The great mass of the Presbyterian Church in Scotland, both Resolutioner and Protestor, was still effectively in operation, had refused to recognise the validity of the military government, and supported the Restoration. The Long Parliament, which had legislated for Presbyterianism, reassembled in England to call for the return of the king. The military administration in Dublin was over-thrown, and a Protestant Convention was held which, in the absence of bishops, also had a Presbyterian hue. The illusion was short-lived, however, and within three years the model of government in church and state which had preceded the civil war was re-established in all three kingdoms. In particular, Laud's programme of church reform, which had precipitated the civil war, was enacted almost in its entirety.

The ease with which episcopacy was restored seems most surprising in Scotland, and it shows that Presbyterianism could not yet be taken for granted as the natural condition of the Scottish Protestant mind. The Scottish Presbyterians were still a faction in the church — a faction that had taken power in alliance with a powerful faction of the nobility. But the Church of Scotland had been an unequivocally Episcopalian church for forty years before the Covenanting movement, which had plunged the country into war follow-ed by an English military occupation. Bishops, as we have just seen, were an important part of the Scottish constitution and of the power of the monarchy, whose restoration was seen on all sides as essential to peace and national unity. The architect of the restoration of episcopacy was James Sharp, a leading spokesman for the Resolutioners during the Cromwellian period. Although Sharp and Robert Leighton, Bishop of Dunblane, were ordained by English bishops to secure recognition by the English church, they did not insist on the Episcopalian re-ordination of Scottish ministers. Presbyteries continued in existence, except that they now had to be licensed by the bishops. The church was decidedly 'low' in its forms of worship, and its doctrine continued to be Calvinist. A strong party within it, of which Leighton was the representative figure, was anxious to arrive at an accom-modation with the principled Presbyterians who had refused to accept the new arrangements.

They were the more anxious because, if Protestant Scotland as a whole was not militantly Presbyterian, particular areas undoubtedly were, and in some of these the restored church had only a nominal existence. The area in which Presbyterianism was strongest was the south-west — Ayr, Galloway, Kirkcudbrightshire, Dumfriesshire — the area facing the north of Ireland.[36]

2. *A Unique Dissenting Church*

The period between the Restoration and the Revolution is probably the most remarkable and heroic period in Ulster Presbyterian history, yet, since they were not able to publish their own opinions at the time, little is known about it. Patrick Adair's *True Narrative*, which is a most interesting account of the origin and development of the church by a man closely involved in its most crucial stages, was intended to take the story to 1690, but finishes in 1670. McBride's *Sample of Jet-Black Prelatic Calumny* and Kirkpatrick's *Historical Essay upon the Loyalty of Presbyterians*, which aim to trace and explain the political behaviour of the Presbyterians in the seventeenth century, and which will be discussed when we come to the controversies of which they were a part, both have more to say about the English and Scottish Dissenters than about the Ulster Dissenters at this time. Yet we know from the results of it that the achievement of the Ulster Dissenters was quite exceptional. They formed an organised Dissenting church — arguably the first unified Dissenting church in the British Isles to incorporate many different congregations.

They were the first set of ministers after the Restoration to be ejected for Nonconformity. If we accept the evidence presented by McConnell in his *Fasti of the Irish Presbyterian Church*, only about five out of about seventy ministers who had been part of the Presbyterian organisation at this period conformed (the confusion of church organisation in this period is such that it would be impossible to give precise figures as to who could or could not be counted as a Presbyterian). By contrast, the great majority of ministers active in the Cromwellian period both in Scotland and in England conformed. There is, of course, a difference in scale. About 300 ministers in Scotland and, according to Baxter, 1,800 in England were ejected. These still constituted minorities. In making the comparison we should also bear in mind that the Ulster Presbyterian Church was a creation of the militant Presbyterian movement of the 1640s, built by young ministers with a missionary zeal for Presbyterianism. The Churches of Scotland and England were Episcopalian churches which had Presbyterianism imposed on them for political reasons. Most Ulster Presbyterian ministers, if they conformed, would have to be regarded as turncoats; the same judgment would not be fair if applied to most ministers of either the Church of England or the Church of Scotland.[37]

Furthermore, the Scottish ministers were not asked to submit to episcopal re-ordination. The Ulster ministers were. The new Archbishop of Armagh was none other than John Bramhall, the former Laudian Bishop of Derry, who had suppressed the fledgeling Presbyterianism of the 1630s. The new Bishop of Down and Connor, the area in which Presbyterianism was strongest, was Jeremy Taylor, one of the most respected figures in the literary history of Anglicanism, but a man strongly committed to a 'high' notion of the rights of bishops. Both Bramhall and Taylor, engaged in controversy with Roman Catholic writers, had argued that the true authority of the church resided in the bishops and that the great apostasy of Roman Catholicism lay in the pope's having given episcopal rights to ordinary priests. Bramhall in the 1640s, opposing the Solemn League and Covenant when it was being introduced in England, had written a powerful polemic against Presbyterianism, especially against its discipline. He argued, in effect, that the power claimed by the kirk session over the individual member of the congregation was an unwarrantable imposition on the freedom of the individual. He explicitly supported the view of Thomas Erastus that the ministrations of the church were rights to be demanded of the priest and only to be withdrawn in very exceptional circumstances after due process of law through the bishops' courts. Presbyterianism was to be suppressed in the name of freedom because it was a petty tyranny over the conscience and conduct of the individual.[38]

The Presbyterian ministers refused to recognise the authority of bishops and, of course, refused to submit to episcopal re-ordination. They were therefore expelled from their livings. It is just possible to imagine a system by which they could have continued to occupy the parishes and receive the tithes of the Church of Ireland while refusing to recognise its national constitution. The English Presbyterian ideal of 'comprehension' within the Church of England implied something of the sort, while in Scotland an experiment along these lines was actually put into practice with some success by means of the First and Second Indulgences of Charles II issued in 1669 and 1672. Under these, Presbyterian ministers were introduced to parishes, receiving their tithes, in areas in which it was impossible to establish the Episcopalian system, but under very tight conditions, basically intended to prevent them from proselytising. Such ideas were not considered in Ireland in 1661, and in the event the Church of Ireland, in the absence of Bramhall and Taylor, both of whom died within a few years of the Restoration, tried, without expressing it as a principle or as a policy, the more radical experiment of a toleration.

The ejection of the Presbyterian ministers was followed by an attempted *coup d'état*, led by Colonel Thomas Blood, which had some old Cromwellian and Presbyterian support. The result was the almost complete scattering and suppression of the ministers. Readers should remember that at this time there was no police, no permanent machinery for enforcing the law (the permanent presence of a massive army had been one of the secrets of Cromwell's success in the art of government). Thus the Presbyterians, like Catholic priests, could be suppressed completely by one military action, but it was more difficult to keep them in a continuous state of suppression. We have seen them suppressed twice before — in the 1630s by Bramhall and his friends, and in the early 1650s by the Cromwellians. On both occasions they came back in added strength. They did so in the 1660s as well, but there was one remarkable difference.

The ministers suppressed in the 1630s had been ministers of the Church of Ireland, with a legal right to its tithes. They had returned under the protection first of the Scots army, then of the parliamentary commissioners, who restored them to the rights of Church of Ireland ministers. After their suppression in the 1650s some returned on the mere basis of what appeared to be a practical toleration, but the main body, consisting largely of new ministers, appeared after a salary was granted in 1655 or, in even greater numbers, after tithes were restored in 1657. Now, in the 1660s, they were returning against continued government opposition and with no prospect of any income other than that voluntarily provided by their own congregation in addition to the tithes they were legally obliged to pay to the established Episcopalian minister. They had no prospect even of a church or a manse other than what could be provided, voluntarily and illegally, by their own congregation. Yet by 1670 they had returned in such numbers that the church was restored to its old strength.

The most extraordinary thing, however, is that they re-established their 'meetings' of ministers, or presbyteries. This, so far as I can see, is unique in the British Isles and flies in the face of one of the most fundamental principles of government policy. The government recognised that it could not legislate for private conscience, and that while it could legislate to prevent individuals from giving and receiving the ministrations of a particular sect, it was very difficult to enforce this legislation. What it could do was to prevent the emergence of churches uniting several different congregations into a coherent organisation, and this was the burden of the fierce Clarendon Code introduced in England in the 1660s. Such an organised, or 'connexional', church, especially if it had a vigorous discipline of its own, could only be seen as a political society within society whose highest religious duties were owed to a structure independent of the state and in some degree antagonistic to it. In the case of the Scottish and Ulster Presbyterians we could say that their antagonism to the state was particularly strong, since they had not repudiated the Covenant which obliged them to 'extirpate' prelacy — now the established form of church government in all three kingdoms.

In England the government was aided by the nature of English Dissent. The Independents, who had the spirit of opposition to the government in a higher degree than the English Presbyterians, were in principle opposed to any connexional form of church organisation. The English Presbyterians, on the other hand, were finally committed to the ideal of a national church, and more prepared than the Scottish Presbyterians to allow the principle of some form of supremacy for the civil government. Their aim was to convert the Church of England, if not to a full Presbyterian system, at least to a 'moderate Episcopalianism' with a much more vigorous discipline, as proposed by Baxter. They had what might be described as fellow-travellers within the Church of England, who were to achieve an ascendancy after the Revolution. They were prepared to a large extent to accept the argument that to organise as a separate connexional church in opposition to the Established Church would be an act of disloyalty. They therefore became *de facto* Independents, distinguished from the principled Independents by their commitment to achieving a national, established, connexional church.[39]

In Scotland the Presbyterians were less inhibited by their own principles. They believed that the church should be independent of the civil government, and the Protestors had already organised in opposition to an established national church. But they too were still strongly wedded to the national church as an ideal and were reluctant to reduce themselves to the level of a sect. The First and Second Indulgences of Charles II gave many of them the opportunity to come back into the Established Church, without acknowledging prelacy, though on condition that they did not attempt to set up presbytery. Others, as Burnet points out, were able to go to Ireland. The great danger faced by the government was the rise of what were known as 'conventicles' and the popularity of 'field preachers' gathering together large crowds of people in the open air to listen to highly emotional sermons on the virtues of the Covenant. But this amounted to a reversion to the 'privy kirk' of the 1620s revivals. The conventiclers and field preachers did not form presbyteries. An attempt to do so in the 1670s foundered on disagreements as to the degree to which they could co-operate with the 'indulged' ministers, and the degree to which they were entitled to use violence against the prelatical establishment. A union, or 'General Correspondence of Praying Societies', was briefly established by the most militant elements in the early 1680s under the fierce persecution of the Duke of York (later James II), but in the almost total absence of ordained ministers this was largely a lay affair.[40]

In general, we may say that Scottish Presbyterianism was divided between those who sought or were prepared to accept an accommodation with the national church, and those who functioned as independents, were determined to settle for nothing short of the full Presbyterian ideal, and found themselves in the 1660s, the late 1670s and early 1680s in a state of war with the establishment.

In Ulster the ideal of a national Presbyterian church was never very realistic, and the Ulster Presbyterians very rarely thought in 'national' terms. They concentrated on organising themselves as a dissenting Presbyterian society. To do this a certain tact was required. To a large extent we must acknowledge that they were being permitted to do it, both by the government and by the Established Church. But they had to operate within certain limits. The ministers of particular localities met as presbyteries, but they did not meet all together as a synod. Reid quotes a passage from the minutes of the Presbytery of Antrim which shows the church going to great lengths to disguise the fact that they were ordaining ministers on their own authority. Ordained ministers were to go to Scotland for some time after they had been ordained, and to return as if they had been ordained there. They had a particular enemy in the person of Robert Leslie, Bishop of Raphoe, son of Henry Leslie, who, as Bishop of Down and Connor, had co-operated with Bramhall in the 1630s. He secured the imprisonment of four ministers between 1666 and 1670 for refusing to answer a summons. An attempt to charge and imprison twelve ministers in Down was defeated by the Primate, and in 1681 the entire Presbytery of Laggan was imprisoned, though for less than a year, for proclaiming a public fast.[41]

As persecutions go, this amounts to toleration, especially since in 1672, the year of the Scottish Second Indulgence, the Ulster Presbyterian ministers were actually given a grant of money by the king — the first instalment of the famous *regium donum*. A major condition of this toleration was that they prevented the militant Scottish Covenanters from agitating in Ireland. Adair describes the embarrassment of the ministers in the 1660s when, with a long political experience to guide them, they declined to work up popular feeling against the re-establishment of the Episcopalian Church and were therefore accused of lukewarmness by many of their own people and by a group of young ministers of whom the most prominent was Michael Bruce, ancestor of the William Bruce whom we shall meet at the turn of the nineteenth century. The agitators were soon rounded up and expelled, only to be replaced later by David Houston, founder of the Reformed Presbyterian tradition which we shall also be meeting again later.[42]

Some of Bruce's sermons given in Scotland have survived, and in one of them is found this graphic description of the life of a Scottish Covenanting minister belonging to the 'privy kirk':

> This is ay the comfort that a poor minister hath to gang out and preach to a people and country-side. Would ye ken what he can promise himself? Nothing: but this. He is sure of the fury of the magistrate in the place he comes to, and he is sure of the fury of the curate in the parish; and he is sure of the fury of a whean graceless folk; and he is sure of the censure of a whean Old Jobb-trot-Christians [*sic*] that hath joined with the curates, and if there be any dunts in dealing he will get his share of them; yet go they must and do their duty they must. (*Six Dreadful Alarms*, p. 18)

In another sermon he attacks the ministers who have taken the Second Indulgence and those Scottish Christians who will only support the church if it is clear that God is actively supporting it:

> Some times thou had a room in Christ's body; thou was either a hand or a foot or something; but now since thou had slipped a buckle, thou is become useless. (*The Rattling of the Dry Bones*, p. 22)

But his view remains optimistic:

Now there are many Christians, because he has given the
house a shake to make the loose stones fall out, they think
the house will all be ruined; no sirs, it is to make the loose
stones fall out that he may gather them together in a rickle
be themselves to be laid aside for they shall never be put in
the wall again . . . and mistake him not when he doth so
for he is about to build. (ibid., p. 38)

It is possible, as Bramhall did, to take the formal position
of the Presbyterians and show that it amounts to a despotic
interference with the individual's private life. It is certainly
possible, and in my view right, to be horrified at the prospect
of an all-embracing national Presbyterian church, thoroughly
convinced of its own rightness and of the sin of tolerating
heresy — an important feature of the argument of the Belfast
Presbytery's *Necessary Representation*. There are many
reasons for being pleased at the dominance of the Episcopalian
Church of England, with all its internal absurdities and contradictions. Yet it is also impossible not to be thrilled by the
moral courage and strength of individual spirit and integrity
of the Scottish Covenanting tradition. Had the Covenanters
triumphed, they would probably have been appalling, but in
opposition they were magnificent, and, believing that they
were fighting for the spirit, they had their spiritual reward.
As Bruce put it, 'So do and wait for Him in His own way,
and ye shall have a brave life of it.' (*Six Dreadful Alarms*,
p. 23)

3. *The First Synod of Ulster*

The Glorious Revolution of 1689 must have looked like a
fulfilment of Bruce's expectation that the Lord was 'about
to build'. It was a different event in each of the three kingdoms in which it took place. In England it was supported by
nearly all sections of effective political opinion, including
many of those supporters of the High Church and absolute
monarchy who were already beginning to be known as
'Tories'. In Scotland it took the form of a civil war, with the
victorious side being identified with Presbyterianism. In
Ireland, taken as a whole, it took the form of a conquest.[43]

It was, of course, first and foremost an event in English politics. It could be described as a successful re-run of the struggle of the Long Parliament with Charles I — successful because it was not, in England, opposed militarily and therefore did not produce an army able to dominate the outcome as the New Model Army did in the 1650s. Bodin and James I had argued that it was desirable that the king should rule in accordance with the wishes of his parliaments, but that it was not a legal obligation. At best it was a requirement of natural and divine law, which could not be enforced by subjects. The Glorious Revolution established the principle that the consent of parliament was legally necessary.[44]

Why did the Tories, at least initially, not resist it? Part of the answer lies in the danger we have already observed in the High Church theory that the church was a body defined by the rule of bishops. So long as the bishops accepted the supremacy of the king as a fundamental principle of church government, this posed no threat to the state. The elevation of their authority was the elevation of the king's most loyal agents, and it also provided a means by which the Church of England was more closely identified with the intellectual principles of continental Catholicism where, at least in France, the authority of the bishops was being asserted to bolster the national church, loyal to the king, in opposition to the pope. But when the king was not a member of the church, the bishops were placed in an embarrassing position, and their dilemma became even more acute when he took what appeared to them to be active measures in opposition to the church. Both Charles II and James II had encouraged the advancement of a hierarchy with very high notions of its own authority. James I would have recognised the danger. Such a hierarchy, faced by direct conflict between their commission from God and their commission from the king, were likely to start behaving like Presbyterians.

The crisis that brought about the Revolution began as a crisis for High Church Toryism. In England, as in Scotland, there was still a problem as to what to do about the Nonconformists — the still substantial and influential body of opinion left over from the Interregnum who were excluded, by their refusal to join the national church, from national political life. There were three options: repression, accommodation and toleration. By 'accommodation' (or 'comprehension') was meant altering the constitution and discipline of the Church of England so that Nonconformists could join it. A radical experiment in accommodation had been attempted, with some success in Scotland, weakening the Presbyterians and thereby leaving the remnant open to a policy of repression, which, however, produced in 1679 a horrifying civil war in which James himself (then serving as royal commissioner in Scotland, having been removed from England by Charles II so that his open Catholicism would not stimulate the efforts to bar his succession to the throne) was deeply implicated. A large section of opinion both among English Nonconformists and Anglicans (who included many former Presbyterians and Independents who had conformed after 1662) favoured comprehension.

Both Charles and James, however, when they were not engaged in repression, favoured toleration. Comprehension or accommodation with Puritan Presbyterianism was a movement away from the Catholicisation of the Established Church; it meant creating an Established Church that was at once stronger and more Protestant. Both Charles and James were engaged in the delicate task of bringing England, and with it Scotland and Ireland, back into the family of Catholic nations. A policy of toleration meant establishing the principle that churches other than the Established Church could operate more or less freely in society. It was politically impossible to demand this freedom for the Roman Catholic Church alone, but it could be demanded for its members in conjunction with the Protestant Dissenters, and once the general principle of toleration was established, it could more easily be extended in favour of the Roman Catholic Church. An indulgence would also have the effect of encouraging those sympathetic towards Protestant Dissent to leave the Established Church, thus facilitating its Catholicisation. Charles had attempted to pursue this policy, which helps to explain his grant of the *regium donum* to the Ulster Presbyterians and his encouragement of a lenient policy towards them (a policy James would soon have reason to regret). James's Declaration of Indulgence of 1687, granting a measure of toleration to all Dissenters, both Protestant and Roman Catholic, was an extension of the same policy.

James's mistake was his attempt to enforce this policy through a Church of England whose anti-Puritanism and high notion of its own authority he and his brother had done everything in their power to promote. He provoked a revolt among his own High Church supporters, and we are confronted with the bizarre spectacle of the champions of absolute monarchy refusing to obey the king and being supported by the Whigs, despite the fact that their cause was to uphold the prerogatives of the church against the rights being given to Dissenters. It is at this point that the world being turned upside down begins to change its shape.[45]

The terms 'Whig' and 'Tory' were beginning to come into general use in the 1680s, referring respectively to the party which wished to exclude James from the throne on account of his religion, and the party which believed that parliament did not have the right to interfere with the lawful succession of its monarch. 'Tory' was a nickname for the Irish bandits led by former Catholic gentry who had been deprived of their lands and were now living by brigandage. 'Whig' was a well-established nickname for the Scottish Covenanters. The Irish Tories had largely come to notice through the exploits of Redmond O'Hanlon in the 1670s, and the Scottish Whigs through the civil war that was raging in parts of Scotland at the same time. Tories were Irish Catholic rebels; Whigs were Scottish Presbyterian rebels. A society dominated by two forces for whom these were seen as appropriate nicknames was an uncomfortable one for an absolute monarch. It is an ironic fact, which becomes clearer after the Revolution, that English Tory loyalism is almost as troublesome a political tradition as Whig parliamentarianism. We may here note in passing what we have already observed in Sir John Davies's defence of absolute monarchy and John Bramhall's defence of the Church of England: that the English rationale for concentrating all power in the hands of the monarch was to free the individual member of the commonwealth from his subordinate obligations. (Hobbes, often but wrongly seen as a father-figure of totalitarianism, also argued that the centralisation of power was the only possible condition for the freedom of the individual.) The merit of the Church of England, as against Presbyterianism and even Independency, was that it did not attempt to regulate the moral life of the individual, who could regard its ministrations as rights to be claimed rather than rewards to be earned. The anarchic streak in English Toryism can be seen at a very early stage in its development.[46]

The Revolution in England created two claimants to the throne and forced the other two kingdoms to choose between them. Scotland was divided. Ireland chose James.

The news of the English Revolution which had brought over a Presbyterian claimant to the throne resulted in a Presbyterian uprising in Scotland, similar in kind to the risings of 1666 and 1679, except that now there was no lawful authority to oppose the insurgents. The success of this rising was not due to any sudden popular conversion of Scotland to Presbyterian principles, but more to the fact that the Presbyterians knew what they wanted and were prepared to fight for it, while the moderate Episcopalians were quite disorientated. Their two basic ideas, loyalty to the king and strong anti-Catholicism, were in conflict. But the rising was only effective south of the Tay. North of the Tay the Episcopalian clergy held on and were defended by their parishioners well into the 1690s.

The Presbyterians controlled Edinburgh when a Convention of Estates met there in March to decide how to respond to the crisis. William's chief adviser on Scottish affairs, William Carstares, was a Presbyterian, and Holland had been a favourite resort for Scottish Presbyterian exiles. The Bishop of Edinburgh on behalf of the Episcopalian Church of Scotland had made a very ambiguous submission to William ('Sir, I will serve you so far as law, reason, or conscience shall allow me'), and an influential part of the Episcopalian nobility quickly withdrew from the Convention to join John Graham of Claverhouse, Viscount Dundee, famous for his part in putting down the Covenanters, in raising the Highland clans for James. What remained of the Convention was then, under pressure both on the ground and, initially at least, from the new king, able to declare for Presbyterianism. The first General Assembly of the Presbyterian Church of Scotland, as we know it today, met in 1690, made up of those ministers still living who had been expelled from the Church of Scotland in 1661. It was an assembly of old men, quite unrepresentative of the religious life of Scotland at the time. Nevertheless, the policy of alliance with the Presbyterians served the Williamites well, since at the Battle of Dunkeld in August 1689, by what appears to have been a military freak, a regiment drawn from the militant Covenanters, or 'Cameronians', broke the back of the unstable Highland alliance that Claverhouse had put together for James.[47]

James's real stronghold was Ireland. He had cultivated Ireland — and an Irish army — as a reliably Catholic centre on which he could fall back, or which could be used if necessary to impose Catholicism on England. Since 1687 an unrestrained policy of advancing Catholics and demoting Protestants had been pursued. The Irish Catholic gentry, who had been encouraged in a more timid fashion under Charles, had rapidly been formed into a coherent national leadership, controlling the town corporations and the army. When the news of William's landing and James's flight arrived, James's Lord Deputy, the Catholic Richard Talbot, Earl of Tyrconnell, hesitated momentarily, but when he threw in his lot with James, the whole country, with the exception of Protestant Ulster, was mobilised in about a month.[48]

It is sometimes suggested that no distinctly Irish interests were represented in this confrontation between a Dutch prince and an English king. William's army was certainly international in character. In addition to its importance in British history, the Battle of the Boyne was, of course, an event of considerable importance in European history. William was locked in a battle against the expansionist policies of Louis XIV, who had ambitions on all his frontiers and whose aggressive intentions concerning the Spanish Netherlands posed a particular threat to the United Provinces. William had helped to form a coalition of all the major European powers against France, a coalition that included the Catholic powers Spain and Austria and was supported by the pope. Louis had pursued a policy of buying the neutrality of England. For William the Revolution was a means of bringing England into his alliance, thus completely encircling France and depriving Louis of a potential ally. Hence the international nature of William's army.

James's army, however was Irish and was enthusiastically committed to his cause. There was, of course, an important French element as well, but Catholic Ireland recognised that this was its last chance to throw over the Cromwellian land settlement and the Protestant ascendancy. There was now no question of a return to the freedoms of the pre-Elizabethan aristocracy. That might have been an element in the Confederation of Kilkenny, and a strong element in Owen Roe O'Neill's army. There was in 1690 a freewheeling parody of Owen Roe O'Neill among the Ulster Gaels in the person of Hugh Ballderg O'Donnell. But in the main the Irish army was royalist. It accepted that Ireland could only exist as a commonwealth under a king, and that the only available king who could be expected to favour Catholicism was James.

The struggle in Ireland was between Catholicism and Protestantism, with Protestantism finding substantial support only in Ulster.

This picture is not at all altered by the pope's support for King William. The pope had great European concerns on his mind, in particular the interests of Catholic Spain and Austria. James's ally Louis had made a declaration of independence from the Roman Catholic Church, with the result that a very large part of the French Catholic Church was under papal interdict. The prospect of England becoming Catholic was no doubt attractive, but it was now clear that James could not achieve it. The fact that Catholic Ireland was engaged in a life-and-death struggle was, necessarily, a minor consideration.[49]

There is no need here to go through the events of the courageous holding operation conducted by the Ulster Protestants against James and Catholic Ireland, or the invasion and reconquest of Ireland by William. What is of interest to us is that the moment it was possible for them to do so — even before the final defeat of Catholic Ireland with the capitulation of Limerick — the Ulster Presbyterian ministers formed themselves into a synod — the Synod of Ulster — the first Protestant Dissenting synod in the British Isles.

The Synod of Ulster was a very different body from the General Assembly of the Church of Scotland. Most obviously, of course, the Church of Scotland was established, while the Synod was dissenting. In some ways this meant that the Synod could be what the Assembly aspired to be. The Assembly aspired to be an independent body whose commission derived directly from Christ the King. In fact it was established, and its constitution determined, by an act of parliament. Throughout the 1690s there was a raging controversy, reminiscent of the quarrels with James VI, over whether or not the Assembly could meet without the permission of the king. It was resolved by an ambiguous formula under which the Assembly would meet at regular times and the king's commissioner would be present; but whether the presence of the king's commissioner was necessary to the existence of a valid, legal Assembly was left an open question. The Synod of Ulster had no such problems. It met on its own authority, when and where it pleased, and no representative of the government was, or was required to be, present.

There were over 900 parishes in Scotland when the General Assembly was established. Over 600 of these, held by Episcopalian ministers, were immediately declared vacant. William wanted the Episcopalian ministers restored, on condition that they accepted a Presbyterian constitution. For most of them, as moderate Episcopalians for whom the form of church government was a matter of indifference, this was no problem; their liturgical practice had in any case been 'low', and their doctrine was Calvinist. But for the doctrinaire Presbyterians who dominated the early General Assembly this was hardly sufficient. The moderate Episcopalians were weak professors who had no real commitment to Presbyterianism, had compromised with the enemy, and had profited while the true Presbyterians had been either forced into a humiliating 'accommodation' or driven into the mountains. The practical problem of supplying parishes was so overwhelming that the Presbyterians were forced to compromise again, allowing Episcopalians back on very stringent conditions. But such compromise was painful to men who believed they had a direct commission from God; and this particular compromise meant that by the end of the decade the Assembly was no longer made up exclusively of militant Covenanting Presbyterians. It was Presbyterian in form, but just as the pre-Revolution Church of Scotland had been dominated by moderate Episcopalians, so the post-Revolution church was dominated by moderate Presbyterians. No such problems were experienced by the Synod of Ulster, which was made up exclusively of people who had held to Presbyterian principles despite repression (even if half-hearted repression) and poverty. We shall see that, ironically enough, this was soon to facilitate a greater theological radicalism among the Ulster ministers.

A third problem experienced by the established Presbyterians but not by the Dissenters in Ulster was to have even more radical effects. This was the problem of patronage, which was to split the Church of Scotland in the middle of the eighteenth century and again in the middle of the nineteenth century. Although the problem did not arise dramatically until after the Union between England and Scotland in 1707, which put the Church of Scotland under the control of a predominately English and Episcopalian parliament, this seems an appropriate point to mention it. In Presbyterian principle, the minister can only take up his office on the basis of a 'call' from the congregation. Yet the parishes of the Church of Scotland, together with the right to collect tithes, constituted a form of property. Much of this property was legally in the hands of 'patrons' — usually drawn from the local gentry — who had the legal right to nominate incumbents. Similar rights were widespread in England and provided a useful variety in the means by which positions in the church could be obtained, against the monopoly of the bishops. One of the first acts of the doctrinaire Presbyterian General Assembly of 1690 was to abolish this right of patronage. But two years after the union the parliament of Great Britain restored it, thus, in principle at least, seriously weakening the General Assembly's right to order its own affairs by treating incumbencies as a form of property to be regulated by the secular law. Presbyterian incumbencies in Ulster, however, had not been a form of legally protected secular property since the ejection of 1661, and the only slightly similar problem they encountered was occasional attempts at interference by (usually Episcopalian) landlords who owned the land on which churches were built.[50]

The Synod of Ulster was a free assembly accountable only to God, that is, to its own interpretation of God's will. Its ministers enjoyed some small royal patronage in the form of the *regium donum*, originally granted by Charles, renewed and increased by William, and suspended for a time by Anne. This came without any conditions. The Synod had no legal status and was subject to periodic harassment by the establishment and its parliament. But this was experienced as harassment from outside, not as any entanglement in a dual sovereignty over the affairs of the church itself. The churches constituting the Synod were in a very real sense a whole community organised according to its own principles, regulating its own affairs independent of the state structure of which the Established Church, with the secular power at its head, was a part. To their opponents in the Church of Ireland, once that church had recovered from the shock of the Revolution, the government's toleration of such a state of affairs was barely credible.

4

Free
to Develop

1. *Distinctive Principles*

Seaton Reid, in his history of the Irish Presbyterian Church, remarks of the Presbyterians after the Revolution that 'from this period their history is, in a great measure, unconnected with that of the country at large' (Vol. II, p. 410).

While that statement requires some qualification, there is a great deal of truth in it. Before the nineteenth century European nations were formed by aristocracies agreeing to sink their differences in a common allegiance to a central power. In the seventeenth century the Irish Catholic aristocracy had been slowly developing in this manner, the high point of the development being the administration of Tyrconnell and the resistance to William of Orange. This was an Irish national unity that had to be opposed by the Ulster Presbyterians. At best it could only offer them the kind of toleration by treaty the Huguenots had enjoyed under the Edict of Nantes, which had shortly before, in 1685, been revoked by James's ally Louis XIV. At worst it held out the prospect of complete suppression, as in all the major European countries, now including France, where a Catholic ascendancy was secure.[51]

Cromwell had introduced a rival, Protestant aristocracy in Ireland whose ascendancy was assured by the success of the Williamite Revolution. In so far as Ireland has a national history, rather than an assemblage of local histories, in the eighteenth century it is the history of this Protestant land-owning class and its parliament. This parliament, however, was a subordinate parliament which under Poynings' Law could only discuss bills whose heads had already been approved in London, where the real sovereignty continued to rest. The Irish parliament also represented only a comparatively superficial caste in Irish society, lacking the common identity with their subordinates which in England was provided by common membership of the Established Church.

Nevertheless, the 1690s is one period in which the Presbyterians might have been able to join in what Irish national life there was. From being virtually a hidden, silent community, they became an open community. Their Synod met openly, and they began to take part in public life, quickly increasing their representation in a number of town corporations (a process that began with James's Declaration of Indulgence) and making efforts to establish congregations outside Ulster. Had this process been allowed to continue, the Protestant ascendancy and its Dublin parliament would have had to take greater account of Presbyterian opinion than they did, and in the 1690s Dublin was indeed the centre of lively disputes between the Presbyterian and Anglican interests.

The leading Presbyterian propagandist of this time was a Dublin minister, Dr Joseph Boyse. Boyse, however, was not a member of the Synod of Ulster. He was an Englishman, born in Leeds, and represents the English rather than the Scottish Presbyterian tradition. Like their English counterparts, Boyse and his southern colleagues were reluctant to organise a distinct dissenting Presbyterian church and wished, as far as possible, to co-operate with the Independents, who had also survived to a small extent in the south. They formed a 'Southern Association', which was a much looser body than the Synod of Ulster and did not claim binding, divinely ordained authority over its members. It was reminiscent of the 'associations' formed by Baxter and others in the English Presbyterian tradition under the Interregnum.[52]

In 1694 William King, Bishop of Derry, published *A Discourse concerning the Inventions of Men in the Worship of God* in the form of a pastoral letter addressed to the Dissenters in his diocese, whom he addressed 'in the spirit of meekness (as one that is appointed by the providence of God and the care of a Christian magistracy to watch over your souls)' (p. 132). In the course of it he describes both Baxter and Boyse as Congregationalists, a description justified by the actual form of church organisation which they implemented (Boyse had in fact preached for a short time in a Brownist church in Amsterdam). He went through the various points in which the worship of the Established and Presbyterian Churches differed, arguing that the Established practice was both more scriptural and better calculated to instruct the people in sound doctrine. Boyse replied the same year with his *Remarks on a Late Discourse*, which, although it was largely a defence of northern Presbyterian practice, indicated that there were certain aspects of it with which he was unhappy, especially the practice of sitting at prayer. Boyse makes it clear that he approves of standing and kneeling, but is opposed to their excessive use and to their being made compulsory. He is himself unconvinced by his own explanation for the northern practice — that people who must travel long distances are too tired to stand, or that the meeting-houses are too small to allow kneeling. But he does not defend it for what it was — a point of principle among the northern Presbyterians. He also argues for more frequent communion, but again points to differences between the English and 'northern' practices.

In discussing the charge that he was a Congregationalist he argues that Christ instituted two churches other than 'particular congregations':

the Catholic Church and such National or Kingdom Churches (as that great light of his age, Mr Baxter, pleads for in his late Discourse on that subject) that is a society consisting of a Christian sovereign magistrate and of Christian subjects worshipping God ordinarily in true particular pastoral Churches, over which the foresaid magistrate exercised coercive government by the sword, as pastors exercise a ministerial one by the Word. . . . What I have asserted in those Reflections is but the common principles wherein both the Presbyterian and Congregational divines are agreed. (p. 150)

He does not think the difference is very great between those (the Presbyterians) who argue that synods have a power of government over the church, and those (the Congregationalists) who argue that they are merely consultative.

Boyse, then, is far from defending the view that the church has a national authority separate from that of the magistrate, and the only connexional church he defends is a national one — co-terminous with the civil society. He is also far from defending a body such as the Synod of Ulster, which was not at all national, yet claimed a right of government. His thinking is in line with the outlook of those English Presbyterians who in the same period had high hopes of reincorporation into the Church of England and who wished to consolidate their strength through agreement with the Independents. In organising the Synod of Ulster the Ulster Presbyterians had set themselves firmly against any such accommodation within the Church of Ireland. In the 1690s there was a Calvinist king; a Presbyterian church had just been established in Scotland; the Church of England was in disarray and under pressure to accommodate the English Dissenters. The Ulster Presbyterians had every reason to believe that they could advance on their own terms.

2. *Understanding History*

Such hopes for progress came to an end with the accession of Queen Anne. William's claim to the throne had been based on his marriage to Queen Mary, daughter of James. He had insisted, however, on being recognised as king in his own right, not simply as Mary's consort. Tories could work out a theory by which Mary could be recognised as a valid sovereign. But in 1694 Mary died, leaving William to rule alone until his own death in 1702. Strict Tories, who fell short of Jacobitism, had to regard that period as a virtual interregnum. But Anne, Mary's sister, was in the rightful succession, provided that arguments could be found for excluding James and his son, the Old Pretender. Whereas Mary was devoted to her Dutch Calvinist husband, moreover, Anne had been raised in England under the care of the Bishop of London, at a time when Charles and James were encouraging the Church of England to be as 'high' and as nearly Roman Catholic as possible. Her accession to the throne gave new life to the Tory case, which mainly took the form of a defence of the Established Church against encroachment by the Dissenters. The effect of this was felt in Ireland in 1704, when a bill prepared by the Irish parliament for the suppression of Catholics was returned from the English parliament with a clause added barring from public office Protestant Dissenters who refused to take the sacrament according to the rites of the Church of Ireland. The bill was passed by the Irish parliament and, despite the formal protests that had been registered against the clause concerning the Protestant Dissenters, was taken as a signal by the Church of Ireland that a counter-offensive against the Presbyterians was now possible. A pamphlet war, in which Jonathan Swift participated in support of the Church of Ireland, now opened, and in the course of it a distinct Ulster Presbyterian political outlook and view of their own history – broadly corresponding to the English 'Whig' view of history – began to emerge.[53]

One of the earliest salvoes in the literary battle came from England in the form of a pamphlet entitled *The Parallel, or Persecution of Protestants the Shortest Way to Prevent the Growth of Popery in Ireland*, published anonymously in 1705 by Daniel Defoe. Defoe had recently become something of a hero in London for his *The Shortest Way with the Dissenters*, published in 1702 after the accession of Queen Anne. This took the form of a call from a 'High Church Tory' to apply to the English Protestant Dissenters the same principles that Louis XIV had applied to the Huguenots: 'Moses was a merciful, meek man, and yet with what fury did he run through the camp and cut the throats of three and thirty thousand of his dear Israelites who were fallen into idolatry; what was the reason? 'twas mercy to the rest, to make these be examples to prevent the destruction of the whole army.' (pp 20-1) Defoe was imprisoned when the pamphlet was discovered to be a satirical imposture.

The Parallel supported the main principles of the 1704 bill to prevent the further growth of popery, but argued that it was an absurdity that such a bill against Roman Catholicism should contain a clause that also discriminated against Protestants. He argued that this could only be explained on the basis of sinister intentions: Ireland was 'a mark, a buoy on the covered rock, a notice of concealed mischiefs, a warning-piece to all the Protestant world' (p. 2), as shown by the 1641 rising and the reign of Tyrconnell. The new bill was a further blow directed against Irish Presbyterianism which would soon be turned against English Protestantism. He then briefly outlined the behaviour and record of Ulster Presbyterians during the seventeenth century, arguing that they had always been loyal to England and to the crown, and drawing special attention to the 1649 protest against the execution of the king.

In 1709 this argument, together with the claim in an address to the queen from the Dissenting ministers in the north of Ireland that they had been loyal to the crown 'in all changes and turns of government', were attacked in a pamphlet entitled *A Sample of True-Blue Presbyterian Loyalty* by Dr William Tisdall, Vicar of Belfast. Tisdall had been a friend of Swift's, though their relationship had cooled when he proposed to Esther Johnson, Swift's 'Stella', in 1704. His pamphlet argued that the Presbyterians had been determined enemies of monarchical government, as their behaviour towards James and Charles and their role in the civil war had proved. Against Defoe's citing the 1649 *Necessary Representation* from Belfast, Tisdall quoted the Presbytery of Belfast's Bangor Declaration of the same year calling on Presbyterians not to support the Royalist army of Viscount Ards. In 1712 Tisdall published *The Conduct of the Dissenters* (the title being a conscious echo of Swift's then very popular attack on the conduct of the European war in which England had been embroiled by William — *The Conduct of the Allies*). Tisdall's pamphlet attacked the behaviour of the Ulster Presbyterians after the Restoration, and especially the political advances they had made in the 1690s, which were now being rolled back.

Two replies to Tisdall were published in 1713: John McBride's *A Sample of Jet-Black Prelatic Calumny* and James Kirkpatrick's *An Historical Essay upon the Loyalty of Presbyterians in Great Britain and Ireland*. Both pamphlets are of special interest to us here, firstly because they are the first substantial pieces of literature published within the Ulster Presbyterian tradition (Adair's *Narrative* was not published until the nineteenth century), and secondly because they both represent a serious effort on the part of their authors to take stock of the experience of the seventeenth century and to explain, in the light of the Glorious Revolution, how loyalty to the king could be reconciled with opposition — even armed opposition — to his laws and his church. Defoe's *Parallel* had offered a far too simple account of the undeviating loyalty of Irish Presbyterianism. It had been easy for Tisdall to demolish it. It was now necessary for the Presbyterians to engage in a much fuller explanation of their principles and recent history.

Both pamphlets argue for limited monarchy — that if the king trangresses the limits of his authority, he can be called to account by his subjects. But both are somewhat vague as to how the limits of the king's authority are to be defined. According to McBride,

> That the reasoning part of mankind have ever declared themselves to be but conditional subjects, to their fellow-creatures, though advanced by divine providence to the highest degree of dignity on earth, is so evident that the contrary cannot be asserted without blasphemy; for we are only obliged to obey the highest human powers on condition they do not command what is contrary to the declared will of the Supreme Divine Power. Nor is our subjection due but upon condition of protection. (pp 77-8)

But neither McBride nor Kirkpatrick go quite so far as to claim that the church has the right to declare authoritatively what 'the declared will of the Supreme Divine Power' is. Both are anxious to refute Tisdall's claim that the kirk claimed authority over the civil magistrate. The church has the right to present petitions and give advice. Church members have a right to withdraw from the church established by the magistrate if they believe it to be in serious error. But they do not insist, as did the Second Book of Discipline or the Church of Scotland in its brief moment of ascendancy in the 1640s, that the church courts constituted a second kingdom or polity, exercising national authority and empowered to suppress dissent, responsible only to Christ. McBride, in fact, while defending the church in its opposition to the Duke of

Hamilton's Engagement with Charles I in 1648, makes the point that it was only offering advice in a matter of conscience; he regrets that it was seen by some as a matter of exercising authority: 'And that others were made publicly to confess the sinfulness of that Engagement is what I know better than I approve.' (p. 35)

Both writers again justify the authoritative, national acts of the Church of Scotland, such as the National Covenant, on the grounds that they were authorised by the civil power, without inquiring too closely as to how the consent of the civil power was obtained. McBride, while all the time arguing that Presbyterians are obliged to respect the legally constituted authorities, is unable to restrain his own disrespect for their persons: 'Lest we should be suspected of disloyalty, in rejecting the testimony of crowned heads, though they be dead and rotten, all due respect shall be paid to them.' (p. 38)

Both McBride and Kirkpatrick assert that James VI and I supported the Church of Scotland before going to England, without discussing his long battle with the church or going into the question of how James established episcopacy in the Church of Scotland even before he went to England. The name of Andrew Melville is not mentioned. In fact both writers seem more at ease with English than with Scottish Presbyterian history. English acknowledgments of the supremacy of the civil magistrate are easier to come by. They write as Dissenters, regretting the fact that they cannot concur with the nature of the church established by the king, but not denying his right to establish a church of that sort, and acknowledging the Episcopalian Church to be a true church. Thus Kirkpatrick, in discussing the church settlement under Elizabeth, complains: 'It is certain the Brownists were a dangerous sect, who carried matters very high and denied the Church of England to be a church and were indeed guilty of extreme contempt.' (p. 123)

The right of dissent is not grounded in a divine right inherent in the Presbyterian clergy deriving from their correct form of church government, but simply in individual conscience; as Kirkpatrick puts it, 'If we once believe that their consciences truly dictated to them the points wherein they differed from the Established Church, they could not (without manifest contempt of the authority of God) forbear to put their principles in practice.' (p. 125) This did not, however, of itself give them a right to overthrow the established order. That right derived from the forcing of conscience by the Laudian reforms, by the excessive repression of Dissent (McBride (p. 78) remarks that the Test Act would not be sufficient to justify disloyalty), by arbitrary government (the king's claim to rule on his own authority without reference to the law of parliament), or by any furtherance of the cause of popery. Kirkpatrick in fact argues that Presbyterianism encourages individual self-reliance in opposition to authority in both church and state, an argument heard more frequently at the end of the eighteenth century:

> The ecclesiastical constitution of presbytery does provide such effectual remedies against the usurpation and ambition of the clergy, and lays such foundations for the liberty of the individual in church matters, that it naturally creates in the people an aversion from all tyranny and oppression in the state also. (p. 152)

Kirkpatrick, more than McBride, enters into a defence of the prerogatives of parliament and especially praises the Long Parliament, quoting from (among many others) Coke and Prynne. Neither McBride nor Kirkpatrick have much to say about the prerogatives of either the Scottish or the Irish parliaments, and indeed Kirkpatrick, in his discussion of the kirk's opposition to the Engagement of 1648, is more explicit than McBride that the Engagement was supported by the Scottish parliament, but 'to press any duty concerning the king's honour, with the neglect or prejudice of the Honour of God, is indeed to use liberty as a cloak of maliciousness' (p. 235).

If Tisdall reached that far in Kirkpatrick's very long, detailed, somewhat rambling but still fascinating book, he might have thought there was an echo in the word 'maliciousness' of the word 'malignancy' — the word used by the Presbyterians of the civil war period to characterise the Royalist Episcopalians. Certainly a change had come over the Presbyterians in the language they used and in the claims they made. It is the language of English Whig parliamentarianism rather than that of the Two Kingdoms. The Kingdom of Christ is now the kingdom of the individual conscience rather than that of the church. Kirkpatrick, and to a lesser extent McBride, seem closer to the moderate Episcopalian tradition of Ussher and Baxter than to the High Presbyterian tradition of Melville and Rutherford. Both like to quote the Anglican Whig bishops Burnet and Hoadly in their support. Kirkpatrick underplays the importance of the Covenant, arguing, rather oddly (p. 324), that the Presbyterians did not make Charles II's subscription to it a condition of their loyalty (though they certainly made it a condition for their preparedness to support his coronation and fight his battles) and stressing (pp 540-1) that it played no part in the ordination of Presbyterian ministers (though he is slightly more ambiguous on the promises to be given by elders, which varied from congregation to congregation). McBride gives a more robust defence, pointing out that the Covenant had been enjoined by parliament and telling Tisdall: 'I hope you are more modest than to impeach the wisdom of the British parliament', but going on to explain that it was a treaty between two countries:

> Since that League was broken by England first under the usurping powers, then by and after the Restoration of King Charles the Second, Scotland is not obliged thereby; and seeing the two kingdoms are united in one, a league is needless and impracticable betwixt them, both being now but one, and if the Union be inviolably preserved, you need be under no panic fear of having your Constitution subverted in England or Ireland. (pp 212-13)

We shall see later that the Covenant was by no means entirely dead, and more immediately we shall see that Kirkpatrick at least was not entirely representative of the Synod in the general development of his English Whig moderate principles.

3. *Latitudinarianism in England*

Kirkpatrick was soon to be one of the ministers at the centre of what has been called the First Subscription Controversy — the first of the two major divisions that occurred within the Synod of Ulster. This controversy followed and was closely related to the Bangorian Controversy in the Church of England and the Salter's Hall Controversy among the English Dissenters. To understand it we must go back and briefly summarise some developments in English church history.

We have seen that Charles II and James II both encouraged a very 'high' or Anglo-Catholic development in the Church of England: an emphasis on ritual, and on hierarchy as a divinely ordained, essential mark of a true church. Underneath this, however, there were still many people arguing for an accommodation with the Dissenters on the basis of 'moderate episcopacy' – the view that forms of church organisation were a matter of convenience rather than of divine ordination. The Glorious Revolution became possible when James came into conflict with his own High Church, and especially with the Archbishop of Canterbury, William Sancroft. Sancroft and his followers, however, were fervently committed to the view that James and his successors represented the true line of royal succession. They had been prepared to oppose him passively, prepared to be imprisoned by him, but were unhappy about his violent overthrow, and were especially unhappy about taking the oath of allegiance to William, in defiance of their earlier oath of allegiance to James. The result was an extraordinary division in the Church of England, when Sancroft, with seven of the bishops and about 400 clergy, known as Non-Jurors, refused to take the oath of allegiance and seceded, eventually forming their own church, claiming it to be the true Church of England. Among the High Church party that remained they excited great admiration. The young Jonathan Swift wrote an ode in praise of Sancroft, and High Churchmen were reluctant to fill the spaces they had vacated. The result was that these places, including the bishoprics, were largely filled by the moderate party, led by Sancroft's successor at Canterbury, John Tillotson, who had been part of the Presbyterian party in the negotiations at the time of the Restoration. William, with his Presbyterian inclinations, was in any case inclined to favour the moderates, and there were high hopes that a comprehension of many Dissenters into the Church of England would be achieved during the 1690s.[54]

High Church sentiment and dislike of the Dissenters remained strong, however, among the clergy and laity and was encouraged by the accession of Queen Anne. The impeachment of the High Church preacher Dr Henry Sacheverell in 1709 by Anne's still largely Whig ministry created a tide of High Church Tory feeling which swept a fully Tory administration under Robert Harley (later Earl of Oxford) and Henry St John (later Viscount Bolingbroke) into power. It was this administration, with its strong bias against the Dissenters, that was in power in 1713 when McBride and Kirkpatrick published their defences of Presbyterian loyalty and of the Glorious Revolution. Their ascendancy came to an end with Queen Anne's death and the accession of George I, which inaugurated the long period of political peace and managed government associated with the name of Robert Walpole. One of the first bishops to be appointed after George I's accession was Benjamin Hoadly, who became Bishop of Bangor in 1715, though he hardly ever visited his diocese.

Hoadly had already made a name for himself first as a defender of episcopal ordination and conformity to the Church of England, then as a defender of the principles of the Revolution. A sermon preached in 1705 arguing that the subject was only obliged to obey good rulers was condemned by the Lower House of Convocation, and Hoadly began what was almost a lifelong struggle with one of the leading intellectuals of the High Church party, Francis Atterbury. In 1717 he was again in trouble with the Lower House of Convocation for his *Preservative against the Principles and Practice of the Nonjurors both in Church and State* (1716) and *The Nature of the Kingdom or Church of Christ*, a sermon published in 1717 by order of the king.[55]

The Convocations of Canterbury and York were the parliaments of the Church of England, going into session every time the secular parliament assembled. The more important Convocation of Canterbury consisted of an Upper House of bishops and a Lower House representing the chapters and the parochial clergy. With the appointment of what was almost a new bench of bishops under William pledged to a policy of bringing in the Dissenters, the interesting situation arose that the Lower House was 'high' — committed to the view that the church was defined by the divine authority given to bishops – and the Upper House was 'low', or, to avoid confusion with the evangelical Low Church that developed later, 'latitudinarian'. In order to defend what they saw as the essential characteristics of the church against its own bishops, the Lower House began to develop an almost Presbyterian view of its own rights and prerogatives; and, especially in the early eighteenth century, many High Churchmen began to develop what we have seen as a distinctly Presbyterian insistence on the independence of the church from the secular authority, since Anne's government, until Bolingbroke's triumph after the impeachment of Sacheverell, was still largely Whig in inclination. Under Bolingbroke the High Church seemed to have triumphed, but its triumph was short-lived, and many of its champions, including Bolingbroke himself, were implicated in an ill-starred attempt at a Jacobite restoration in 1715. Nevertheless, the Lower House of Convocation continued in its High Church sympathies. In launching an attack on Hoadly, who may be described as the representative figure of the Hanoverian church settlement, they were engaged in a very dangerous enterprise.[56]

Hoadly argued in his *Preservative* that the Church of England had put itself at a disadvantage with regard to the Non-Jurors because it accepted so many of their fundamental ideas. He aimed to show that the Revolution settlement in church and state was not just an extraordinary product of an exceptional and unpleasant necessity, but was firmly based on principles. James had been expelled not because he was an exceptionally bad king, but because he was a Catholic, and the nation had a right to choose its king and to set conditions for the monarchy. Hereditary monarchy was not, as many High Churchmen liked to argue, a divinely ordained institution:

> Search with your own eyes and see whether you can possibly find a plain and express passage of Scripture in which God instituted any particular form of humane government for any nation in the world; unless you except one [the Jews] which first wilfully and resolutely chose it for themselves; or, in which he commands all nations either to keep firm to that one form; or, when once they have for any length of time been under subjection to a race of princes,

that they are obliged, upon pain of damnation, not to put by the next in blood, even though the destruction of the whole be unavoidable without it. (pp 9-10)

He went on to attack the view, advanced by the Non-Jurors, that the power of bishops was independent of that of the civil power, that it was inherent in their persons once ordained and could not be taken away from them, and that therefore the Non-Juring bishops still had the right to 'regular and uninterrupted successions; authoritative benedictions; excommunications or absolutions' etc. (pp 58-9). Such claims were emphatically countered by Hoadly:

> As to this particular branch of our constitution it is manifest that, whatever power or authority is conferred upon bishops by spiritual persons at their consecration; yet the right of exercising this in their particular dioceses, ariseth only from the nomination of the king. (p. 20)

He argues against the doctrine of episcopal succession on the grounds that it was evident that the succession had often been interrupted and therefore could not be part of God's plan; and he propounds the view that the test of Christianity lies not in an authority inherent in particular fallible men but in the sincerity of the individual's private conscience:

> The favour of God therefore follows 'sincerity' considered as such and consequently equally follows every equal degree of sincerity. If any persons, rather than agree to be happy in the company of others, choose to hazard their own salvation upon their own infallible certainty; or the salvation of others upon the indispensable obligation of all men to see what they see: I do not envy them a pleasure which hath nothing but imagination and absurdity to support it. (p. 55)

Hoadly further developed this last point in his sermon, *The Nature of the Kingdom or Church of Christ*, in which he maintains that Christ is the only king in his church:

> He hath, in those points [of law], left behind him no visible human authority, no viceregents who can be said properly to supply his place, no interpreters, upon whom

his subjects are absolutely to depend; no judges over the consciences or religion of his people. (p. 11)

The sermon then proceeds to show how all attempts to establish a church discipline were invasions of the prerogatives of Christ, whose rewards and punishments are not of this world. Anyone sincerely disposed to follow Christ must be seen as a Christian. Christ's church is 'the number of men whether small or great, whether dispersed or united, who truly and sincerely are subjects of Jesus Christ alone, as their lawgiver and judge, in matters relating to the favour of God and their eternal salvation' (pp 16-17). Hoadly then moves on to attack passion in religious worship, saying that prayer should be a reasonable address to God, and he concludes that

> All his [God's] subjects are equally his subjects; and as such, equally without authority to alter, to add to, or to interpret his laws, so as to claim the absolute submission of others to such interpretation . . . and it is easy to judge whether of the two is most becoming a subject of the Kingdom of Christ, that is, a member of his church: to seek all these particulars in those plain and short declarations of their king and lawgiver himself; or to hunt after them through the infinite contradictions, the numberless perplexities, the endless disputes of weak men in several ages till the enquirer himself is lost in the labyrinth and perhaps sits down in despair or infidelity. (pp 30-1)

Hoadly's pamphlet and sermon gave rise to a fierce controversy in the Church of England, and a *Report of the Committee of the Lower House of Convocation* condemned it as tending 'to subvert all government and discipline in the Church of Christ and to reduce his Kingdom to a state of anarchy and corruption' (p. 2). 'If no one method of religion be, in itself, preferable to another, the conclusion must be that all methods are alike, in respect to salvation, of the favour of God.' (p. 8) As a result of the controversy and of this report, Convocation was suppressed, that is to say, it was prorogued by royal authority indefinitely, and until the 1850s the clergy of the Church of England had no central corporate representative body of their own, apart from the bishops in the House of Lords. The Convocation of the Church of Ireland was also suppressed at the same time.

Hoadly's arguments, of course, were not new. The idea that there is no intrinsic authority in the persons of the clergy which could not be taken away from them was basic to the first phase of the Reformation (which took power away from the Catholic clergy), especially to Luther and his concept of the 'priesthood of all believers'. We have seen the Dutchman Coornhert arguing against making creeds and articles a condition of membership of the church. A theory of toleration based on the rights of the private conscience had been worked out by the Independents during the Interregnum and had formed a large part of Milton's reply to the *Necessary Representation* of the Belfast Presbytery. Milton too had ridiculed clerical claims to intrinsic authority. And the great theorist of the Revolution, John Locke, had declared in his *Letters on Toleration* in the 1690s that

> No man can so far abandon the care of his own salvation as blindly to leave it to the choice of any other, whether prince or subject, to prescribe to him what faith or worship he shall embrace. For no man can if he would, conform his faith to the dictates of another. All the life and power of true religion consists in the inward and full persuasion of the mind, and faith is not faith without believing. . . . A church, then, I take to be a voluntary society of men, joining themselves together of their own accord, in order to the public worshipping of God in such a manner as they judge acceptable to him and effectual to the salvation of their souls (pp 9, 14)

The exaltation of the rights of the private conscience, and the absolute separation of the Kingdom of Christ and the world, with no human authority having the right to speak for the Kingdom of Christ, would cut through the Gordian knot of the conflicts between Dissenters and the Established Church. Churches would become simply private worshipping societies, membership of which was to carry no political implications. What was remarkable about Hoadly's writings was that this ideal was being proclaimed by a bishop of the Church of England, a bishop, moreover, who had the full support and confidence of the king and his ministers; and that the representative body of the Church of England was suppressed in order to prevent it from condemning him.

Hoadly, in addition to arguing that there was no scriptural prescription for the nature of the church, or for the nature of civil government, had also condemned 'the infinite contradictions, the numberless perplexities, the endless disputes of weak men'. The spirit of agnosticism in questions of church polity was also abroad in the same period in questions of doctrinal theology, not just in the Church of England but also among the Dissenters. Coornhert had argued back in the sixteenth century that much theological truth was simply unknowable and that therefore to make such knowledge a condition of faith was to commit an absurdity. Such ideas were behind the disputes which split the English Dissenters in the Salter's Hall Controversy which quickly followed the Bangorian Controversy.

The Salter's Hall Controversy broke out in 1719, though it had been in prospect for a long time previously through the spread in England of 'Arian' or 'Socinian' ideas. Arianism and Socinianism will be looked at more closely when we come to discuss the Arian Controversy in the Synod of Ulster in the 1820s; briefly, the Arians and Socinians saw the traditional Christian doctrine of the Trinity as confusing, irrational and unwarranted by Scripture. They argued that the Son and the Holy Ghost were persons separate from God the Father and proceeding from him. The Arians took the view that nevertheless the Son (Christ) was divine, while the Socinians (called after the sixteenth-century Italian reformer Fausto Sozzini, who finally settled in Poland to become a leader of the already anti-Trinitarian Minor Reformed Church of Krakow) argued that, while he had a divine mission, Jesus was not a divine person.

There had been an Arian controversy in Dublin in 1701, when Thomas Emlyn, assistant to Joseph Boyse, whom we have already met, admitted holding Arian views and was deposed from his Wood Street congregation (though he had already offered to resign). There followed a pamphlet dispute with Boyse on the doctrine of the Trinity, but the expression of anti-Trinitarian views was at this time a punishable offence, and, to Boyse's distress, Emlyn was charged in 1703 and imprisoned by a court which included the Archbishops of Armagh and Dublin on the bench. After his release in 1705 Emlyn returned to England, where he continued his still illegal controversy on the Trinity.[57]

Other writers arguing a similar case included Thomas Firmin, William Whiston, the Irishman John Toland and, most importantly, Samuel Clarke, whose highly influential *Scripture Doctrine of the Trinity*, arguing that the doctrine was not held by the early church, was published in 1712. To the great suspicion of the High Church Anglicans, Firmin and Clarke especially seemed to be favoured by the latitudinarian bishops (Hoadly was to write a life of Clarke). Their theories were attractive to those who wished to minimise the differences between the Established Church and the Dissenters. Those differences turned on questions of church government and doctrine, but could be overcome by a respect for private conscience; this became easier to achieve if adherence to particular doctrinal views — especially on matters that were abstruse and mysterious — were not insisted on as necessary to salvation. Hoadly stressed the rational side of Christianity. Toland's book, burned by the common hangman in Dublin, was called *Christianity Not Mysterious*. This tendency was as threatening to orthodox Calvinism as it was to High Church Anglicanism.

Salter's Hall had since 1694 been the venue for a weekly Presbyterian lecture held under the auspices of the Presbyterian merchants in London. In 1719 a conference of Independent and Presbyterian ministers was held there to discuss an Arian controversy which had broken out among the 'United Brethren of Devon and Cornwall' (a loose association of Presbyterian and Independent ministers similar to the Southern Association in Ireland). The controversy turned around Dr James Pierce, a minister in Exeter who had been prominently engaged in writing on behalf of the Dissenting interest (he is quoted several times in Kirkpatrick's *Presbyterian Loyalty*, and he was also involved in controversy with the Anglican Dr Andrew Snape, a leading antagonist of Hoadly's). Pierce did not actually promote Unitarianism in his preaching, but he never made any reference at all to the doctrine of the Trinity. When challenged on the matter by a committee of the Exeter ministers, he replied that he saw the Father's divinity as the source of the divinity of the Son and Holy Ghost. The Exeter ministers appealed to the London ministers for their advice, and at the Salter's Hall conference it was proposed that ministers should be required to subscribe to the first of the Thirty-Nine Articles and to the answers to questions 5 and 6 in the Shorter Catechism drawn up by the Westminster Assembly — the articles and questions dealing with the Trinity. The proposal was narrowly defeated, and Hoadly proclaimed that this was the first Convocation or assembly of divines since the time of the Apostles that had carried a question for liberty. The controversy, however, sharply split the English Dissenters into two parties: the Subscribers, broadly corresponding to the old Independents, and the Non-Subscribers, broadly corresponding to the Presbyterians. Edmund Calamy, widely seen as Baxter's successor as leader of the Presbyterians, had opposed holding the conference at all — that is to say, he was opposed to interfering with the private conscience of ministers. In 1709 he had visited the General Assembly of the Church of Scotland and complained that the process of examining an 'unsound minister' was a revival of the Inquisition.[58]

4. *Latitudinarianism in Ulster*

These two disputes formed part of the background against which, in 1719, John Abernethy, minister at Antrim, preached a sermon published under the title *Religious Obedience Founded on Personal Persuasion*. Abernethy, son of one of the Commonwealth and Restoration Ulster ministers, had worked for some time in Dublin as a coadjutor to Boyse. He was a leading member of the Belfast Society, a group of ministers who had been meeting since 1705 to discuss theology and exchange books. The Belfast Society was to be the core of the movement against subscription in the 1720s. The year of its foundation, 1705, was the year in which, partly in response to Emlyn's trial, the Synod introduced the requirement that its ministers subscribe to the Westminster Confession. This had been a requirement in the Church of

Scotland since 1690, when it was incorporated into the act under which the church was established. Abernethy came into conflict with the Synod when, in 1717, he had been sent as a minister to Ussher's Quay in Dublin, one of three Dublin congregations attached to the Synod under the care of the Presbytery of Belfast. After three months he had returned to Antrim without the Synod's permission. A sceptical attitude towards the rights of church courts, and especially of the Synod, was to be a feature of the Non-Subscribers' arguments.[59]

Abernethy's sermon on *Religious Obedience* was almost pure Hoadly: 'Religion, according to our most obvious notions of it, is a reasonable service performed to the supreme intelligent Being, who observes the most secret thoughts of his creatures in order to recompense them. . . . Reason . . . is our greatest excellency. . . . Actions done with freedom and understanding and they only are human actions.' (pp 233-4) It is the Christian's duty to examine all the evidence carefully and dispassionately and to accept and act on it only on the basis of his own private conscientious conviction. To act insincerely against his own conviction is sinful, even if that conviction should be mistaken. The sermon was based on Romans 14 : 5: 'Let every man be fully persuaded in his own mind' — a text which, Abernethy argued, plainly showed 'that matters of conscience are not under human jurisdiction' (p. 240). The magistrate had power over the 'whole extent of outward human actions which regard the public peace' (p. 246), and the church could refuse communion for scandalous or immoral behaviour, but neither the magistrate nor the church had any authority over the individual conscience or over individual belief. Christians could not be judged according to their belief in certain doctrines because this was out of their control:

> It is not in our power to refuse or so much as suspend such an assent or dissent; not from any faulty impotence, but, as far as I can see, from the essential Frame of the Soul itself, and in that wherein by the very constitution of our nature, we have no liberty, there can be neither moral Good nor Evil. (p. 225)

This was a serious assault on the central Protestant doctrine of justification by faith alone. Calvinism had always argued that justification was an area in which 'by the very constitution of our nature we have no liberty'. It was not by our own moral goodness or sincerity that we were to be saved, but by the choice — arbitrary as far as mankind was concerned — of God. The function of the church was to provide comfort to the elect by the repetition of Gospel promises; those who received comfort from them were likely to be of the elect. But in this view of the matter, correct doctrine was everything. Correct doctrine, or 'Gospel truth', was the starting-point, and it was up to men to come up to it. By contrast, in Abernethy's view the starting-point was the human heart ('the foul rag and bone shop of the heart', as Yeats puts it) and the human virtue of sincerity.

Despite its important implications, Abernethy's sermon only excited a small controversy which seemed, at the 1720 Synod, to be resolved in favour of the Non-Subscribers. The Synod was acutely aware of the breach that had just opened among the English Dissenters at Salter's Hall and was anxious to avoid the same problems. It was justly proud of the fact that the Ulster ministers, through the Act of Bangor against importing the Scottish Resolutioner/Protestor disputes, had managed to maintain a remarkable degree of unity even under the very difficult circumstances of the Restoration period. The 1720 Synod agreed a 'Pacific Act' which allowed candidates for the ministry who had doubts about particular passages in the Westminster Confession to moderate their subscription with an explanation of their doubts. The Synod then wrote an unduly smug letter to Salter's Hall, deploring their divisions.

Subsequent events in the Non-Subscription Controversy are complicated, and I only intend to summarise them here, since it is with the arguments rather than with the history that we are chiefly concerned.[60]

Two Ulster ministers, the Rev. John Dunlop and the Rev. Samuel Haliday, had been in London at the time of the Salter's Hall dispute. Haliday had been appointed to the First Congregation in Belfast (Kirkpatrick was minister of the Second Congregation), but Dunlop wrote to say that he was suspected of Arianism. He was cleared of this charge at the 1720 Synod,

and the Belfast Presbytery proceeded to admit him. He refused, however, to subscribe to the Westminster Confession,
arguing that he was not bound by the terms of the Pacific
Act as he was already an ordained minister. He had been ordained in Geneva in 1708, a circumstance to which we shall
return, and had joined the Synod in 1712. Four members of the
presbytery protested, and the matter was taken up by a Belfast
sub-synod in 1720 and by the 1721 Synod. By now a vigorous
pamphlet war had begun, the first real examples of the literary
genre in which Ulster Presbyterianism was to excel.

At the 1721 Synod ministers were called on to make a
voluntary declaration of their belief in the eternal Sonship
of Christ (the Arians argued that the Son, though divine, had
emanated from the Father at a specific point in time and was
therefore not co-eternal with him) and to renew their subscription to the Westminster Confession under the terms of
the Pacific Act. Those who refused were the 'Non-Subscribers',
and it should be noted that their refusal was on the grounds
that the Synod had no authority to require them, not that
they disagreed with the doctrines in question.

The dispute dragged on for the next three years. A section
of Haliday's congregation left to form the Third Belfast congregation. (All three Belfast congregations met in Rosemary
Street. The First is still there; the Second is now All Souls'
Church in Elmwood Avenue; the Third is now Rosemary
Church on the North Circular Road.) In 1725 the Synod
resolved to gather all the Non-Subscribers together in one
presbytery — the Presbytery of Antrim — and in 1726 this
presbytery was expelled from 'juridical communion' with the
Synod. This meant that the Non-Subscribers could not sit,
deliberate or vote with the Synod. They were still, however,
recognised as valid ministers, so that the Synod's ministers
could, if they wished, share pulpits and join in communion
with them. The Non-Subscribers received the full support,
throughout the dispute and afterwards, of Joseph Boyse and
the Southern Association.

Much has been written about whether or not the Non-
Subscribers were really Arian. The question, however, may
be misconceived. Whether they actually believed in the doctrine of the Trinity or not, they certainly had a different

attitude towards it from that of the Subscribers. They regarded it as a point of speculative theology, an area of secondary importance, in which precise knowledge was impossible. There could be no doubt that Joseph Boyse believed in the doctrine of the Trinity. He had defended it at great length in controversy with Thomas Emlyn, and he had argued against the Socinians that if Jesus were a mere man, he could not redeem from sin or act as a mediator between God and man. But the Presbytery of Antrim's *Narrative of the Proceedings of Seven General Synods* (1727) quotes him as saying that the doctrine of the Trinity was not a fundamental article of belief. By a fundamental article was meant 'that without the explicit belief of it a man cannot be saved but must perish everlastingly' (p. 61). Although 'the doctrine of our Saviour's Divinity ran through the Christian scheme and did animate our Faith', still it was nowhere stated in Scripture that those who did not believe in it were damned. The Non-Subscribers had raised the controversy at a time when Arianism was very much in the air. The obvious anxiety of the Subscribers was that Arianism should be prevented from getting a foothold in the ministry — as it already had in Dublin and in Exeter. The Non-Subscribers were prepared to concede that a candidate for the ministry should give an account of his faith to his brethren before ordination. But the Synod was to trust to the decision of the presbytery, and no objective rule was to be allowed. They clearly did not have the feeling of the Subscribers that the rise of Arianism was a dangerous crisis in the affairs of the Dissenters, for which a remedy was to be found.

Both Robert Allen and Godfrey Brown in their excellent theses on the subject conclude that if the Non-Subscribers were not Arian, they were probably Arminians. Brown shows that Boyse had a position not far removed from that of the original Arminians in that he believed that grace was freely available to all who sought it by proper means (p. 201). Arminianism, in the Ulster Presbyterian mind, was of course associated with Laud, and as such it is strongly condemned by Kirkpatrick in his *Presbyterian Loyalty*, though Kirkpatrick was a member of the Belfast Society and a leading writer for the Non-Subscribers:

> The evil councillors of that unfortunate Prince [Charles I]
> were not satisfied with all the countenance Papists got
> under him; but to complete the danger of religion must
> put him upon methods for corrupting the Protestant
> doctrine by spreading the poisonous infection of the most
> rigid tenets of Arminianism. (p. 188)

Nevertheless, if Arminianism is taken in its broadest possible
sense as the view that the virtue of the individual has a role to
play in the work of salvation, there can be no doubt that the
whole thrust of the Non-Subscribers' argument was Arminian.
They found it impossible to believe that a sincere Christian
could be damned, and they regarded religion as, in Abernethy's
words again, 'a reasonable service performed to the supreme
intelligent being, who observes the most secret thoughts of
his creatures in order to recompense them'. In other words,
man was a free being, saved or damned by God's judgment of
his free thoughts and actions. The judgment follows the
individual's behaviour and is contingent upon it.

But the central point in the actual dispute was the same as
the point at issue between Hoadly and the English Convocation: the power and authority of church courts.

In the Subscribers' view, doctrine was of supreme importance, and the church had the right and duty to define it
and to ensure that its preachers preached it. Charles
Mastertown, one of the leading Subscribers, argued in his
Christian Liberty Founded in Gospel Truth (Edinburgh 1727)
that

> Scripture doctrines are not speculative in their own nature:
> it is true men may treat them speculatively, that is, they
> may consider them abstractedly from the connection they
> have with Christian practice, but such as rest in the mere
> contemplation of Christian doctrines, they use them con-
> trary to their original design, which is to promote a holy
> life, a conformity to the divine Image, both in our mind
> and manners . . . that religious obedience is founded
> merely in personal persuasion; I choose rather to say that
> the freedom of a Christian in his religious obedience is
> founded in the conformity of his sentiments to divine
> revelation. . . . Unless they [preachers] had agreed in the

public profession of a competent number of divine doctrines contained in that law of truth, the people could not
have sought the knowledge of sound principles at their lips.
(pp 6, 31, 35-6)

He invokes the idea, familiar to anyone who has read much in
the way of Roman Catholic apologetics, of 'right reason'
(p. 30).

Another Subscriber, perhaps their best writer, Gilbert
Kennedy, argued in his *A Defence of the Principles and Conduct of the Reverend General Synod of Ulster* (1724) that

The conviction of the mind is no further a rule to any than
as it is agreeable to God's word. If it be not according to
this, there is no light in it (Isa. viii. 20). Conviction of the
mind is a necessary antecedent of religious obedience and
may be motive to it, but it is the authority of God that
binds us to duty. (p. 56)

The Non-Subscribers would have agreed that the personal
persuasion they talked of should harmonise with God's Word.
The sufficiency of Scripture was a fundamental doctrine with
them. Their quarrel was with the claim of the Synod, or any
other church court, to make an authoritative interpretation
of Scripture. This they saw as the essence of popery. The
Protestants had been forced to part company with the Roman
Catholic Church because it imposed numerous terms of communion on top of what was required in Scripture. The right
to impose a test on the conscience could become a right to
impose heresy (Haliday, *Reasons against the Imposition of
Subscription*, pp 112-13), and this could best be guarded
against by allowing freedom of debate. The test was necessarily a 'human' test, contrived by fallible men.

The dispute can be seen to some extent as the product of
the unique status of the Synod of Ulster as a dissenting connexional church. In England there was little question of
terms of communion, scriptural or otherwise, being imposed
among the Dissenters, because there was no church court
claiming the authority to impose them. In terms of church
government, the only difference between the Presbyterians
and the Independents was that the Presbyterians required the

presence of more than one minister at an ordination. But these ministers did not constitute a formal presbytery. In 1724, in the middle of the dispute in Ulster, Alexander Colville, called to Dromore but refused ordination by the Presbytery of Armagh, went to London and was ordained in Calamy's church by ten English Presbyterian ministers. When the Presbytery of Armagh still refused to accept him, Calamy threatened to use his influence to cut off the Synod's *regium donum*. Colville refused to appear before the Synod or to recognise its right to hear the case. He was then installed by the 'Presbytery of Dublin' (which was not a presbytery in the Scottish use of the term: three of its members were attached to the Synod of Ulster, under the Presbytery of Belfast; three were members of the Southern Association).[61]

The Non-Subscribers, then, were behaving like English Presbyterians, who had themselves adopted much of the principle as well as the practice of the old Independents. The Independents, the reader will remember, had argued against the idea of the church as a corporate institution. They had recognised a right in the civil magistrate to order religious affairs to prevent the churches contributing to civil disorder, but that was the only authority they recognised above the level of the congregation. This had been the principle under which the English Puritans had been organised during the Interregnum; it had necessarily continued as the practice of the Dissenters following the Restoration, forbidden by law to exercise any corporate jurisdiction; it had now become a matter of principle among the Presbyterians to the extent that, at Salter's Hall, the Non-Subscribing, mainly Presbyterian, majority had argued against the Subscribing, mainly Independent, minority, that ministers had no right to interfere in each other's congregations, even for the purpose of merely offering advice.

There can be little doubt that the Non-Subscribers at this time, unlike their Arian successors in the 1820s, had the spirit of the age with them. Their central thesis — that faith required a subjective personal conviction — was almost universally accepted. It probably strikes the modern reader as self-evident. Yet it is by no means self-evident. A church which regards itself as a divinely ordained teaching authority does not require each of its members to decide on all of its propositions for themselves. The individual member of the church accepts its authority to decide these matters for him. The Roman Catholic Church is such a church. A large section of the Anglican Church had always held a similar view. And from the Non-Subscribers' point of view, the Subscribers in the Presbyterian Church were making a similar claim.

The Subscribers did not, however, argue for implicit faith in their own teaching authority. Kennedy in fact used an argument based on the rights of private conscience, which was to be frequently reiterated during the 1820s dispute. He argued that the Non-Subscribers were imposing on the private conscience of the Subscribers. The Subscribers believed that an objective test, based on scriptural arguments, was necessary to preserve the church against heresy. They were in a majority in this particular worshipping society. The Non-Subscribers were forcing them to co-operate with men whose principles they either did not know, or, if they did know them, could not approve. Referring to the opposition to a voluntary subscription to the Confession in 1721, Kennedy wrote:

> Those that opposed such an allowance and protested against their [the Subscribers'] acting according to the light of their conscience at that time were the greatest imposers upon conscience. And could they, in an imperious manner, endeavour to restrain others from obeying the light of their consciences, and not destroy Christian liberty, the right of private judgment, and undermine that darling but dangerous notion that RELIGIOUS OBEDIENCE IS FOUNDED UPON PERSONAL PERSUASION? (*Defence of the Principles and Conduct of the Reverend General Synod of Ulster*, p. v)

Implicit in that was the view that although the Synod had the right to impose terms of communion on its members, still the Synod was only one worshipping society among many, and those who could not accept its terms could go elsewhere. Kennedy confirms that this is what he thinks:

> Indeed if the Synod declared that they were the only church of Christ upon earth and that there was no sal-

vation out of their communion, their depriving a person
of it were a damning him to Hell. But though they be
persuaded that their society is as pure as most others:
yet they dare not, nor do not, pronounce others' societies
damned; persons are saved in other societies that differ
from them in many things. And therefore the synodical
decrees relating to this are no more than in effect this:
a person disagreeing with them in some principles, as for
example, concerning the power and authority of the church
etc. is to join with such as are of the same opinion, that he
may not stumble others and hinder their edification. He's
never in this case likely to be so acceptable and useful
among them as elsewhere. Let, as for example, him that
denies the authority of Synods join with the Independents.
(p. 33)

Kennedy is taking for granted Locke's definition of a
church as 'a voluntary society of men, joining themselves
together of their own accord' etc., which of course was not
the definition of the Second Book of Discipline or of the
Covenanted Church of Scotland in the 1640s, or indeed of
the Belfast Presbytery's *Necessary Representation* which protested against 'a promiscuous toleration'. His book, like those
of the Non-Subscribers, has something of an English feel to
it: he makes great use of a quotation from Baxter to the effect
that the Westminster Shorter Catechism is 'a fit test to try
the orthodoxy even of teachers themselves' (the Westminster
documents are themselves, of course, English documents
taking some account of Independent principles and of an
Erastian parliament, and less assertive about the rights of the
church than the Scots commissioners would have liked).

There is a missionary zeal about the Non-Subscribers which
is lacking among most of their Arian successors in the nine-
teenth century. They felt that they had uncovered the prin-
ciples under which the religious warfare which had bedevilled
Europe for the previous two centuries could be resolved.
Hoadly's argument that there were two Kingdoms and that
the magistrate could not interfere with the Kingdom of
Christ was, thus far, simply a repetition of Melville's view.
The crucial difference was that for Hoadly and the Non-
Subscribers the Kingdom of Christ was not a corporate body

with an authority derived from Christ, but the kingdom of the individual conscience. Each man was individually accountable to Christ for his own spiritual life, but this had no political implications. The principles of the Earthly Kingdom were to be entirely earthly.

Similar ideas were spreading in Europe. Haliday, who had travelled widely, pointed out that George, as Elector of Hanover (who was now George I of England), the King of Prussia and the Diet of Ratisbon had opposed the imposition of subscription to a formula of faith. Moreover, the 'Formula Consensus' in Geneva had been abolished in 1705 by the civil authorities, a final victory for the state in its long battle with Calvin's church (*Reasons*, p. 70). Haliday himself had chosen to be ordained in Geneva in 1708 because subscription was no longer required. To qualify under William's Toleration Act, English Dissenters had to subscribe to certain of the doctrinal articles of the Church of England (including the doctrine of the Trinity). In 1718 and 1719 Queen Anne's Schism Act (depriving English Dissenters of certain rights such as the right to run schools) was repealed, and, for the first time, the Toleration Act was introduced in Ireland. As part of these measures there was a strongly supported, though unsuccessful, move to end the requirement of subscription. During the course of the dispute over subscription in Ulster the Non-Subscribers published, under the title *The Royal Peacemaker*, an appeal against religious division and unreasonable forcing of conscience written by George I.

The policy of the English Presbyterians had been to press for a widening of the constitution of the Church of England to incorporate them. Now the hope was that with a virtual abolition of terms of communion, religious divisions would become an anachronism. Disagreements would become merely private and personal affairs. It would be accepted that a great variety of theological views could coexist without endangering the work of salvation. The only motive for suppressing particular religious views would be if they threatened the public order; and only a church which claimed a corporate, extra-national authority over the consciences of its members — the Roman Catholic Church, for example — was likely to do that.

This was a great vision — and it was a vision central to religious life in England, and even to some extent in Scotland, throughout the eighteenth century. Of course, distinctions and even acrimonious divisions between sects were not abolished. But a right to differ was widely accepted. And although the Non-Subscribers were defeated in the Synod of 1726, their ideas continued to spread until by the end of the eighteenth century there was little distinction in principle between the Presbytery of Antrim and the majority of presbyteries attached to the Synod of Ulster.

5

The
New Dissenters

1. Evangelicalism and Calvinism in Scotland, England and America

In the preceding chapter I stressed the importance of English influence, especially on the Non-Subscribers. At the same time as the Non-Subscription Controversy in Ulster, a long dispute was taking place in the Church of Scotland concerning John Simson, Professor of Divinity at the University of Glasgow. I have seen no references to Simson in the Ulster controversy, though there are numerous references to the Salter's Hall debates. Simson became Professor of Divinity in 1708, three years after the Belfast Society was formed, and although he came into conflict with the 'Marrow Men' (a term which will soon be explained) in 1714, it was not until after 1722, by which time the Ulster controversy was well established, that he was suspected of heterodoxy on the question of the Trinity. Any influence he might have had was probably through his pupils on a later generation of Ulster ministers. The dissidents who formed the Third Belfast congregation in protest against Haliday collected some money in Scotland, and the advice of the Scottish church was sought. Apart from that, the lack of Scottish involvement is quite remarkable. In this chapter we shall be looking at a resurgence of Scottish influence, in the form of the Secession and Reformed Presbyterian Churches.[62]

The predominance of English rather than Scottish influence may be partly attributable to the lack, throughout the seventeenth century, of a substantial Scottish theological literature. The great works of the Calvinist Church of Scotland are its authoritative documents — chiefly the First and Second Books of Discipline. Knox was not notable as a theologian. His best-known work is his largely political *History of the Reformation in Scotland*. Melville's works consist largely of Latin verse. The principled Presbyterians in their opposition to James VI were more noted for their powerful preaching in defence of the rights of the church than for their theology. Perhaps the most distinguished Scottish theologian in the early seventeenth century was John Cameron, but he was based in the University of Saumur in France and heavily involved in the French disputes of the time, where he took the more 'heterodox' side (if we take Beza's Calvinism as a standard of orthodoxy). The most memorable literature of the period of Presbyterian ascendancy in the mid-seventeenth century is to be found in the private journals of Robert Baillie and Archibald Johnston of Warriston. Blair and Livingstone published little in the way of theology, and their best-known writings are their autobiographies. The leading theologian of the period was Samuel Rutherford, but his great attack on the Arminians was published in Latin, while his controversial works of the 1640s were written in England as part of the English disputes surrounding the meeting of the Westminster Assembly. Throughout the Restoration period the Scottish universities were in the hands of the moderate Episcopalians and theological controversy was discouraged. The literature of the Covenanters turned more on the rights and sufferings of the church than on the nature of grace. By far the most distinguished Scottish writer of the period was the moderate Episcopalian Gilbert Burnet, who, despite his continuing interest in Scottish affairs, spent most of his career in England. It was Burnet who provided the most widely read theoretical and historical justification for the Glorious Revolution, and he is quoted extensively by both McBride and Kirkpatrick (who do not mention Locke).[63]

This absence of a Scottish theological literature helps to account for the uncertain note struck by the Ulster Subscribers. They do not stand on the foundation of a clearly understood Calvinist theology of grace. They were still a church intellectually dependent on the Church of Scotland, which had not produced a literature that was of great assistance to them. The Belfast Society had seen the lack, and for fifteen years its members had devoted themselves to a comprehensive process of self-education. Kirkpatrick's longwindedness and wealth of authorities are the marks of a self-taught writer (McBride, who was not a member of the Belfast Society, is, as it happens, the more self-confident and better writer). The great idea, which the Belfast Society was to seize upon, was the irrelevance of theological controversy, an idea which appealed to a church which had not greatly engaged in it. The most notable – indeed the only – theological writers in Irish Presbyterianism in the period were the Dublin-based Englishmen Emlyn and Boyse, neither of whom were members of the Synod. As we have seen, Emlyn was an Arian and Boyse a Non-Subscriber.

In the light of this it will not seem surprising that when a resurgence of orthodox Calvinism took place in the Church of Scotland it turned on an English book – Edward Fisher's *The Marrow of Modern Divinity*, first published in 1646 while the Westminster Assembly was sitting. It is a comparatively simple and readable exposition of the covenant theology which had such an influence on the Westminster Confession. It consists of a discussion between four characteristic Christians: Nomista, Antinomista, Evangelista and Neophytus. Neophytus is a young Christian bewildered by the controversy between Nomista and Antinomista, which is resolved by Evangelista. Nomista argues that the Christian must be saved by strict observance of the law; Antinomista that the Christian saved by the grace of God is free of the law and can do as he wishes without regard to it. Evangelista explains that it is indeed impossible to observe the law fully and that observance of the law cannot serve as a means of salvation; but that the Christian saved by Christ thereby becomes a servant of Christ, and it will be in his nature to observe the law, albeit imperfectly, not as a means of salvation but as a manifestation of his love for his Lord.

God's relations with man are explained in terms of two covenants, both made with Adam: the Covenant of Works made before the Fall, and the Covenant of Grace made after the Fall. Under the Covenant of Works, Adam, and all mankind in him, lived in conformity with God so long as he obeyed his law, summed up in the command to avoid the forbidden fruit. When Adam, and all mankind in him, broke that law, he committed a sin which, because directed against an infinite eternal goodness, required an infinite eternal punishment. Thenceforth the moral law, which runs through the Old Testament and is summarised in the Ten Commandments, became nothing more than a reminder of the standard to which man could not attain — a reminder, therefore, that man, under the Covenant of Works, was damned eternally. Under the Covenant of Grace, however, the Second Person of the Trinity took on himself the sins of all believers, and, as all mankind was damned in the person of Adam under the Covenant of Works, so Christ suffered the infinite punishment of all believers, under the Covenant of Grace.

The Marrow of Modern Divinity was reissued in Scotland in 1718, and two years later one of its leading champions, Thomas Boston of Ettrick, published his *Human Nature in Its Fourfold State*, perhaps the masterpiece of Scottish popular Calvinism. John Macleod says of it in his *Scottish Theology*:

> There is no book of practical divinity, not even William Guthrie's *Trial of Saving Interest in Christ*, nor Rutherford's *Letters*, that was more read in the godly homes of Scotland than this treatise. It did more to mould the thought of his countrymen than anything except the Westminster Shorter Catechism. Such a pre-eminence earned for it the distinction of being a favourite target for the sharp-shooters of the Broad Church School. Thus, for example, George MacDonald made one of his heroes hide his aunt's copy of it in his fiddle-case, where the worthy lady would not be likely to look for the book of which she was so fond and which the scapegrace so heartily disliked. (p. 146)

The point is not that the ideas in *The Marrow* and *Human Nature* were new, but that they were the beginnings of a new popular literature in Scotland concentrating not so much on the rights of the church as on the theology of grace. Such a literature already existed in abundance in England, where 'High Calvinism' was becoming increasingly moribund (and where the new trend was to contribute to the rise of Methodism, though it was not its initiating impulse). In Scotland, with the Marrow Controversy and the emergence of the Secession, the theology of grace was about to undergo a renaissance.[64]

The Marrow of Modern Divinity was condemned by the General Assembly of the Church of Scotland for Antinomianism, despite the fact that a large part of it is taken up with an attack on Antinomianism. The propositions condemned in it included the view that fear of eternal punishment and hope of reward were not Christian motives (though they are described as motives that can turn the Christian to Christ) and that the believer is not under the law. Most significantly, perhaps, it was accused of teaching that the saved Christian would have an assurance of salvation. This last idea – a knowledge of grace – is perhaps the great mark that distinguishes what we may now loosely call 'Evangelical Christianity' from what the Evangelicals would call formal Christianity, and it is again an idea that was more firmly rooted in seventeenth-century English Congregationalism than in Scottish Presbyterianism. We have already seen how discerning signs of grace became an important part of the thinking of the gathered churches within the Church of England before the civil war, and what influence this thinking had in America.

The Marrow Controversy was also connected with the more traditional disputes over the nature of church government. The triumph of Presbyterianism in 1690 was more a triumph in appearance than in reality. With the admission of the old conforming clergy under pressure from William, the principled Presbyterians were outnumbered and also outweighed intellectually in that the conformists had had control of the universities. The General Assembly and Scottish parliament in 1690 abolished the right of lay patrons to dispose of livings, though they replaced it with a complicated system dividing responsibility between the elders and local lay powers – magistrates and 'heritors' – giving the congregation only a right of veto. Thomas Boston, for one, had to wait a long time before he could find a heritor prepared to approve him. With the Act of Union of 1707 the Scottish parliament was folded into an overwhelmingly Episcopalian parliament of

Great Britain which, despite safeguards for the church written into the act, exercised a right of appeal in ecclesiastical matters, including disputes over patronage. In 1711 the united parliament restored patronage. In reaction both to the suppression of the Marrow theology, and to the General Assembly's recognition of the rights of patrons, the 'Associate Presbytery' was established in 1733. Its ministers were still notionally members of the General Assembly and still had legal rights to their livings, but they set up their own discipline independent of that of the Assembly. They were expelled in 1740, when the Secession began in earnest.[65]

It is in 1740, then, that the Ulster Presbyterians ceased to be the only Protestant Dissenting connexional church in the British Isles.

Parallel to the rise of the Secession in Scotland were the Methodist revival in England and the Great Awakening which to a large extent took place among people derived from Ulster Presbyterian stock in America. I have said in passing that Methodism did not take its initial impulse from the English Congregationalist tradition, despite the very great literature on the theology of grace already developed in that tradition in the seventeenth century. I am basing that comment on the career of John Wesley, but Wesley is so central to Methodism that it seems permissible. In the person of John Wesley Methodism can be said to take its origins from a most surprising source — High Church Anglicanism. Wesley's father, Samuel Wesley, was a noted High Churchman and opponent of the Dissenters. The original 'method' of John and his brother Charles was a series of strict devotions in accordance with the rubrics of the Church of England — a justification by works with a vengeance.[66]

Something of what we might call an 'Evangelical' spirit was, however, already evident on the High Church side in the Bangorian Controversy. Hoadly's opponents included the High Church divine, William Law, who greatly influenced Wesley. His *A Serious Call to a Devout and Holy Life* (1727) is one of the classics of Anglican devotional literature. In his *The Bishop of Bangor's Late Sermon and his Letter to Dr Snape in Defence of it Answered* (1717) Law strikes a note which seems to me to be missing in the replies of the Ulster

Subscribers to Abernethy. Hoadly had argued that prayer was a reasonable address to God and had argued against 'heat and flame' — a view repeated by Abernethy. Law replied:

> Prayer chiefly consisteth of confession and petition. Now to be calm and free from worldly passions is a necessary temper to the right discharge of such duties: but why our confession must be so calm and free from all perturbation of spirit; why our petitions may not have all that fervour and warmth, with which either nature or grace can supply, is very surprising. . . . If therefore any should happen to be so disturbed at his sins as to offer a broken and contrite heart to God, instead of one calm and undisturbed; or like Holy David, his soul should be a-thirst for God, or pant after him as the hart panteth after the water brooks, this would not be prayer [according to Hoadly] but superstitious folly. (pp 23, 28)

In the 1730s the Wesley brothers and their fellow High Church Anglican, George Whitefield, seized upon the idea that this thirsting after God (a very different concept in itself from 'reasonable service') could not be satisfied by endless religious observances (works) but only by what is described in *The Marrow of Modern Divinity* as the 'passive' obedience of the Christian — the recognition that grace is a free gift of God and that it is the duty of the Christian to be open to receive it.

Under the pressure of this idea, although Wesley and Whitefield wished to be regarded as faithful members of the Church of England and to relate their activities to its traditions, all distinctions among churches, rituals and observances became very secondary matters. The duty of the preacher was to preach the free availability of grace on all possible occasions to all possible audiences. Methodism stressed that this grace was knowable: it was an emotional experience. Wesley and Whitefield differed on whether that grace was perpetual: Whitefield held to a Calvinist view that grace was only obtainable by Christians saved for all eternity, while Wesley held an Arminian view that grace once gained could be lost again. Both, however, stressed that it could be experienced and that without such a 'warm' or 'lively' experience it was doubtful if a man could be called a Christian.

The Methodists, and especially the Calvinist Whitefield, recognised a similarity between their movement and the Scots Secession, but when Whitefield went to Scotland in 1741 to form an alliance with the Seceders, the differences soon became clear. The Seceders remained firmly wedded to the traditional Presbyterian ideal of a true church that would ideally be co-terminous with the civil society. They did not approve of a freewheeling evangelism across church boundaries and did not trust an enthusiastic preaching that seemed to offer grace as an emotional moment experienced under the influence of powerful preaching. Preaching for them was still a matter of expounding doctrine, and although *The Marrow* and Boston both argued that the Christian could have assurance of his election, it was as a result of a long process of self-examination; and it was not a judgment to be made by the church, which could only judge the quality of a Christian by his outward actions and his understanding of doctrine.

Whitefield found more sympathetic colleagues in America, which he also visited at about the same time, and where a revival had been taking place since 1735. Here we are principally interested in the involvement of the Presbyterians.[67]

American Presbyterianism was centred in Pennsylvania, the state that had been founded by the Quaker William Penn in 1682 on the principle of religious tolerance. The Presbytery of Philadelphia had been established at the beginning of the century by a group of Scots-Irish ministers who included Francis Makemie, from Ramelton in Donegal, often called the Father of American Presbyterianism. In 1716 the Synod of Philadelphia was formed, with four presbyteries and about seventeen ministers.

This small synod could be said to have been in a similar position to the Synod of Ulster in that it was not an established church, and was functioning entirely on its own authority and free to organise its affairs. It differed in that there was no established church in Pennsylvania for it to react against. In the next fifteen years the church spread more into New England, an area with a strongly Congregationalist tradition. It was still, however, largely supplied by ministers from the north of Ireland, and in 1724 subscription

to the Westminster Confession of Faith was introduced because of suspicions about their orthodoxy. As with the
Synod of Ulster's Pacific Act, ministers were allowed to record
their scruples. Some doubts arose in particular over what the
Confession had to say about the power of the civil magistrate
to punish heresy and regulate the affairs of the church.[68]

This American Presbyterian Church split in 1740 under
pressure from the Great Awakening. Within the Synod a
group had emerged, mainly associated with William Tennent,
formerly an Episcopalian minister, and his academy, the 'Log
College' in Neshaminy. The Great Awakening had originated
in 1735, in Congregationalist New England, where it was
largely associated with Jonathan Edwards in Northampton.
Like English Methodism, it stressed the free gift of God's
grace as something that could be experienced. It offered,
instead of hard doctrine, an opportunity to feel spiritual
exaltation, the feeling of being saved, under powerful
preaching. William Tennent and his son Gilbert were especially influenced by this thinking and began to insist on
the need for a 'converted' ministry which would show visible
signs of grace. The Synod on the whole, however, reacted
against it. There were moves to insist on proper university
qualifications for candidates to the ministry, which seemed
to be an attack on the Log College. And rules were introduced against ministers preaching in one another's parishes.
These were opposed by the Tennents and their supporters
on the grounds of the need for converted ministers to preach
the Gospel wherever possible. In 1740 Gilbert Tennent read
a paper to the Synod condemning his fellow-ministers as
'unconverted' and saying that those who believed they could
be saved through their own efforts were 'rotten-hearted
hypocrites, and utter strangers to the saving knowledge of
God and of their own hearts'. In 1741 Tennent's presbytery,
the Presbytery of New Brunswick, seceded from the Synod
of Philadelphia, and in 1745 the Synod of New York was
formed with the Presbyteries of New Brunswick, New York
and Newcastle.[69]

There are two main points I want to make here: first, the
resistance of the Presbyterian tradition, as represented by
the Philadelphia Synod, to the Great Awakening; secondly,

the presence in America, to a greater extent than in England, of the Congregationalist or Independent tradition. Charles Hodge, whose *Constitutional History of the Presbyterian Church in the United States of America* has been my main source for the above account, argues against the view that the division in the Synod represented a Scots Presbyterian/English Congregationalist division. Nevertheless, the existence of a strong Congregationalism, with a substantial tradition of literature on the theology of grace, and of searching for visible marks of grace, as well as an aversion to authoritative church courts, represents one common denominator between Methodist England and revivalist America. A modern scholar, J. D. Walsh, in an article on 'Élie Halévy and the Birth of Methodism', after stressing that the first Methodist converts came from the small High Church religious societies of which the Wesleys' 'Holy Club' was one, goes on to comment on the importance to the movement's success of Dissenters who were 'uneasy at their failure to produce, in a cooler religious climate, the classic marks of regeneration demanded of them by Puritan doctrine and Puritan forebears' (p. 6). Such classic marks of regeneration had not been demanded by the doctrine and forebears of the Scottish Presbyterians, except in the 'privy kirk' tradition which had been briefly influential in Ulster in the 1620s.

This view may be confirmed by a brief look at the second major secession that occurred later in the century, in 1761, in the Church of Scotland — the Relief Church. The leading figure in the Relief Church was Thomas Gillespie, who had been converted under Thomas Boston and was much influenced by *The Marrow of Modern Divinity*. He was dissatisfied with his training at the hands of both the Church of Scotland and the Seceders. He went instead to England, where he studied under the Congregationalist Philip Doddridge at Northampton. He then returned to Scotland and joined the Seceders. But he quarrelled with the Seceders on the question, much agitated in America too, of the power of the civil magistrate in the church, and on their opposition to Whitefield, whom he approved. With Whitefield, he argued for 'open communion', against the insistence of both the Church of Scotland and the Seceders on confining communion to members of their own churches. He functioned like an Independent. He formed an alliance with Boston's son, Thomas Boston junior, who was also in dispute with the Church of Scotland and who, according to Gavin Struthers's *History of the Rise of the Relief Church*, 'planted his standard as an English Presbyterian dissenting minister'. In 1761 Boston, Gillespie and the Rev. Thomas Colier, a Scotsman who had been minister of Ravenstondale in Westmorland, England, formed the Relief Presbytery to draw in members of the Church of Scotland dissatisfied with its system of patronage and its unenthusiastic preaching. Their principles were outlined by Patrick Hutchinson of St Ninian's in his *A Compendious View of the Religious System Taught in the Relief Synod*, which was based on covenant theology but declared: 'It is the distinguished excellence and glory of the Gospel that it offers Jesus and his salvation fully and freely to every sinner who hears this joyful sound' and 'That church-state, or establishment of religion, which is constituted by human authority, or cannot consist without it, is not for Christ, it is not his Kingdom, nor has the least connection with it.' It offered open communion to all 'visible saints' and, naturally, quarrelled on these points with the Seceders (a quarrel in which, as we shall see later, the principles of the Relief Church eventually triumphed).[70]

Again we can see both the dislike of mainstream Scottish Presbyterianism for the freewheeling doctrine of grace, and the influence of English Congregationalism. The Relief Church did not organise in Ulster, where Congregationalist theology and theories of church government had never taken root. If we arrange England, America, Scotland and Ulster in order of their openness to such 'Evangelical' preaching, Ulster will come last in the list and the order will correspond roughly to the extent of English Congregationalist influence, even though the English Congregationalists themselves were not at the head of the English movement. (This view will be strengthened further when Scottish Congregationalism appears on the scene and attempts to move into Ulster.) Ulster did receive the Secession. The Secession had a theology of grace, but it was a matter of doctrine, not a matter of highly charged emotional experience.

2. *Seceders and Covenanters in Ulster*

Anyone embarking on a study of the history of Ulster Presbyterianism is likely to have an impression that it has split in many directions, especially when we come across such exotic groups as the 'Primitive Anti-Burghers'. On closer acquaintance, however, that impression fades, and one is struck by how surprisingly stable the Synod of Ulster was, at least if we consider only its ministers. Until the present century the main body of Presbyterians in Ulster sustained only two splits: the Presbytery of Antrim in the 1720s and the Remonstrant Synod in the 1820s. Both were in a 'liberal' direction (the pattern was broken in the 1920s when the Evangelical Church split in an orthodox direction). The Seceders were certainly to prove fissiparous, but they organised in Ulster as a new church. They took their laity from the Synod of Ulster, but, although some were more sympathetic to them than others, they took no ministers.

This stability was not due to a uniformity of sentiment. Quite the contrary. The Non-Subscription Controversy continued after the expulsion of the Presbytery of Antrim throughout the eighteenth century, until by 1800 most presbyteries did not require subscription. This division was related to, but did not exactly coincide with, a division between 'Arminians' (in the most general sense of the word), for whom sincerity and virtue could expect to be rewarded in eternity, and 'Calvinists', who held that election was a gift of grace — not the consequence, though it could be the cause, of virtuous behaviour. Towards the end of the century ministers were divided into two camps in what, at the time of the United Irish rebellion, was virtually a state of civil war. Even after the Arian Controversy of the 1820s, when the Synod became more uniformly Calvinist in its theology, there continued to be divisions on such matters as the interdenominational National Education System, the introduction of unqualified subscription to the Westminster Confession, and the question of co-operation with or outright hostility to the Church of Ireland. Nor were these divisions smoothed over by a policy of not agitating controversial questions. They were fiercely discussed in a lively pamphlet literature which continued through to the present century.

Such disagreements would not be remarkable in a great national church, such as the Church of England, Ireland or Scotland, or indeed in the great international Roman Catholic Church. They were remarkable in a small dissenting church, especially one organised according to the Presbyterian model which required ministers to meet together and exercise authority in a corporate manner. Strain was imposed on particular presbyteries. In 1743 the Presbytery of Armagh divided after a series of skirmishes between Subscribers and Non-Subscribers. The Subscribers were put into the new Presbytery of Dromore (a reverse of the 1725 policy when the Non-Subscribers were put into the Presbytery of Antrim). Both presbyteries remained attached to the Synod. A similar division at the level of the presbytery occurred in 1774 when the Presbytery of Bangor was divided over the ordination of a minister who refused to subscribe to the Westminster Confession, and those who insisted on subscription were gathered into the new Presbytery of Belfast.[71]

This policy was rather in line with the arguments of Abernethy and his friends, who had insisted on the rights of presbyteries against the authority of the Synod, which was becoming very loose. But the main thing to observe is that the Synod was behaving like a broad national church, not like a small purposeful sect. The Westminster Confession of Faith in Scotland and the Thirty-Nine Articles in England were imposed by the secular parliament. It would require an act of parliament to remove them. But ministers in both established churches felt free to take a rather relaxed attitude towards them. They were like ritual practices, part of the tradition of the church, but they were not a programme of action. The churches were not bodies dedicated to promoting those particular ideas. The Westminster Confession of Faith was not imposed by act of parliament on the Synod of Ulster. The Synod was quite free to abandon it if it so chose — as many presbyteries did, in defiance of the Pacific Act, which was not repealed until the 1820s.

The Synod also continued to have friendly relations with the Presbytery of Antrim. Proposals for closer relations were made in 1747 and 1758. When a fund was established in Dublin to support the widows of ministers, both the Synod and the Presbytery of Antrim joined it. Loyal addresses were made on the death of George II in 1760 and on the birth of the Prince of Wales in 1762 by the Synod and the Presbytery of Antrim jointly as 'the Presbyterian ministers of the Northern Association in Ireland' — a clear concession to the kind of Presbyterian Independency which predominated in England and among the Presbyterian ministers of the Southern Association.[72]

Membership of the Synod of Ulster was therefore not membership of a church preaching a uniform doctrine or with a uniform idea of itself. The points in which the Synod differed from the Established Church were, in the eyes of many of its ministers, matters of secondary importance — dislike of vestments, a fixed liturgy, an ambivalent attitude to the eucharist (as a commemoration or as a 'mystery'), the hierarchical system, the political role of churchmen in the House of Lords. They were questions of style and social organisation rather than fundamental questions of theology. After the early eighteenth century, when its attempts encountered strong resistance from the Church of Ireland, the Synod made hardly any effort to expand outside Ulster. In fact, until the period of the Volunteers, the Ulster Presbyterians showed an extraordinary lack of interest in Ireland as a whole. Their pamphlet literature of the mid-eighteenth century is almost entirely concerned with disputes among themselves and with the Seceders and the Covenanters. They never showed very much interest in the Roman Catholic majority in Ireland, and in this period they show little interest even in disputing with the Church of Ireland. They functioned rather like a nation, a self-contained political unit. The church was a form of social organisation, with its own legislature — a highly democratic and intellectually lively political unit which had as little as possible to do with the all-Ireland institutions of church and state (Abernethy engaged in a vigorous dispute with Swift in the 1730s, but he had moved to Dublin and was now part of the Southern Association).

This did not suffice for the Seceders. They did see themselves as a purposeful and uniform community defined by their commitment to a distinctly religious end. The immediate occasion of their secession from the Church of

Scotland — patronage — did not exist in Ulster, though the Synod had introduced a system of electing ministers biased towards the more wealthy members of the congregation (who contributed more to the stipend). But, as in Scotland, the Seceders appealed to those who disliked the 'broad' range of opinions which is almost a necessary characteristic of a national church, and who wanted instead to be members of a 'true' church — the church that was preaching the doctrine from which true Christians could obtain comfort, the promises made by Christ to his elect. Being a 'true' and purposeful church, the Seceders were much more prone to division than the Synod. In Scotland they divided very shortly after their establishment over the lawfulness of taking what was known as the Burgesses' or Freemasons' Oath, into 'Burghers', who held that it was lawful, and 'Anti-Burghers', who held that it was unlawful. The Burgesses' Oath required jurors to 'profess the true religion presently professed within this realm and authorised by the laws thereof'. The Burghers insisted that they themselves represented the true Church of Scotland, authorised by the laws of the realm, from which the main body of the church had fallen away; the Anti-Burghers held that the oath referred, as it presumably did, to the Established Church from which they had seceded.[73]

The dispute indicates the continued importance, in the eyes of the Seceders, of the Presbyterian ideal of church/state relations. They were a church which ought to be co-terminous with the state and preserved by its laws, not a body of Christians who felt themselves to be saved and therefore separated from the political society. As part of this national ideal, they practised the renewal of the Solemn League and Covenant, committing themselves to the same aims for which their forefathers fought in the 1640s. Their 'alienation' from the Episcopalian Church establishments was therefore much greater than that of the Synod of Ulster. The overthrow of episcopacy was for them a religious duty, and they necessarily had a hostile attitude towards the government that supported episcopacy. The Westminster Confession authorised obedience to infidel or heretic authorities: 'Infidelity, or difference in religion, doth not make void the magistrate's just and legal authority, nor free the people from their due obedience to him: from which ecclesiastical persons are not exempted' (chap. XXIII, iv); and that provided the basis and extent of their loyalty.

The division between Burghers and Anti-Burghers had occurred in Scotland before the Seceders had managed to organise in Ulster, and since the Ulster Seceding ministers were still responsible to their Scottish Synod, the importation of the division was unavoidable, even though the Burgesses' Oath, which had been the occasion of it, was not imposed outside Scotland. At the turn of the century the two Scottish 'Associate Synods' each split again, using the terms 'Old Light' and 'New Light', which had been used in the Ulster Non-Subscription Controversy of the 1720s to describe the difference between the Subscribers and Non-Subscribers. Interestingly enough, and helping to confirm the view that Evangelical revivalism had little appeal in Ulster, this division was not reproduced among the Ulster Seceders. The immediate issue was over the right of the civil magistrate to punish heresy, an issue that was discussed at very great length in Ulster. But although the Ulster Seceders seem to have leaned towards the 'New Light' position (that the magistrate should not punish heresy), the Scottish New Lights were Evangelicals, promoting personal conversion experiences and visible signs of grace, and greatly influenced by the thinking of the Relief Church and of the Congregationalist movement led by the Haldane brothers which was particularly active in the north of Scotland. The attempt to import this movement among the Ulster Seceders in the form of the Evangelical Society of Ulster at the end of the eighteenth century was successfully suppressed by the Ulster synods. Some of the minsters who were attached to it left the synods in protest, but they did so as individuals, and therefore as Congregationalists, not as a separate New Light Synod.[74]

Insistent as the Seceders were on the rights and importance of 'true churches', the need for Covenant renewal and the ideal of the church co-terminous with the civil society, they were but a band of freethinkers by comparison with the Reformed Presbyterians or Covenanters.

The Reformed Presbyterians derived from those Presbyterians who refused to recognise the Revolution settlement of 1689-90 for a variety of reasons, but principally because it entailed the establishment of prelatic churches in England and Ireland. They argued that this was a denial of the Covenant and its obligation to 'endeavour the extirpation of popery and prelacy'. John McBride, in his *Sample of Jet-Black Prelatic Calumny*, had regarded the Solemn League and Covenant as a treaty between the nations of England and Scotland, which was no longer binding on Scotland because England had broken it. For the Covenanters it was a covenant between the various nations and God, and it was perpetually binding. As the Church of Scotland had refused to support Charles I or Charles II until they had subscribed the Covenant, so the Covenanters could not recognise William III or any of his successors. The Revolution is described in the Reformed Presbytery's *Act, Declaration and Testimony* of 1761 as 'a turning aside like a deceitful bow'. By establishing both presbytery in Scotland and prelacy in England, William had 'proclaimed himself destitute of . . . truth and religious fear' (p. 49).

The Covenanters can be compared, little though either side would relish the comparison, to the Non-Juring Church of England, which similarly refused to recognise the Revolution settlement, believed itself to be the true Church of England, and was in principle opposed to the existence of any church in the nation beside itself. Like the Non-Juring Church of England, the Covenanters took the view that the Bible contained clear principles of government which were to take precedence in all political arrangements. For the English church this meant obeying the rightful king, his right being determined by the succession, whatever his nature, even if he was a heretic or a tyrant. The utmost resistance permissible was a refusal to execute unjust laws, together with a preparedness to suffer passively the consequences. For the Scottish Covenanters, by contrast, the king must be a 'brother', that is, a member of the 'true church':

> The Christians have a right to set a king over them, yet it is evident they are not left at liberty to choose whom they please, but are, in the most express and positive terms, limited and circumscribed in their choice to him whom the Lord their God shall choose. (p. 99)

God's choice was signalled by the possession of 'scripture qualifications', which include a complete adherence to the moral law of the Old Testament. It was his duty to suppress heresy:

> No less wicked is it for a magistrate to protect, by a pro-miscuous toleration, all heretics, heresies and errors. . . . Experience has in every age taught that a toleration of all religions is the cut-throat and ruin of all religion – it is the most effectual method that ever the policy of Hell hatched to banish all true godliness out of the world. (p. 99)

Needless to say, the Covenanters had little time for the Synod of Ulster:

> The presbytery view them (complexly considered) as unworthy of their regard or notice in these papers, as to engaging in any particular or explicit testimony against them, in as much as they have denuded themselves of almost any pretence to the Presbyterian name, but having also fallen from the belief and profession of the most important and fundamental truths of Christiantiy . . . deserving rather to be termed a synagogue of Libertines, a club of Socinians, Arians, Pelagians, etc. banded together against Christ and the doctrines of his cross, than a Synod of the ministers of the Gospel. (p. 93)

While the Non-Juring Church of England was a church made up of clergy without a laity, the Covenanters started as a laity without a clergy. The most fiery of the pre-Revolution Covenanting preachers, such as Alexander Shields, joined the Church of Scotland at the Revolution, and the Covenanters, of course, had strict ideas as to the proper process of Presbyterian ordination. They had only one minister, David Houston (based in Ireland), but he died in 1696, and they had to wait until 1706, when they were joined by a properly ordained minister of the Church of Scotland, John MacMillan. Even then, MacMillan could not ordain on his own authority, so that it was not until 1743 (when he was joined by another minister) that they were able to establish a presbytery in Scotland, and not until 1763 that a presbytery was formed in Ireland. The Irish presbytery collapsed under pressure from emigration in 1779, and it was not until 1792 that the Covenanters in Ireland were able to constitute a presbytery which proved permanent. Numerically, therefore, the Reformed Presbyterians were a very marginal church, but they had an importance that went beyond their numbers, because of their logical consistency and their refusal to compromise. And as the division of Presbyterianism with the most impressive record of a principled refusal to recognise the legitimacy of the secular government, they were about to acquire a new impetus and importance in the heady days of the Volunteers and the United Irishmen.[75]

6

Political
Ambitions

---

1. *An Armed People*

The Ulster Presbyterians had, throughout the eighteenth century, been a distinct people who were excluded from participation in the politics of the state in which they lived but
who had developed a social structure of their own in many
ways more vigorous and cohesive than that of the state and
its Established Church. The appearance of a whole political
society distinct from the political society governed by
Westminster and Dublin was if anything reinforced by their
divisions. The Synod of Ulster, incorporating within itself a
wide variety of theological and political views, had the appearance of a national church surrounded, like the Church of
England, by a dissenting fringe – the Presbytery of Antrim,
the Seceders and the Covenanters.

The differences among Presbyterians turned largely on
those matters in which religion overlaps with politics – the
relations that ought to exist between church and state. The
Ulster Presbyterians never, at any stage in their development,
produced a substantial devotional literature. The polemical
theology in which they specialised turned largely on the
degree to which a true church could recognise, co-operate
with or accept the assistance of a state which supported a
prelatic establishment. By comparison with the English and
Scottish Dissenters, they occupied a rather privileged position.
The English Dissenters received a small grant of money from
the king to support their ministers' widows. The Synod of
Ulster received a much more substantial grant to help support
the ministers themselves.

Their attitude to government varied from a thoroughgoing support to outright opposition. John Cameron, minister of Dunluce, a former Reformed Presbyterian who had adopted an extreme New Light position of advocating full inter-communion between all Christian denominations, including the Roman Catholic Church, praised Ireland, in *The Catholic Christian, or The True Religion Sought and Found* (1769) as 'a land of light and liberty, where different professions of religion, even the most obnoxious, either enjoy a full toleration, or are connived at and live unmolested' (p. 3). The Reformed Presbyterian William James, on the other hand, in his *Homesius Enervatus* (1772) complained that the government tolerated heresy and argued that the only merit in the British con-stitution was the fact that the Roman Catholics were excluded from the throne. The Synod of Ulster's William Campbell, a Non-Subscriber, in his *Vindication of the Principles and Char-acter of the Presbyterians of Ireland* (1787) objected that under the constitution the clergy had too much political power, and he made it clear that he would object equally to such power being exercised by Presbyterian ministers.

The government was thus praised for its tolerance, attacked for not being sufficiently tolerant, and abused for being too tolerant.

In the 1770s this population, which had long organised itself as a distinct political society and been engaged in an intense debate on the nature of the state, was transformed, in an extraordinary set of circumstances, into a citizen army.

The circumstance of the arming of the Ulster Presbyterians was the American Revolution and the war declared by France in support of it. The army was stretched beyond its resources, and Ireland, vulnerable because of its large Catholic popul-ation, was left undefended. The government therefore author-ised the Irish aristocracy to raise and arm battalions of Volunteers, who were, however, not under the direct control of the Dublin Castle administration. Throughout Ireland this meant the establishment of armed Protestant garrisons sur-rounded by an unarmed Catholic population. In Ulster it meant the arming of a whole people, including the Presby-terians, despite the fact that they had good reason to sym-pathise with the Americans.[76]

There was a substantial Ulster Presbyterian contribution to the American Revolution. A comparison with the Fenian support for Irish nationalism in the second half of the nineteenth century would, however, be misleading. The Ulster Presbyterians who emigrated to America in the eighteenth century were not, like the famine victims of the 1840s, motivated by a burning hatred of Britain. They were exchanging a situation in which their ambitions were cramped for one in which opportunities appeared to be boundless. They had been virtually excluded from politics, they were living under and required to support an alien church establishment, and in many cases, especially in the period immediately preceding the American Revolution, they had been engaged in intense agrarian warfare to establish rights as tenants in opposition to their landlords. But they were not in principle national separatists, or even, despite their antipathy to the king's claim to be supreme governor of the church, anti-monarchists.

In this they corresponded with and contributed to the American mood. The Americans had long been deeply dissatisfied with their relations with the British government. They were now exercising what they saw as their right as free and loyal citizens to protest against what had become an intolerable despotism. Their position as loyal rebels resembles that of the Ulster Protestant rebels of the 1790s, of 1886, 1912, 1974 and, at the time I am writing, 1986. On all these occasions, as in the American Revolution, national separatism was considered as a last resort rather than as a primary purpose.[77]

Considering the advantages of national separatism, which appear very obvious in retrospect, the loyalism of the Americans before 1776 seems rather surprising. The crucial consideration seems to have been defence. Britain had recently been engaged in a long and costly war to defend the Americans against their new allies, the French. The British saw the American opposition to taxation as a profoundly ungrateful refusal to pay for their own defence. The American principle was 'No taxation without representation' — that the British had no right to make decisions concerning America, however moderate or reasonable those decisions may have been, without the involvement of the Americans themselves in the decision-making process. But there was, naturally, considerable confusion on the American side caused by the benefits to be derived from British protection. In this situation, the journalist Tom Paine had a crucial role to play in clarifying the issues and giving a sense of purpose to the American agitation, and Paine was shortly to become popular among the Ulster Presbyterians as well. The parallel with the present (1986) situation of the Ulster Protestants is remarkable. They too are excluded from the political process by which they are governed through being refused membership of the major British political parties. Like the Americans, they too are being denied access to a government to which they wish to be loyal, and are faced with the possible prospect of having to engage in a fight for national separatism as the only tolerable alternative to the full participation in the political process that they have been denied.

The rise of the Volunteer movement in response to the American Revolution put the Ulster Presbyterians into a completely new situation. As an armed people, even if armed under the patronage of the aristocracy, they were now a force to be reckoned with. The Anglican ascendancy had clearly indicated that they were dependent on Presbyterian support, and, in the whole spectrum of the Irish Volunteer movement, the Ulster Presbyterians, with a popular base, a coherent identity and long experience of independent social organisation, were the most substantial part. The possibility of participating in politics was now open to them, especially since the ascendancy itself was acquiring new political ambitions.

The Ulster Presbyterians were governed by two parliaments, from both of which they were effectively excluded: the sovereign parliament at Westminster and the devolved Anglican ascendancy parliament in Dublin. The Irish ascendancy were not represented at Westminster, which therefore had no need to consider Irish interests as its own. Yet the Irish parliament was wholly dependent on the Westminster parliament. Under the fifteenth-century Poynings' Law the Irish parliament could debate no bills that had not previously been approved by the king, to whom also the executive, the administration in Dublin Castle, was responsible. Theoretically such a system might have been less obnoxious under an absolute monarchy in which the king had a will independent from that of parliament, but under a constitutional monarchy the king was almost wholly dependent on the Westminster parliament with its primarily English interests. In 1703, in the aftermath of the Glorious Revolution and the intense political debate that it had generated, the Irish parliament had petitioned for a full incorporating union — involving its own abolition and full representation for Irish ascendancy interests at Westminster. This had been refused, and the ascendancy sank into a long century of what may be described, using a modern term, as 'second-class citizenship'.[78]

Presbyterians were not formally excluded from membership of the Irish parliament, though they were excluded from positions of profit and public trust under the crown. In practice, however, the system of representation gave them very little opportunity to participate in parliamentary life. This at least had the merit of protecting them from the system of parliamentary corruption. Ireland was governed by the Castle, but the Castle required the consent of the parliament and had to buy that consent with honours and government sinecures. The same system prevailed to a large extent in England and is associated with the name of Sir Robert Walpole. But it was more distasteful in Ireland to the extent that the corruption of one society by another society is more distasteful than the corruption of a society by itself. It was also more distasteful in that the Anglican ascendancy was a caste recently imposed on Irish society by military force, and was lacking the ties of a common religion and traditional loyalty and affection which gave their English counterparts some title to be regarded as the 'representatives' of the areas which returned them to parliament.

The political programme of the Ulster Presbyterians was straightforward enough, and was formulated in the *Letters of Orellana*, published in the *Belfast News-Letter* in the 1780s by William Drennan, son of a Non-Subscribing Presbyterian minister, who performed for Ulster something of the service performed by Tom Paine for the Americans. In the same decade the Dublin parliament was given greater control of the government of Ireland through the repeal of Poynings' Law. This coincided with the demands of the ascendancy and had been granted in 1782, shortly before the publication of Drennan's *Letters*, by the British parliament, alarmed by the spectacle of armed Protestant unity. A vigorous reform movement then followed, aimed at making parliament more directly representative of 'the people', including the Presbyterians, though not the Roman Catholics, who were to be content with a relaxation of the penal laws. The demand for reform brought the Presbyterians, with substantial Anglican allies, into conflict with the ascendancy, and its failure resulted in the 1790s in the rise of the United Irishmen.

The political possibilities opened up by the power of the Volunteers generated a fierce political enthusiasm among the Ulster Presbyterians, almost to the exclusion of religious concerns, though, in the millenarian atmosphere of the times, the two could not be easily separated. It was seen in the energetic campaigning of Presbyterian ministers in the Co. Down elections of 1783 and 1790 on behalf of the Stewart family, who supported reform, against the conservative Hill family, who opposed it. The enthusiasm for politics of the period was to be a continual source of reproach among writers in the early nineteenth century. Nor was it universally supported at the time. The Seceders registered a protest against the fall into the ways of worldly politics by supporting the Hill family interest, for which they were rewarded by — for the first time, and in startling contrast to their treatment in Scotland — being given a grant of *regium donum* (though, in fact, Lord Hillsborough complained in private correspondence that the government had been over-generous). The well-known United Irish leader Jemmy Hope had been a Seceder and has left an account of his disillusionment with them over this incident.[79]

There is another political aspect to the arming of the Ulster Presbyterians in this period, apart from the new political power it gave them, and that is its connection with 'republicanism'. In current usage in Ireland the term 'republicanism' means little more than militant national separatism, but in the eighteenth century it referred to a political and moral ideal which to a large extent, whether or not they used the term itself, was shared by the Ulster Presbyterians. It was the ideal of a society composed of strong, self-reliant, men, distinguished by the possession of particular skills, associating and deciding matters of common interest together on a voluntary basis, and leading simple and frugal lives, rejecting the pompous splendours and self-indulgence of the aristocracy. The ideal had been formulated earlier in the century by the French-Swiss philosopher Jean-Jacques Rousseau, taking his own birthplace of Geneva as a model. The emphasis on 'men' is not accidental, since Rousseau in his *Discourse on the Sciences and Arts*, the work that first established his reputation as a writer, attacks what he sees as the effeminacy of the age, brought about by the progress of the arts and sciences, which have undermined 'virtue'. 'Virtue' he defines as military virtue – the ability to defend oneself, which is essential to self-reliance, and the discipline and self-control that is necessary to armies.

I cannot say that I have found direct references to Rousseau in the literature of the Volunteer or United Irish movements, but his writings are an important key to understanding the radicalism of the time, while the ideal he outlines bears a striking resemblance to the actual political community created by the Ulster Presbyterians, especially in the 1780s, when it became armed. Rousseau's model was, as we have seen, Calvinist Geneva, which he praises in the dedication to his *Discourse on the Origins and Foundations of Inequality among Men*, in which he describes it as a self-policing society of equals. At the beginning of the eighteenth century Geneva, by an act of the secular legislature which marked an end to clerical domination, had adopted the principle of Non-Subscription. We have seen how Samuel Haliday, whose induction as minister of the First Belfast Presbyterian congregation provoked the eventual expulsion of the Presbytery of Antrim from the Synod of Ulster, had chosen to be ordained in Geneva for that reason.[80]

The Ulster Presbyterians were a society that included many independent craftsmen and businessmen, who had voluntarily, through their participation in the church, accepted a strong social discipline which was agreed and enforced in a relatively democratic manner. They did not at this time have many very wealthy adherents, and their religious culture, as well as their financial circumstances, discouraged frivolity, excess and, in particular, the visual arts. One imagines, however, that they might have approved the austere, heroic, neo-classical style of painting which accompanied the French Revolution, had they been acquainted with it. From its outset, of course, they supported the French Revolution, which had taken Rousseau and his Roman/Spartan/Genevan republicanism as its inspiration. Presbyterian ministers became enthusiastic champions of the volunteering cause, and a number of 'Volunteer sermons' have survived which sing the praises of training in arms as a means of teaching youth the virtues of moral discipline, self-reliance and resistance to the will of despots. William Steel Dickson, later to be imprisoned for his associations with the United Irishmen, argued in his *Three Sermons on the Subject of Scripture Politics*, published in 1793, that taxation was unnecessary, since the only serious purpose of taxation was to pay for the defence of the country, and an armed people could defend itself (p. 63).[81]

The problem for the Presbyterian radicals was that, although their own community constituted a virtual republic in its own right, they were now demanding full participation in the politics of a country in which they were a small minority. In a long-term view, their very strength can be seen as a source of weakness. The English reformers of the same period, though motivated by similar ideals, had none of their cohesiveness. The Dissenters who supported them were organised on Congregational principles and did not have the same sense of being a distinct, organised community as the Ulster Presbyterians. Nor did they have the same geographical concentration; and nor, of course, were they armed. Armed rebellion seemed a feasible proposition to the Ulster Presbyterians, especially in the areas in which they were strongest, in Antrim and Down. The possibility of armed rebellion was implicit in the 1783 Volunteer Convention, when the Volunteers camped outside the Dublin parliament with the explicit intention of intimidating that assembly to introduce measures of reform. In the event their bluff was called, but the same threat was again present in the 1790 Volunteer Convention in Dungannon. These conventions were, of course, by no means exclusively Presbyterian affairs, but it was in Ulster, and mainly through the Presbyterian presence, that they could credibly appear as conventions of an armed people demanding a renegotiation of its contract with the government. The Presbyterians were a people, but they were not the Irish people. Their strength lay in their existence as a distinct community, but this was of itself an obstacle to the formation of a truly national movement. What appearance the Volunteer movement had of being a national movement was due to the participation of sections of the Anglican ascendancy, which, despite its comparative lack of a popular base, was at least dispersed throughout Ireland.

The English radicals could not mount anything so impressive as the Volunteer conventions. They were scattered as a small and unpopular element throughout English society. But by that very token they could act as a leavening throughout English society, and they eventually had their reward in the social turmoil which produced the 1832 Reform Act, to which the Ulster Presbyterians, though in general they supported it, contributed very little. To quote Isaiah: 'Fear not, thou worm Jacob. . . . Behold, I will make thee a new sharp threshing instrument having teeth: thou shalt thresh the mountains, and beat them small, and shalt make the hills as chaff.' (Isa. 41: 14-15)[82]

The need to establish a national movement to achieve reform raised sharply the question of relations with Catholic Ireland. The question had already been raised in the immediate aftermath of the achievement of legislative independence in 1782 by Henry Grattan, for whom the idea of an independent democratic Irish nation that excluded the Catholics was an absurdity. Henry Flood, on the other hand, who presented the demands of the Volunteer Convention to parliament in 1783, argued that if Catholics were admitted to an independent reformed parliament, they would quickly dominate it. It was not until the 1790s that Grattan's ideas on the subject began to be seriously entertained among the Ulster Presbyterians, and the turning-point in their view of the matter was the French Revolution.[83]

2. *Alliance with the Catholics*

There was nothing natural about an alliance between Irish Presbyterians and Roman Catholics, despite the fact that they had a common enemy in the Anglican ascendancy. The main traditional objection of the Presbyterians to Anglicanism was precisely its resemblance to Roman Catholicism, and a section of Presbyterian opinion, represented in its most militant form by the Reformed Presbyterians (who were, as we shall see shortly, active in the United Irish agitation), objected to the ascendancy on the grounds that it was too tolerant towards Roman Catholics. All Presbyterians were agreed that Roman Catholicism had a deplorable history and absurd doctrines. And even those who took a benign and tolerant attitude could hardly feel confident that their benevolence and tolerance would be returned if Roman Catholics assumed political power.

Furthermore, there was a great difference in the condition of the two populations. The Presbyterian radical leaders had taken up republican ideals because they had the opportunity to do so, chiefly through the Volunteer movement. Their radicalism was a product of high spirits and self-confidence. They felt themselves to be free men, whose rights were invaded by a despotic and corrupt government. They wished to be able to participate in a simplified decision-making process, purged of its corruptions. And their ideals flowed naturally from their own self-developed mode of social organisation and from their own cultural traditions. They were already, as Lord Castlereagh and his secretary, Alexander Knox, were to complain, republicans.

The Catholic population, on the other hand, were for the most part what was left of a highly aristocratic society after its aristocracy had been finally wiped out or exiled in what the most radical sections of Presbyterian opinion still saw as a 'Glorious Revolution'. Its most lively political ideal through the eighteenth century, still alive in popular sentiment though now quite hopeless, was Jacobitism, involving support for the principle of absolute monarchy — the very reverse of Presbyterian republicanism — and identified with the Stuarts, who were the traditional Presbyterian enemy. Their principles of church government were wholly hierarchical, even though they had been prevented by the penal laws from forming a church structure as cohesive or as public as that of the Synod of Ulster. Over much of Ireland they were still largely Gaelic-speaking and steeped in a culture that had long ceased to be functional.[84]

It is, however, arguable that the very hopelessness of the majority Catholic population facilitated the radicals in believing that an alliance with them might be possible. They had, or appeared to have, no distinct political existence of their own, outside the Catholic Committee, based in Dublin, which had been formed in the mid-eighteenth century on a basis of accommodation with the Hanoverian settlement, and which had developed a modern outlook, parallel to that of its English equivalent. In the 1790s, when Wolfe Tone became its secretary, it even acquired a republican appearance through having been taken over by a distinctly bourgeois party based in Dublin. Unlike the English Catholic Committee, it was far from being representative, but so long as it was not repudiated by the Catholic bishops, it was the only political spokesman Catholic Ireland had, and when the Presbyterian radicals found that they could, for a brief period at least, control it, they concluded that the prospects for Catholic Ireland acquiring republican ideals were bright.

In the 1780s William Drennan had asserted in the *Letters of Orellana* that 'a reform attended by an equal participation of civil rights with the Catholics' would be worse 'than to continue without a reform' until such time as the Catholics had acquired that 'self-estimation, conscious dignity and, in short, that Republicanism of soul which will announce to the world that the people who possess it are stamped by the hand of Heaven, heirs of Independence' (pp 30-2). But by 1792 he argued that that very development had occurred, because

To commercial interest, a middle and mediating rank has rapidly grown up in the Catholic community and produced that enlargement of mind, that energy of character and that self-independence which men acquire whose interests do not hang at the mercy of this or that individual, but on general and necessary consumption. . . . The Catholic mind has cast off its 'feudality'.[85]

It is doubtful if the kind of radical transformation in the social base of Irish Catholicism Drennan describes had actually occurred in the intervening six years, and he is probably referring simply to the change in the composition of the Catholic Committee. But a radical transformation had occured in the way in which Roman Catholicism could be perceived as a world power, and it is probably this change, brought about by the French Revolution, which enabled Drennan to accept the representative nature of the Catholic Committee so uncritically. Wolfe Tone, in his *Argument on Behalf of the Catholics of Ireland*, published in 1791, is more explicit:

> It is not six months since the Pope was publicly burned in effigy at Paris, the capital of that Monarch who is styled the eldest son of the Church. Yet the time has been when Philip of France thought he had a good title to the crown of England from the donation of the Holy Father. The fallacy lies in supposing what was once true in politics is always true: I do believe the Pope has now more power in Ireland than in some Catholic countries, or than he perhaps ought to have. But I confess I look on his power with little apprehension because I cannot see to what evil purpose it could be exerted; and with the less apprehension as every liberal extension of property or franchise to Catholics will tend to diminish it. Persecution will keep alive the foolish bigotry and superstition of any sect, as the experience of five thousand years has demonstrated. Persecution bound the Irish Catholic to his Priest and the Priest to the Pope; the bond of union is drawn tighter by oppression; relaxation will undo it. The emancipated and liberal Frenchman may go to mass and tell his beads; but neither the one nor the other will attend to the rusty and extinguished thunderbolts of the Vatican, or the idle anathemas, which indeed his Holiness is nowadays too prudent and cautious to issue. (pp 24-5)

The French Revolution was a republican revolution conducted by Catholics (I am taking the term 'republican' as

referring to the ideal of a state managed by the representatives of the people meeting as equals, not as a dogmatic
insistence on the overthrow of monarchy. Belfast tended to
be Girondin rather than Jacobin in its sympathies). One of
its first acts was the reorganisation of the French church on
democratic lines through the 'Civil Constitution of the Clergy',
promulgated, by a happy coincidence, on 12 July 1790. Two
days later Belfast celebrated the first anniversary of the fall
of the Bastille. France had been seen from Britain as the most
formidable of the continental Catholic powers, even if the
Gallican church had already, to a large extent and for a long
period of time, come under effective state control. The
Revolution, and the reorganisation of the church along lines
analogous to Presbyterianism, could easily be seen as a new
Reformation, radically altering the balance of power between
Protestantism and Catholicism in Europe. It was welcomed
by all sections of Ulster Presbyterians, including the most
rigorously Calvinist. The Burgher Synod (Seceders) in 1791
issued a *Reasons for a Fast* which proclaimed that 'the wonder-
ful revolution in France seems to hold out that event as a
hastening in the holy Providence of God'; while the recently
reconstituted Reformed Presbytery (Covenanters) in its
Causes of Fasting, issued in 1792, suggested that the pouring
out of the last vial of wrath on the Beast and his Kingdom
was imminent.[86]

The early 1790s, then, was a period of immense revolutionary optimism, in which the recently flagging impetus of the
Volunteer movement was renewed with redoubled force by
the inspiration of France. It was a period in which the struggle
between Christ and Antichrist became identified with a
struggle between liberty and despotism, and it was possible
for the quasi-republican society in Ulster to see itself as the
spearhead of British radicalism. In these new circumstances,
brought about by Catholics in France, Tone's arguments
struck a chord, especially in Belfast, where Catholics were
experienced as a small bourgeois element caught up in the
radical mood which surrounded them. The fact that the
Dublin Catholic Committee could adopt Tone as its secretary
on the basis of a pamphlet which welcomed the burning of
the pope's effigy in Paris was most encouraging. To clarify

the question of the political allegiance of Irish Catholics to the pope, the Belfast Society of United Irishmen requested the Catholic Committee to make a declaration similar to that issued by the English Catholic Committee, disclaiming the right of the pope to interfere in relations between the sovereign and his subject. The Catholic Committee duly obliged. A town meeting to discuss the admission of Catholics to the full rights of citizenship was held in Belfast in 1792 and voted in favour.

A more cautious observer of Catholic politics would have pointed out, however, that unlike the aristocratically based English Catholic Committee, the republican Dublin committee had made no effort to canvass a wider opinion on the subject. Furthermore, the English committee had admitted that the pope's right to exercise authority in internal national politics had been a part of Catholic doctrine, but went on to assert, as Wolfe Tone did, that this had now changed (Tone, it may be noted in parenthesis, ascribes no change to the pope himself; he takes it for granted, possibly with the French example long before the Revolution in mind, that it was possible for Catholics to differ from the pope in principle and to sustain those differences both in practice and in argument). The Dublin Catholic Committee indignantly repudiated as slanderous the suggestion that the church had ever taught any such thing. The Dublin declaration was therefore considerably less substantial a document than that of the English, as was pointed out at the time by a correspondent in the *Northern Star*.[87]

A more cautious approach towards the extension of the franchise to Catholics was advanced in the Belfast town debate by William Bruce, minister of the Non-Subscribing First Belfast congregation, and by Henry Joy, proprietor of the *Belfast News-Letter* (and uncle of Henry Joy McCracken), both using arguments similar to those of Drennan in the 1780s — that Irish Catholics had not yet undergone the process of social transformation that could enable them to make good use of the rights of free men. It is interesting to note how the position of the Ulster Presbyterians with regard to the Catholic population forced them to think of republican rights as a product of historical or social development, whereas Locke, Rousseau and even Paine talk of these rights as belonging to man in the abstract, basing a large part of their argument on the premise that such rights are an original possession of man in his most primitive state.[88]

Although defeated in the Belfast town debate, the tendency represented by Bruce and Joy continued to have a voice in the *Belfast News-Letter*, while the *Northern Star* was founded in reaction against the *News-Letter* and to argue the radical case. The *News-Letter*, readers will remember, had carried Drennan's *Letters of Orellana*. It had shared in the initial enthusiasm over the French Revolution and, like the *Northern Star*, had continued to follow with close interest all the developments of the French experiment. Both papers came to adopt a more critical line. Tone, in France, continued in a high state of revolutionary enthusiasm throughout the terror, but the *Northern Star* in Belfast, while still supportive, increasingly adopted an apologetic note, arguing that these excesses had been the result of the intolerable despotism which preceded them and would not be necessary for the reform of the British mode of government which already, in the House of Commons, contained a republican element. The *News-Letter* became more straightforwardly hostile, following the kind of reasoning adopted by Edmund Burke, who had likewise previously supported the Americans (though the *News-Letter* did not follow Burke in his continuing support for the Irish radicals).

The radical wing of the Volunteer movement in Ulster was therefore split on the Catholic question by 1792, and in 1793 the enthusiasts for the French Revolution found themselves in even more radical opposition to the government when, following the execution of Louis XVI, Britain joined the war on France in alliance with the continental Catholic powers. In the war between Christ and Antichrist, liberty and despotism, Britain had now unequivocally joined the ranks of Antichrist and despotism. The Moderator of the Synod of Ulster in 1793 was William Steel Dickson, who was to be imprisoned in 1798. A sermon was preached to the Synod by Thomas Ledlie Birch, who was to be exiled to America in 1798, in which he said:

We must think that the final overthrow of the Beast, or

opposing power, is almost at the door; and especially as we may observe in a certain contest the seemingly literal accomplishment of the Battle of Armageddon, in which the Beast and his adherents are to be cut off, as a prelude to the peaceful reign of 1,000 years.[89]

The 'certain contest' is clearly the French war, and we know enough about Birch to know that Britain was now on the side of the Beast.

Britain entered the war with an armed population at its back, a substantial section of which (largely concentrated in Ulster) was militantly committed to the French cause. Under those circumstances the disarming of the Volunteers and their replacement by a militia directly responsible to the Castle was a military necessity. At the same time Pitt saw that it was necessary to break the connection between the Catholics and the Irish radicals, and he therefore put pressure on the supposedly independent Irish parliament to admit Catholics to the franchise with an exceptionally low property qualification. It was an astonishingly radical move which probably went beyond even what many of the United Irishmen envisaged (Tone's *Argument* had suggested that the dangers of a Catholic ascendancy would be minimised by preserving a high property qualification), though its potentially radical effect was soon to be weakened by the Act of Union, while it could also be argued — and was undoubtedly the case — that the poorest Catholic voters were those most at the mercy of their landlords. Whatever its longer-term dangers, Pitt's device had the desired effect of detaching the Catholic Committee from effective participation in the United Irish movement.[90]

At the same time the disarming of the Volunteers ended the appearance Ulster had of a society of free men armed for their own and their country's defence. The ideal which had been almost universal in the 1780s was now impossible so long as Ireland continued to be attached to Britain. The disarming was by no means complete, and weapons in large numbers continued to be held and manufactured, but they had to be kept hidden. The armed society had to operate clandestinely. Eventually there was a much more thorough and brutal disarming in 1797 which contributed mightily to the angry mood of the 1798 rebellion, while depriving it of some of its military potential.

It would, of course, be very misleading to suggest that the whole Presbyterian community supported the United Irish movement. We have already seen that the Belfast liberals divided in 1792 on the question of extending the vote to Catholics. Bruce and Joy pursued an intellectual path similar to that of Robert Stewart, soon to become Viscount Castlereagh. Stewart had been elected for Co. Down with energetic Presbyterian support, which included Dickson and Birch, in the very year — 1790 — when enthusiasm for the French Revolution was at its highest. Castlereagh was soon to become the *bête noir* of the radical Presbyterians, the man who supervised the suppression of the United Irish rising (and, incidentally, prevented it from taking a much nastier course than it did), and eventually went on to conduct the war against Napoleon and bring it to a successful conclusion. Many Presbyterians were involved in what was virtually a running war with Catholics in areas in which the Catholic population was substantial. Once it became clear that the Catholic Committee was unable or unwilling to act as an organising centre for Catholic Ireland, the United Irishmen, looking for Catholic allies, were forced to enter into direct negotiations with the agrarian terrorist societies which were fighting the Catholic side of this war — the Catholic counter-parts of the Protestant Peep o' Day Boys and the fledgeling Orange Order.

The United Irishmen were an alliance of three elements: Presbyterians, representative of a substantial section of a well-organised community; Anglicans, scattered throughout the country and therefore in a position to extend the con-spiracy on an all-Ireland basis, but still in themselves un-representative of a wider community; and Catholic secret societies, some of them long established and with a clearly defined leadership, but with no particular knowledge of or interest in republican or French revolutionary ideas. From the government point of view, it was a formidable and frightening combination, and its most formidable as well as its most conscious point was Presbyterian Ulster. It may have been only a minority of Presbyterians and Presbyterian ministers who were directly involved in the United Irish organisation, but when an armed revolt is in careful and determined preparation over a period of five years and the surrounding community does not exert itself to help the government suppress it, we may safely assume that there is widespread, if tacit, support for it.

3. *Defeat and Demoralisation*

The year 1793 saw the end of the Volunteer movement and the pride and hopes that went with it. The year 1798 saw the final defeat and discrediting of the United Irish movement. The rebellion was discredited by the Catholic sectarian form it took in Wexford, where the supposed ascendancy leadership lost control. The Wexford rising confirmed the worst fears of those who, like Bruce and Joy, believed that the Protestant republicans could not establish and maintain hegemony over Catholic Ireland. Nevertheless, Presbyterians have held and still hold an ambivalent attitude to the 1798 rising. The historian W. D. Killen, in his continuation of Reid's *History of the Presbyterian Church in Ireland*, is uncompromisingly hostile and seeks, unconvincingly, to minimise the Presbyterian involvement, which, he suggests, was almost entirely confined to the New Light, or quasi-Unitarian, section of Ulster Presbyterianism, later to be cut off in the Arian disputes of the 1820s. Some of the leaders, including Dickson and the laymen William Tennent and William Orr, undoubtedly held New Light views. Orr, however, was accompanied to his execution by the Reformed Presbyterian, William Stavely, who was a contributor to the *Northern Star*, while Tennent, a proprietor of the *Northern Star*, was the son of one of the first Anti-Burgher ministers to settle in Ulster. The Rev. John Tennent supported the *Northern Star* in its early days, though he disliked the union with Catholics. Another of his sons, John Tennent junior, fled to France and eventually died in the service of Napoleon, while yet another son, Dr Robert Tennent, was involved as a ship's surgeon in the Table Bay mutiny and had a hand in all the radical movements which developed in Ulster until his death in 1836. Robert Tennent was devoutly — even, in his younger days, rather morbidly — orthodox in his theology. Two other leading figures, Thomas Ledlie Birch and Sinclare Kelburn, were members of the Presbytery of Belfast, formed, as we have seen, as a Subscribing presbytery when the Presbytery of Bangor adopted the principle of Non-Subscription.[91]

On the other side of the coin, the most consistent opponent of the United Irish movement in Belfast was William Bruce, minister of the First Congregation and a member of the Presbytery of Antrim, who became in the 1820s one of the leading advocates of Arianism. By a pleasant irony, he prompted the masterpiece of Ulster Presbyterian polemical theology, the *Refutation of Arianism* by the Reformed Presbyterian minister John Paul, who more than anybody else in that period embodies the United Irish spirit. We shall encounter Paul later, but suffice it to say here that it is possible to imagine him coming out in '98, whereas the very idea of his contemporary, the Arian leader Henry Montgomery, with a pike in his hand is ludicrous. The leading opponent of the United Irishmen in the Synod of Ulster itself was the Rev. Robert Black of Londonderry, who was also latitudinarian in his theological views and generally believed to be an Arian. The attempt to link New Light theology with radical politics and orthodox theology with conservative politics may have served the controversial purposes of both Henry Montgomery and the orthodox leader Henry Cooke, but it is untenable in the actual history of the period.

Despite Killen's dismissal of the '98 rebellion, however, a certain pride in it exists, if only in the folk memories of Ulster Presbyterianism. It may have been futile and caused much unnecessary bloodshed, but at least a stand was made, and all the drilling and self-flaunting of the Volunteers did not issue merely in an abject surrender to a government edict. There is a sense, moreover, in which it can be argued that the rebellion succeeded, or at least did not entirely fail. It was a rebellion against the Dublin parliament — against a corrupt ascendancy masquerading as an independent power but in fact still controlled by and receptive to the favours of Westminster. The Ulster insurgents' primary objective of an independent Ireland under Presbyterian republican hegemony may have been decisively thwarted in 1798, but at least the rising achieved its secondary aim in that the despised Dublin parliament was swept away. The rebellion had a radical political outcome in the form of the Union, which the Presbyterians quickly and without any very great difficulty took to their hearts, despite a not entirely rational hatred for its architect, Lord Castlereagh, which has persisted to the present day.[92]

The experiment of giving autonomy to the ascendancy had been tried and had failed. The ascendancy, still committed to supporting Britain in its battles, had been quite incapable of controlling Ireland in the circumstances of the French war. The United Irish conspiracy had terrified and paralysed them, and the revolt had to be suppressed by the British army under the direction of Pitt and the Dublin Castle administration. The liberal wing of the Dublin parliament had opted out of politics, and what was left was virtually demanding the massacre of the whole population. With the Union, the new experiment was to be tried of making Westminster the centre of Irish politics. Ireland was to be governed as part of a national unit with Britain and no longer to be treated as a foreign dependency.

To this end Pitt and Castlereagh set themselves political aims surprisingly similar to those of the United Irishmen. The political monopoly of the ascendancy was to be ended, and the sectarian divisions among Irishmen broken down. Catholics, who already had the vote, were to be admitted to parliament, and the loyalty of both the Catholic and the Presbyterian Churches was to be secured by new arrangements which would give them a semi-establishment status. In the event the ameliorating measures proposed for Catholics failed through the opposition of the king in a rare exercise of his personal prerogative, but the arrangements made for the Presbyterians were more successful.

We should not underestimate the difficulty of Castlereagh's task. If the Irish parliament was not to be abolished by an act of force, it had to be persuaded to dissolve itself, and in so doing renounce a widespread network of power, vested interests, patronage and sinecures. Places in parliament had been bought for immense sums of money and carried with them great material benefits. They were in many cases simply a form of freely negotiable property. Castlereagh had to persuade the parliament to part voluntarily with a source of wealth and influence which the United Irishmen would have taken away by force. This could only be done by bribery on a large scale, a task for which the Lord Lieutenant, the uncourtly soldier Cornwallis, was quite unsuited. It was Castlereagh's achievement, and unless one prefers the perpetuation of a wholly unrepresentative assembly which now stood in vicious opposition to the society it was responsible for governing, or its now impossible overthrow by revolutionary force, it is an achievement that has to be admired.[93]

As regards the part of Castlereagh's scheme which failed — the arrangements for the Catholics — it must be borne in mind that the British constitution was based on the premise that the king, who was now little more than the servant of his parliament, was in charge of the church. The Established Churches of England and Ireland had no independence from the political society around them. They could not meet separately to determine their own affairs. They were subject to their own laity meeting in parliament. We have seen something of the debates on these issues in the seventeenth and eighteenth centuries, and we have seen how deeply ingrained in English political culture was this conviction that an established church should have no independent existence. A major problem of principle had arisen with the Act of Union with Scotland, when Scottish Presbyterians were included in what had become the supreme legislature of the Church of England. The inclusion of Roman Catholics posed much greater problems, and we shall see in the 1830s, when O'Connell's Catholic M.P.s allied with English Whig and Radical tendencies in opposition to the Church of Ireland, that Protestant worries on this score were not completely groundless. Nevertheless, the inclusion of Roman Catholics was an essential part of the programme of incorporating Ireland as thoroughly as possible into a union of interests with Great Britain, and the failure to achieve it in the first thirty years of the Union was a serious weakness.

Castlereagh wished to bind the substantial Irish churches more thoroughly into the British system through government support of the clergy. This was to give them a semi-established status, and had already been done, in the case of the Roman Catholic Church, in Canada. It was one thing, however, to do it in the case of a colonial dependency and quite another in the case of an integral part of the national state. It naturally raised the question of the Catholic Church and the Protestant Dissenters in England. Again the Catholic question was deferred, and again this was regrettable, since this was the last point at which that church might have been amenable to government management. The Synod of Ulster had the advantage, however, that it had already been in receipt of the *regium donum* for a long period of time. Alexander Knox, who conducted negotiations with the Synod, worked out an elaborate justification as to why the Ulster Presbyterians had a right to government support which could not be extended to Dissenters in England and Scotland. On the basis of the historical account in Kirkpatrick's *Presbyterian Loyalty*, Knox argued that the Presbyterian ministers had been introduced in Ulster as part of the plantation scheme by government policy and that the government therefore had a responsibility to them. The argument forgets that the Church of Scotland at the time was episcopal and that the founders of Ulster Presbyterianism were a dissenting and disruptive element both within it and within the episcopal Church of Ireland, but it served to provide some basis in principle for this earnest Evangelical Protestant, who later served as treasurer to the Royal College in Maynooth. He was unable to extend his principle to include the Seceders, who, as we have seen, had been in receipt of the *regium donum* since 1783, when they supported the Hillsborough interest in the Co. Down election.[94]

The Presbyterian ministers had no objection to receiving more money, but they had considerable objections to the conditions under which it was given. The old system by which the Synod received the money and distributed it as it saw fit was changed. The money was to be distributed by an agent appointed from within the Synod by the government. Each minister was to apply individually for his grant and, in doing so, had to sign a profession of loyalty. The grants were to be unequal, divided into three classes to be determined by the government.

There can be no doubt that Castlereagh's intention was to undermine the 'democratic' nature of Ulster Presbyterianism and, with it, the status of the Ulster Presbyterians as a distinct political society. In Castlereagh's *Memoirs and Correspondence* the original scheme, drawn up in conjunction with the Rev. Robert Black of Londonderry, is entitled 'A Plan for Strengthening the Connection between the Government and the Presbyterian Synod of Ulster' with the aim of 'rendering the ministers of the Synod more independent of popular caprices and the arts of factious members of their congregations' (p. 172). In 1802, after his resignation over the Catholic question, he wrote to Pitt's successor as Prime Minister, Henry Addington, to insist that he refuse to bow to pressure from the Synod of Ulster to change the scheme. To accede to these demands 'would surrender the authority of the body very much into the hands of its worst members, by accomplishing the whole of what they have from the first contended for. The distribution and government of the fund is a natural engine of authority.' Power over the grant had to be vested in the state, not in the Synod itself, since ministers' dependence on the government and independence from the congregations 'are the only means which suggest themselves to my mind for making this important class of Dissenters better subjects than they have of late years proved themselves'. Presbyterian sympathy for Jacobinism derived from the principles of ministerial equality and accountability to congregations of their own church. It was therefore desirable not only to make ministers less accountable to their congregations, but also to introduce a principle of inequality: 'Having a hierarchy of their own, they [Roman Catholics] are less alive upon the principle of subordination than the Presbyterians, whose Church is Republican in all its forms and too much so in many of its sentiments.' (pp 223-6)

In fact, even before the new system of distributing the *regium donum*, ministers' stipends, paid by voluntary contributions from their congregations, were not equal. Wealthier congregations paid larger stipends, and, with few exceptions, the classification of the new government grant, when it was finally offered and accepted in 1803, corresponded to the already existing division. The exceptions do not provide any evidence of discrimination against ministers whose names were associated with the United Irishmen, nor was it ever subsequently withheld from any minister on political grounds, with the one – albeit important – exception of William Steel Dickson, who was installed in 1803 in a new congregation (Second Keady) which had not been part of the original scheme. Knox seems to have acted as an intermediary between Robert Black, Castlereagh's leading supporter in the Synod, and the Addington administration. When the Synod accepted the grant on the new conditions, he wrote enthusiastically to Castlereagh:

> Never before was Ulster under the dominion of the British crown. It had a distinct moral existence and moved and acted on principles of which all we could certainly know was that they were not with the state, therefore when any tempting occasion occurred ready to act against it: now the distinct existence will merge into the general well-being, the Presbyterian ministers being henceforth a subordinate ecclesiastical aristocracy, whose feeling must be that of zealous loyalty, and whose influence on their people will be as surely sedative when it should be so and exciting when it should be so, as it was the direct reverse before. (Castlereagh, *Memoirs and Correspondence*, p. 287)

Knox believed that the Synod's agent for the *regium donum* would become 'a kind of permanent Moderator to whom in all matters of a public nature infallible attention and deference will be paid'. This view was somewhat over-optimistic. Robert Black, the Synod's agent, encountered fierce opposition and dislike until he finally committed suicide after his defeat over the Belfast Academical Institution. Thereafter the agent for the *regium donum* did not play an important part in the Synod's affairs.

One of the opponents of the new system, John Sherrard of Tullylish, asked in his pamphlet *A Few Observations on the Nature and Tendency of the Changes Lately Proposed to be Made in the Constitution of the Protestant Dissenting Church* (1803):

> In a word, must not everyone see that these changes go to dethrone the true king and head of his church, to give up

that liberty whereby he has made his followers free, to overturn the constitution of the Presbyterian Church, and to substitute in its place a completely human establishment? (pp 21-2)

But if feelings were running high in the Synod of Ulster, and if their acceptance of the grant was proportionately humiliating, this was all the more the case among the Seceders. They had exulted in the Synod's embarrassment and had received many new members on the strength of it. By 1810, however, both the Burgher and Anti-Burgher Synods had accepted a greatly increased grant, divided into three classes on terms similar to those of the Synod of Ulster. Only the Reformed Presbyterians, who were never likely to receive any money from a government they refused to recognise, held out. They greatly increased their strength in the first decade of the nineteenth century, and in 1810 were able to form a small Synod with twelve ministers and around twenty congregations divided into four presbyteries.[95]

The first years of the Union, then, were years of demoralisation and defeat for the Ulster Presbyterians. The great hopes of the Volunteer movement which had acquired a revolutionary millenarian character in the 1790s had been dashed. The policy of alliance with Catholic disaffection had been an embarrassing failure. The ministers had accepted government money on conditions which they had earlier indignantly refused and which were designed to break down their cohesion as a distinct social unit. From being a substantial minority, arguably a majority if the Protestant monopoly of political life had been maintained, in Ireland, they had become an insignificant minority in the United Kingdom. The future envisaged by Castlereagh lay in subsuming the divisions of Catholic, Protestant and Dissenter into a common British citizenship. But in the event the Ulster Dissenters were to recover their sectarian spirit and sense of purpose in the Arian Controversy of the 1820s, and their quarrel with the Church of Ireland was not composed until after they had managed to rid themselves of Castlereagh's classification system. Even before the 1820s a counter-attack to Castlereagh was launched by the old United Irish leadership in the remarkable form of the Belfast Academical Institution.

Retrenchment
and Reorientation

1. Retrenchment: The Belfast Academical Institution

In the eighteenth century there had been the appearance of a united Irish nation through the all-Ireland Anglo-Irish ascendancy caste, which had a coherent centre in the Dublin parliament. The aim of the Volunteer and United Irish movements was to create a more popularly based Irish nation through a reform of parliament that would make it more representative of the propertied classes, including Presbyterians and, more problematically, Roman Catholics. In opposing this aim the Irish parliament put itself in militant opposition to the people it governed and whom it had itself armed, and had to be rescued from its difficulties by Westminster, alarmed at the very real prospect of an alliance between a revolutionary Ireland and France.

The Ulster Presbyterians had participated in the struggle against the Irish parliament on the basis of a coherent understanding of history and political theory, derived from the struggles between king and parliament in the seventeenth century. They shared the political ideas of their American cousins and of the original English Whigs. The right of the people to organise in opposition to an unrepresentative despotism had been asserted in their own literature on the seventeenth-century struggles — Kirkpatrick's *Presbyterian Loyalty* and McBride's *Sample of Jet-Black Prelatic Calumny*. It was combined with an assertion of the right of civil society to organise its own religious life, independent of the government. To this Whig outlook, which was shared by elements of the ascendancy and by the English followers of Charles

James Fox, was joined the militant traditional Calvinism whose most extreme representatives were the Covenanters, fired by the prospect of overthrowing their traditional Anglican enemy. They too produced a political literature, one of the most interesting examples of which is *A View of the Rights of God and Man*, written by the Rev. James McKinney in exile in America, which attempts to marry Tom Paine's understanding of the 'rights of man' with his own ideal of a political state in a direct covenant with God (he manages it by equating the covenanted state with the millennium — the thousand-year personal rule of Christ, which will be so self-evidently just that the question of dissent will not arise).

The tradition to which the Ulster Whigs looked was a British tradition: it lay in the struggles of an English parliament and an English king (both Kirkpatrick and McBride had deflected attention away from the struggles between the Scottish church and the Scottish king, portraying the church as a representative of the people rather than as a body claiming an independent divinely ordained authority of its own). There was little in the history of the Irish parliament itself to inspire enthusiasm, except its apparent vulnerability. It was an easier target than the English parliament.

Thus the nationalism of the Ulster Presbyterians involved in the United Irish movement did not run deep. The defeat of the Volunteer movement, the Act of Union, and the surrender to the new terms on which the *regium donum* was given were profoundly demoralising events, but they did not give rise to a substantial demand for the repeal of the Union. William Drennan had been the most active of the Ulster Presbyterians in opposing the Act of Union. In 1808 he launched a new journal in opposition to the government, the *Belfast Monthly Magazine*, modelled on and borrowing articles from the *London Monthly Magazine*. The *Belfast Monthly Magazine* could not be accused of timidity. It opposed the continuation of the war against Napoleon, including the campaign of Sir Arthur Wellesley (later the Duke of Wellington) in the Spanish peninsula. While condemning Napoleon as a despot, the paper welcomed the revolutionary effect his campaigns were having in Europe. In particular, it welcomed the revolution which broke out in Spain in 1808. The similar articles in support of the Spanish revolution, jointly written by Henry Brougham and Francis Jeffrey under the pseudonym 'Don Cervallos' had marked the conversion of the *Edinburgh Review* to a liberal-democratic rather than simply a Scottish Whig journal.[96]

But the *Belfast Monthly Magazine* also saw Drennan supporting 'a faithful union' of Ireland and Great Britain, albeit on the as yet unfulfilled condition of Catholic Emancipation:

> As the Scotchman has gradually melted into the North Briton, so may the Irishman into the West Briton if . . . the good sense of an English public can shake off the panic of being invaded and overrun by the potatoe republic with the Pope at its head. (I, 5 (1808))

Drennan's principal concern, during the period in which there was no prospect of a new popular movement for reform of Westminster, was to maintain the independence of civil society from government patronage. In the absence of the Volunteer movement, the most substantial ways in which civil society was independently organised were the non-established Roman Catholic and Presbyterian Churches. Drennan had always been strongly opposed to the *regium donum*, and he naturally opposed its increase under new conditions. He also opposed the proposals put forward by Grattan to allow the government a veto on the appointment of Roman Catholic bishops as an adjunct of the projected legislation for enabling Roman Catholic M.P.s to sit in Westminster. In both cases he was opposing the government on measures designed to overcome the potency of sectarian division in Ireland.[97]

It was as a means to preserve the independence of the Presbyterians and to contribute something to undoing the ill effects of classified *regium donum* that Drennan supported the Belfast Academical Institution.

The Institution still survives as a school in the centre of Belfast, but originally it combined the functions of a school and college, and it was its collegiate or higher education function which caused controversy. The project was astonishingly ambitious, not only in the almost unique proposal to combine a school and college, but also in the scope of the collegiate department considered by itself. The last university established in the British Isles had been Trinity College, Dublin, at the end of the sixteenth century. The immediate precedents for the Belfast college were the English 'dissenting academies', of which the most successful were the Warrington Academy and its successor, the Manchester Academical Institution. At its height in the 1780s the Manchester Academy had four tutors, but these were reduced to one by 1803, when its resources were used to open Manchester College in York, which had grown again to four tutors in 1809. By contrast, the Belfast Academical Institution's collegiate department opened in 1815 with professors in Moral Philosophy; Logic and Belles Lettres; Natural Philosophy; Mathematics; Greek and Latin; Hebrew and Oriental Languages. By 1818 they had been joined by professors in Irish and Anatomy, together with two Professors of Divinity, one for the Seceders and one for the Synod of Ulster. In addition, there was a teacher of elocution and a secretary to the faculty, making eleven in all (since there was an overlap between the chair of Greek and Latin and the chair of Hebrew and Oriental Languages). University College, London, with vastly greater financial and political resources, started in 1827 with fourteen professors, two of whom did not take up their posts, though it quickly expanded.[98]

There were two other important ways, apart from its scale, in which the Belfast Academical Institution can be seen as a precursor of University College, London. It was run by boards of management elected by its subscribers; and it applied no religious tests. Oxford, Cambridge and Trinity College, Dublin, were Anglican. Trinity allowed non-Anglicans to take its courses but not to take its degrees. Edinburgh, St Andrews, Glasgow and Aberdeen were Presbyterian and required all their professors to subscribe to the Westminster Confession of Faith.

The non-sectarianism of the Belfast Academical Institution is the more remarkable when we consider that the only possible basis for its collegiate department attracting sufficient students was the education of the Presbyterian ministry, and this had been decided as part of its policy when it was being planned in 1808. The idea was to provide a general course of education which could be used by all denominations, but to invite the different churches, including the Catholics and Anglicans, to appoint their own Professors of Divinity for needs peculiar to their own ministers. In practice there was no question of the Catholic Church (supplied by Maynooth) or the Anglicans (supplied by Trinity) agreeing to such an arrangement, and 'Inst' — as it has come to be known — became simply a Presbyterian seminary over which the Presbyterian denominations had little control. It was to be a Presbyterian seminary founded and to a large extent run by former United Irishmen and their sympathisers. These included William Tennent, Robert Callwell and William Simms, who had been proprietors of the *Northern Star*; Robert Simms, who had been a state prisoner together with William Tennent; Tennent's brother, Dr Robert Tennent; William Drennan; and the Rev. Henry Henry, the Presbyterian minister of Connor, who had been suspected of complicity in the rebellion and who had taken a leading part in the opposition to classified *regium donum*. John Barnet and Robert Grimshaw, close political associates of Dr Robert Tennent, were also involved, as was W. B. Neilson, son of Samuel Neilson, editor of the *Northern Star*. With such directors, it was evident that little importance would be attached to inculcating the virtues of loyalty to the government.

The attraction of the proposal to the Synod of Ulster was that aspiring ministers would no longer have to go to Glasgow, away from the supervision of their own community and church, for their education. This attraction became all the stronger when it was discovered that, owing to a resolution passed in the Church of Scotland in 1799 against the rise of non-denominational Evangelicalism, ministers ordained by the Synod of Ulster were no longer admitted to Church of Scotland pulpits. Although this had not been the purpose of the General Assembly's motion, they showed no willingness to change it. Ministerial communion between the Synod of Ulster and the Church of Scotland was not restored until 1836, after the Synod had agreed to require from its ministers an unqualified subscription to the Westminster Confession of Faith.[99]

Another factor contributing to the Synod's support for

the Institution was probably the mere fact that Castlereagh and his supporters, 'the two Doctors', Robert Black in the Synod and William Bruce in the Presbytery of Antrim, were opposed to it. Black and Bruce could be said to belong to the same Whig tradition as Drennan. Bruce, indeed, was Drennan's minister. They had both been leading figures in the Volunteer movement, but they had opposed the United Irish movement. Although Bruce had spoken against admitting Catholics to the franchise in the Belfast debate of 1792, he had advocated it as a long-term measure, and Black had supported a resolution in favour of admitting Catholics to sit in parliament which was passed in the Synod of Ulster in 1813. They were both latitudinarian in their theological views, and indeed the implicit Unitarianism of Bruce's *Treatise on the Being and Attributes of God* (1819) was an important stimulus to the Arian Controversy of the 1820s. But they agreed with Castlereagh, and indeed had been largely responsible for the policy themselves, that the Presbyterians should become, through government patronage, a respectable and loyal part of the existing constitution. They could see no benefit in the policy of Drennan and of the old Covenanting tradition, of keeping alive a perpetual state of disaffection in readiness for future opportunities for radical change. In this they showed their similarity to the English Presbyterian tradition, which also tended both towards Unitarianism and respectability.

It may be useful to insert here a word on Castlereagh himself, since he too had connections with the same tradition. His grandfather, Alexander Stewart, had been apprenticed to a merchant in Belfast and became a Presbyterian and an elder in the First Belfast congregation, where Bruce was later to be minister. Castlereagh's father, Robert Stewart senior, who had fought the 1783 election with support from Presbyterian ministers, had been educated in Geneva. Castlereagh himself appears in the baptismal register of the Strand Street Presbyterian congregation in Dublin, attached to the Non-Subscribing Southern Association. It would not, however, be accurate to describe him as an 'apostate Presbyterian'. What apostasy there was had already been committed by his father, later created first Marquis of Londonderry, who belonged to the section of Ulster Presbyterian opinion that was closest to Anglicanism.

We have seen Castlereagh as a radical Whig in 1790, and then as the architect of the Act of Union and of the policy of incorporating the Presbyterians into the new political structure. After the death of Pitt it was probably Castlereagh more than anyone else who had the will and determination to maintain the war against Napoleon. It was Castlereagh who patronised his fellow-Irishman Arthur Wellesley, later the Duke of Wellington, and supported him during the long and apparently fruitless skirmishing in Spain. He therefore deserves much of the credit for making the Battle of Waterloo possible, and he played a leading role in the conferences which reorganised Europe after the defeat of Napoleon. In this capacity it was largely Castlereagh who rescued the pope from his dependence on Napoleon and restored him to the Papal States, an achievement for which he has not been given sufficient credit by Irish Catholic historians. He is by far the most distinguished product of any Ulster Presbyterian family.[100]

But he presided over a period of defeat and demoralisation for the Ulster Presbyterians, and his success as a statesman was based on the failure of hopes which had been vested in him at the 1790 election. In 1805 he stood again for Co. Down and was defeated through Presbyterian influence, including that of his supporter in 1790, William Steel Dickson. The controversy over the Belfast Academical Institution gave the Presbyterians a further chance to assert their opposition to him. Black and Bruce had opposed the project from the start, Bruce partly on the grounds that its school department competed with his own Belfast Academy. Wellesley, as Chief Secretary in 1807-9, had described it, in correspondence with the Prime Minister, Lord Liverpool, as a 'democratical establishment' which would 'separate to a greater degree this numerous sect (the Presbyterians of Ireland) from the inhabitants of Great Britain and from their own countrymen' and which would be pervaded by 'the republican spirit of the Presbyterians'. Nevertheless, it secured an annually renewable parliamentary grant in 1815, after which the Synod of Ulster formally agreed the connection. The collegiate department was opened in November. The grant, however, was thrown into doubt again following 'disloyal toasts' given at a St Patrick's Day dinner in 1816, attended by several of the Institution's teachers and managers. Castlereagh took a personal interest in the matter, as did Sir George Hill of the Hillsborough connection which had opposed Castlereagh in 1790. Hill had earlier supported the granting of a charter of incorporation to the Institution. The main issue they raised was the connection with the Synod. Castlereagh wanted the connection broken and the Institution remodelled to give the government a right of veto over the appointment of teachers, and to provide for visitation rights for the Provost of Trinity College, Dublin, and the Church of Ireland Primate of Armagh. Black argued furiously against the connection at the 1816 Synod, but found only three supporters. In 1817 the grant was withdrawn, but the Synod proceeded regardless with the appointment of a Professor of Divinity, Samuel Hanna. Black, after seventeen years of unpopularity and isolation which seemed to have ended in defeat, drowned himself in the River Foyle some months later.

The Institution, interestingly enough, was saved largely through the aid of Lord Moira, now Governor-General of India, who had been one of the Whig members of the Irish parliament sympathetic to the Volunteer and United Irish movements.[101]

The constitution of the college did not allow for any government influence over the appointment of its joint boards of managers and visitors. But neither did it allow for any academic superintendence. This had been a principal argument of Black and Bruce. Sovereignty lay with the subscribers, and anyone could be a subscriber. Whether the joint boards were loyal or disloyal, orthodox or heretic, competent or incompetent, was entirely dependent on the nature of its financial investors. The control of the joint boards was absolute, and when in the wake of the 1816 St Patrick's Day dinner they attempted to prove their loyalty, a long controversy began with one of the schoolteachers, the English master, James Knowles, who complained that he 'would have preferred living on bread and cheese' to living under the powers he now knew the joint boards to possess under their act of incorporation.[102]

The education of the Presbyterian ministers was thus wholly in the hands of a committee responsible only to the business community of Belfast. The Synod of Ulster and the Secession Synod (the Burghers and the Anti-Burghers had united into one 'Presbyterian Synod of Ireland' in 1818) had as few rights in the matter as the government and the teachers. The Synod of Ulster as a whole, however, did not feel this as a grievance until the case of the Professor of Moral Philosophy, John Ferrie, arose in the 1830s. It provided the occasion for the beginning of the Arian Controversy which brought Henry Cooke to prominence in the 1820s, but his attack on the Institution as such attracted little support.

In acquiescing to the Belfast Academical Institution's constitution the Synod of Ulster was effectively accepting the view that most of the education necessary for its ministers was religiously indifferent. This view harmonised well with the concept of the Ulster Presbyterians as a community united by a common discipline and mode of social organisation rather than by adherence to a particular doctrine, which is how I have described them at the end of the eighteenth century. It is more surprising to see the support given to the Institution by the Seceders, who were more distinctly a religious sect. But the Seceders had long had to use the Scottish universities, even though they believed that the subscription to the Westminster Confession required of them was an empty formality. John Barnet, one of the Institution's managers, who was a Seceder and a political radical, explained to the commissioners of the Irish education inquiry investigating the Institution in 1826 that they were less concerned than Cooke about the orthodoxy of the colleges because they were more strict than the Synod of Ulster in testing the orthodoxy of candidates for their ministry.[103]

Through the Arian Controversy, however, the Synod of Ulster was to become more like the Secession Synod. It became less of a political society and more of a religious society.

2. *Reorientation: The Arian Controversy*

The Arian Controversy did not, as is often suggested, mark

the triumph of political conservatism over political liberalism
in the Synod of Ulster. The terms 'conservative' and 'liberal'
are, of course, complicated, but broadly speaking I refer to
alignments with the Tory and Whig parties in Great Britain,
though I am, of course, aware that they were themselves in
flux, especially after the 1832 Reform Act. In particular, I
refer to attitudes to the Established Church. One of the
constituent parts of British Liberalism was the Nonconformist
Free Church movement, which wanted to see the disestablishment of the Church of England. It had a strong, militantly
orthodox, sectarian and anti-Catholic bias. Despite alliances
with the Irish Catholic interest in parliament, British Liberalism continued to regard the Roman Catholic Church as an
enemy to its own first principle of the right of the individual
conscience, and this was shown in Lord John Russell's
reaction to the establishment of a Roman Catholic hierarchy
in Britain in 1850 and Gladstone's reaction to the declaration
of papal infallibility twenty years later.[104]

In pointing to the development of a Liberal and anti-
establishment tendency in Ulster Presbyterian thinking after
the Arian Controversy we must bear in mind that these were
Liberals faced with the permanent threat of a strong, militantly
Roman Catholic movement demanding a repeal of the Union
which would put them under the control of a Roman Catholic
majority. The 'threats' to which Russell in 1850 and Gladstone
in 1870 were responding were trivial by comparison.

Henry Cooke was himself decidedly and explicitly a Conservative. Like Robert Black before him, he was concerned
to establish the loyalty and respectability of the Synod. He
tried to achieve a relationship with the Conservative leader,
Sir Robert Peel, similar to that between Black and Castlereagh.
In the 1830s he took a scornful attitude towards the Synod's
efforts to end the classification of the *regium donum*. He was
especially anxious to establish a close working alliance
between the Synod and the Church of Ireland in face of the
upsurge of militant Catholicism.[105]

In fact, however, the consequence of his victory in the
Arian Controversy was to restore the Synod's confidence in
itself, a development that was as unfavourable to closer
relations with prelacy as it was to closer relations with

popery. The tradition within the Synod that had developed into Arianism was the Hoadlyite English Presbyterian tradition represented by Black, Bruce and Castlereagh, the tradition that found transition to the Established Church easiest because it attached little importance to denominational boundaries. It was precisely to pacify the government and its supporters that the Institution appointed openly Arian professors — Bruce's son, also called William Bruce, and Thomas Dix Hincks, former principal of the Royal Cork Institute, regarded by the government as a model of what an Irish grammar school should be.[106]

What, then, was Arianism? It was a theory of the nature of Christ, arguing that he was distinct from, and subordinate to, God the Father. The Son, or second person of the Trinity, had, according to the Arians, been created by God at a point in time, the first and greatest of created beings. He was not 'co-eternal' with the Father. This view of the nature of Christ had been widespread at the time of the conversion of the Emperor Constantine in the fourth century. Its leading spokesman had been Arius, a preacher in Alexandria. The controversy had split the Eastern churches, and Constantine held the Council of Nicaea in 325 to try to resolve it. The champion of the Trinitarian view which prevailed at Nicaea was Athanasius. The dispute on the nature of Christ continued over a long period of time after the Nicene Council, and the first conversions among the barbarians in Europe (those who were outside the Roman Empire but were soon to overrun it) were achieved by Arian missionaries.

The appeal of Arianism was its apparent rationality. The doctrine of the Trinity — that God the Father, Son and Holy Ghost were three persons with one substance — appeared abstruse and meaningless. Arianism appeared to simplify the doctrine, while still retaining for Christ a very exalted position. The leading Ulster Arians — Bruce in the Presbytery of Antrim and Henry Montgomery in the Synod — insisted that they did not wish to agitate the question, as they were 'High Arians', with such an exalted view of the person of Christ that they were quite content with most of the Trinitarian formulae. Montgomery was to say in 1828: 'I have heard nothing but Arian prayers since I came to the Synod.'[107]

The objection to the Arian view, however, seems so obvious that it is difficult to understand how anyone could have held the doctrine for any length of time. If the Son is divine, and if prayers and petitions can be offered to him, but he is regarded as a being distinct from the Father, even if he proceeded from him, then Christianity ceases to be a monotheistic religion. The doctrine of the Trinity is essential to reconcile monotheism with the divinity of Christ. The 'High Arianism' of the nineteenth century was a half-way house between Trinitarianism and the more logically consistent Socinianism, which taught that Christ was fully human.

This half-way house was very important for the Ulster ministers. Their strength lay in the commitment of the Synod of Ulster to the practice of Non-Subscription. Ministers of differing views could co-operate in the presbyteries and in the Synod so long as no great importance was attached to their differences. Such a state of affairs facilitated the political interests of the late eighteenth century, but greatly inhibited the development of theology, whether orthodox or radical. The first Ulster Presbyterian minister to publish an open avowal of his Arianism was William Bruce, in his *Sermons on the Study of the Bible* (1824). But the main thrust of the *Sermons* is the argument that theological precision was neither desirable nor attainable. He encourages a selective approach to the Bible, concentrating on its moral and devotional aspects and discouraging the reading of commentaries. He was answered by the Reformed Presbyterian minister John Paul in what I regard as the masterpiece of Ulster Presbyterian literature, the *Refutation of Arianism* (1826), which argues that such an approach is incompatible with the spirit of free scientific inquiry.[108]

The impetus for the dispute came from outside the Synod, principally from a preaching tour by the English Socinian John Smithurst in 1821. This open preaching of a hard Unitarian position (as opposed to the quasi-Trinatarian preaching of the local 'High Arians') was what first alerted Cooke to the dangers. Smithurst had been invited over by the Rev. W. D. H. McEwen, who had been Cooke's predecessor in Killyleagh but who subsequently joined the Presbytery of Antrim. McEwen was teacher of elocution at the Belfast Academical Institution, where he gave volumes of the works of the English Unitarian Dr Richard Price as prizes to his pupils. Cooke's campaign against Unitarianism began with an attack on McEwen, William Bruce junior and Thomas Dix Hincks in the Belfast Academical Institution, but he made very little progress until 1825 when, as Moderator of the Synod of Ulster, he raised the question in his evidence to a major government inquiry into the state of education in Ireland. The Synod and the Institution had hoped that as a result of his evidence the government would restore the Institution's grant, and Cooke's evidence was widely seen as an act of betrayal. Cooke seemed at his weakest and most isolated in the 1826 Synod. But as a result of his evidence to the education commission, the government conducted a special inquiry into the Institution, and when its report was published in 1827 it was found that two of the Synod's ministers, Montgomery and the Synod's clerk, William Porter, had for the first time openly declared their Arian sympathies. The etiquette of Non-Subscription had been broken, and the dispute began in earnest, though its eventual outcome could not be in any doubt. The most surprising feature was the continued liberalism of the Subscribers. Ministers who refused to declare their adherence to the doctrine of the Trinity were not expelled, but measures were taken to ensure the Trinitarianism of all future entrants to the ministry, and under the circumstances the Arians felt that it would be dishonourable to remain. They formed a new Remonstrant Synod in 1830. One curious feature is that, although both the Presbytery of Antrim and the Remonstrant Synod were now openly Arian or Socinian in their sympathies, they both continued to receive government support through the *regium donum*, a state of affairs that would have been unthinkable in any other part of the United Kingdom, where until 1813 (1817 in Ireland) impugning the doctrine of the Trinity was a punishable offence.[109]

The dispute is often seen as a product of the rise of militant Evangelicalism in the Synod. In fact the two figures who could most easily be identified with Evangelicalism, James Carlile and Samuel Hanna, both opposed Cooke in the early stages of the dispute and defended the principle of Non-

Subscription. Carlile succeeded Cooke as Moderator, and his moderatorial sermon of 1826 was a plea for the open discussion of religious differences, praising the Synod of Ulster because its constitution allowed ministers to differ.[110]

The term 'Evangelicalism', however, is open to different interpretations. In Ulster Presbyterian literature it tends to be identified with orthodox Trinitarianism. But in the wider Protestant world it had three main characteristics, none of which were well developed in the Synod of Ulster in the 1820s: an interest in social improvement; an eagerness to proselytise; and an emphasis on the importance of the experience of being converted.

I have already discussed the last of these in my chapters on the eighteenth century, and I have argued that it belongs more to an English Congregationalist than a Scottish Presbyterian tradition. It was a force to be reckoned with in the American Great Awakening and through English Methodism, but it made little impact in Scotland and less in Ulster. The most likely candidates in both places, the Seceders, emphasised correct doctrine and the rights of the church rather than personal experience.

The turn of the eighteenth and nineteenth centuries saw a considerable interest in Evangelical ideas, partly in reaction to the problem, forced on the attention of 'polite society' by the nearness of revolution in the late eighteenth century, of the great mass of the rootless poor, who were outside the existing structures of society, including its churches. In part the problem was created by the gap between the 'agricultural revolution' of the seventeenth and eighteenth centuries and the full flowering of the 'industrial revolution' of the nineteenth century. A large population no longer had a place on the land, but had not yet been converted into an industrial working class. They resembled all too clearly the *sans culottes* on whom the strength of the Jacobins in the French Revolution had been based. The result was the growth throughout the British Isles of societies dedicated to various aspects of social reform, especially popular education.

The principle that such matters were a responsibility of government was still far from being established. The revolutionaries in fact had tended to argue for less government interference and less taxation. The main impetus came from private individuals in civil society and was stimulated by — and stimulated — a greater religious earnestness. The problem was largely seen as a problem of morality — to cultivate civilised behaviour and the discipline necessary for work and self-help. Thus far, the Evangelical initiative was non-sectarian. It encouraged co-operation among seriously minded people of all denominations. We may even represent the Utilitarians in England and Scotland as a non-religious intellectual wing of the same movement — the old revolutionaries turning their energies to theory and social improvement while the prospects of revolution were dim. Henry Brougham, who was active in the campaigns against slavery and for popular education based on the principles of Joseph Lancaster, helped to form a tenuous alliance between the Evangelicals and the Utilitarians.[111]

In Ireland the problem was even more pressing, and was more easily recognised by the government as part of its own responsibility. Rebellion had actually occurred, and a great feat of social engineering was necessary to incorporate the country into the United Kingdom after the Act of Union. Here, however, the problem arose that the mass of the population was at least nominally Roman Catholic and, although the power of the Roman Catholic hierarchy was not yet fully established, Ireland was well supplied with a priesthood. It was not simply a question of incorporating a population that considered itself Protestant but was outside the pale of the churches. Either a struggle would have to be conducted with the priests for the soul of the people, or the Roman Catholic Church itself would have to become, or be made, the medium of social development in Ireland, an idea that struck against the deep-rooted anti-Catholicism of British culture.

Numerous proselytising agencies developed in Ireland in the early nineteenth century, mainly supported by members of the Church of Ireland — the Protestant ascendancy at last waking up to the responsibilities it had neglected in the eighteenth century. There was also a Methodist and Congregationalist input, including the unsuccessful attempt, in the immediate aftermath of the 1798 Rebellion, to evangelise the Ulster Presbyterians through the Evangelical Society of Ulster. In general, the southern agencies concentrated on popular education and the distribution of the Bible 'without note or comment'. They were non-sectarian as regards the Protestant denominations, and even on occasion co-operated with Roman Catholic priests. The need for popular education was widely felt, and in the early days the societies, with financial resources not available to their Roman Catholic competitors, seemed to be very successful.[112]

Among the Ulster Presbyterians, however, the problem was not felt so keenly. They were almost a complete society in themselves, and the very lack of an Evangelical initiative testifies to their continued relative cohesion. They did not feel under much moral obligation to look outside their own community and take responsibility for the souls of Roman Catholics. A connection was formed with the Hibernian Bible Society, but this was largely to distribute Bibles among their own members. Some ministers opened schools, but this seems to have been more with the aim of supplementing their own income than of reforming society. The Seceding Presbyterian Synod of Ireland formed a missionary society after the union of the Burghers and Anti-Burghers in 1818, but its annual reports consist largely of complaints about the lack of support it was receiving, especially from Seceders in their heartland in Ulster. Such strength as it had lay in Dublin. It would be difficult to argue that orthodox Presbyterians contributed more than Non-Subscribers to the array of benevolent societies that appeared in Belfast in the early nineteenth century.[113]

In the 1820s the conflict between the proselytising agencies and the Roman Catholic Church became more intense, largely through the greater confidence and militancy of the Roman Catholic side, organised in a new, popularly based Catholic Association in support of the demand for Catholic Emancipation. Public debates were staged between Catholic priests and Protestant ministers under the auspices of the mainly Anglican New Reformation Society, but again, although Cooke and his leading adjutant, Robert Stewart of Broughshane, were interested in and supported this development, and although the *Ulster Guardian*, which appeared briefly in Belfast in the late 1820s as a mouthpiece of the New Reformation Society, supported the orthodox side in the Synod's dispute, Presbyterian involvement was marginal. We may say that the Arian Controversy stimulated a more distinctly Evangelical Presbyterianism in the 1830s, but it was not a product of an existing Evangelical impetus.

The departure of the Arians, at the end of a series of fierce theological debates, enabled both the orthodox and heterodox wings of Ulster Presbyterianism to develop their thinking much more freely. They were no longer constrained by the need to reconcile their differences in a common social structure. Montgomery and Carlile had both argued that the Synod of Ulster was a unique body, Presbyterian in its organisation and moral discipline, but Independent in its theology. John Paul from outside the Synod had agreed with Cooke that this meant simply that ministers attempting to build a theological edifice were forced to co-operate with other ministers engaged in pulling it down. The *Christian Moderator*, a Unitarian paper co-edited in London by William Porter's son, the Rev. John Scott Porter, shortly to become prominent as minister of the First Belfast Presbyterian congregation, published letters arguing that ministers in Ulster were so inhibited by the social pressures of the Presbyterian system that there was no prospect of the development of radical thinking. The Arian Controversy provided a great stimulus to the intellectual life of Ulster Presbyterianism which can be seen in the wealth and variety of the periodical and pamphlet literature of the 1830s. A distinctly Presbyterian periodical literature in fact started with the departure of the Arians. All the major Presbyterian divisions in this period began to produce their own journals: the *Orthodox Presbyterian* was produced by the Synod of Ulster; the *Bible Christian* by the Presbytery of Antrim and Remonstrant Synod; the *Christian Freeman* by the Seceders; and *The Covenanter* by the Reformed Presbyterians. Ulster Presbyterianism was again finding for itself a role in the world.[114]

8

Parliamentary Politics

---

1. *Two Tactics: Protestant Union and Radical Sectarianism*

The period between 1832 and 1886 provided the best opportunity the Presbyterians were ever to have since the seventeenth century to engage in what might be called 'normal British politics' — that is to say, politics based on divisions of opinion as to the right policies to be adopted by a stable central government. Between 1886 and 1920 they were forced into a united Unionist front to resist Home Rule and the prospect of domination by Catholic Ireland. Between 1920 and 1972 Northern Ireland was divided from the rest of the United Kingdom through the establishment of a devolved parliament, and in the face of a substantial nationalist movement the Unionist bloc had to continue in existence. From 1972 until the time of writing this state of affairs has been perpetuated by Westminster's insistence on a policy of trying to restore a local devolved parliament. Between 1886 and the present day, therefore, the development of politics based on parties committed to differing social ideals has been impossible.

Before 1828 English Dissenters were theoretically excluded from sitting in parliament by the Test Act. In practice, however, they had been able to sit by virtue of Indemnity Acts passed every year since 1747. The agitation to repeal the Test Act in the 1820s had been greatly inhibited by the widespread opposition among English Nonconformists to the admission of Roman Catholics. In 1825, for example, there were many petitions against admitting Roman Catholics to parliament from English Nonconformist congregations. Contrary to what is frequently asserted, Henry Cooke, in his evidence to the House of Lords select committee inquiring into the state of Ireland in the same year, supported the bill for the admission of Roman Catholics which was before parliament at the time. The contrast between the opposition from English Nonconformists and the lack of opposition from Ulster Presbyterians is the more striking when we consider that Catholic Emancipation posed a much greater threat to Ulster Presbyterian than to English Nonconformist interests.[115]

The annual Indemnity Acts, the repeal of the Test Act, and the Catholic Emancipation legislation that followed in the next year made little immediate difference to the composition of the unreformed parliament. The Ulster Presbyterians were still not in a position to influence the choice of candidates for parliament. In Belfast, for example, where a distinct Ulster Presbyterian anti-ministerial politics was strongest, the nomination of M.P.s was tightly controlled by the Marquis of Donegall on the strength of the system of town government that had been established in the seventeenth century. The 1832 Reform Act and the election that followed it provided Presbyterians with the first opportunity to participate in parliamentary politics on their own terms (rather than on the basis of an alliance with a liberal section of the Anglican ascendancy such as was briefly possible in the 1780s and 1790s).

Even as early as 1832, however, the problem that was to plague them to the present day was already evident. Their opportunity was also Catholic Ireland's opportunity, and Catholic Ireland, under the leadership of O'Connell, was committed to a policy of Repeal. The old liberal caucus which had maintained an anti-ministerial tradition since the 1790s, which had published a regular newspaper, the *Northern Whig*, since 1824, and whose most notable achievement had been the Belfast Academical Institution, was poised for victory. Their candidates were Robert James Tennent, son of the seasoned campaigner Dr Robert Tennent, and William Sharman Crawford, an Anglican landlord who was to become an outstanding figure in the history of radicalism both in Ireland

and in Great Britain. They were defeated by the Donegall candidate and by a defection from their own ranks, supporting James Emerson Tennent, William Tennent's son-in-law.

Emerson Tennent was to become a Peelite Tory, an ally of Cooke's and, ultimately, Governor of Ceylon. The group which supported him, the Belfast Society, soon became the Belfast Conservative Society. But the defection was not initially Tory in character. It was led by James MacKnight (or MacNeight, as he was known at the time), who subsequently became an ally of Crawford and of the Catholic Young Ireland leader, Charles Gavan Duffy, in the struggle for tenant right, and who left the Belfast Society, before it changed its name, on the issue of the National Education System. One of the main grounds on which Emerson Tennent won the election was the refusal of R. J. Tennent, with an eye on the growing Catholic vote in Belfast, to declare his policy on Repeal. A further cause of dissatisfaction with 'the old firm of Barnet, Grimshaw & Co.', as the Seceding minister John Edgar called them, was probably the unequivocal support given to the Unitarians in the Synod's controversy by the *Northern Whig*, whose editor, Francis Dalzell Finlay, was himself a Unitarian. The Belfast Reform Soceity, which backed R. J. Tennent and Crawford, were attempting, like many of their liberal or radical successors, to minimise both the substantial religious divisions which had developed within Protestantism, and the great politico-religious gulf which separated Protestant Unionists and Catholic Repealers.[116]

In England, it can be argued, politics developed precisely through the clarification of such divisions. The non-sectarianism of the Belfast Reform Society corresponded to the same Old Presbyterian / moderate Episcopalian Whig tradition in England which had collapsed about the same time. The most prominent Nonconformist M.P. in the years before the Reform Bill was William Smith, a Unitarian. But the nineteenth century saw a division developing between Unitarian and orthodox that was very similar to the Synod's dispute. It was less dramatic, because of the Congregationalist nature of English Nonconformity. It took the form of disputes within and between congregations, not the division of an organised connexional church. As early as 1816, well before the Arian Controversy had begun in Ulster, the Wolverhampton Case had raised the issue of whether or not Unitarian ministers were entitled to use meeting-houses and other property originally given to Dissenting congregations for the promotion of orthodox Trinitarian doctrine. The question was raised in the Manchester Socinian Controversy of 1824 and became a major issue with the Lady Hewley Bequest Case, when the orthodox Dissenters saw the prospect of making a virtual clean sweep of Unitarian properties. The central political representative body of the Nonconformist interest — the Protestant Dissenting Deputies — was split on the issue, and the Unitarians, who had previously dominated it in the person of William Smith, were expelled. The process coincided with a new militancy on the part of the Deputies in opposition to the Established Church of England, which itself was being greatly agitated by a rich and stimulating exercise of controversial theological problems.[117]

In Ulster, however, the battle of the Protestant sects took place within the shadow of the growing power of the Roman Catholic Church and the very real possibility of being submerged in a Catholic-dominated parliament. This was Henry Cooke's central idea, which prompted his call for a sinking of Protestant sectarian and political differences — an alliance of Presbyterian and Church of Ireland, tenant and landlord — in face of the common enemy. Presbyterian radicalism, on the other hand, personified by MacKnight, attempted to chart a course similar to that of their English Nonconformist counterparts: an orthodox Presbyterian sectarianism opposed to the Unitarian, Catholic and Church of Ireland interests, but prepared to ally with Unitarians, Catholics and Anglicans in pursuit of particular social and economic demands such as tenant right and the abolition of tithes, it being clearly understood that they would stand in a solid Protestant bloc with the Church of Ireland if and when the great issue of the Union was at stake.

Clearly the Catholic and Repeal interest, even if it secured a substantial majority of opinion in Ireland, still represented a small minority in the united parliament. The problem for the Ulster Presbyterians was that periodically that minority was large enough to hold the balance of power, and that it was able to enter into alliances. The problem specific to those committed to reform was that the alliances were usually with the English reforming interest, and were sometimes made with a view to achieving changes with which the Ulster reformers were themselves in sympathy. The 1830s were a case in point. O'Connell held a very powerful position in the reformed parliament, and he used it to launch a sustained attack on the property of the Church of Ireland, in concert with the 'tithe war' which had broken out spontaneously and violently in parts of the south of Ireland. The Ulster Presbyterians had no love for the Church of Ireland, and they too experienced the payment of tithes for its support as a grievance. But they could not be unambiguous or united in support of a campaign directed against the Irish Protestant interest and led by a man whose ultimate goal was Repeal.

The division of Ulster Presbyterian opinion is represented in its hardest form by the division between two men who had been allies on the orthodox side in the Arian Controversy — Henry Cooke and the Reformed Presbyterian John Paul, both masters in their own field, Cooke in the spoken word, Paul in the written word. The fact that neither won the main body of Presbyterian opinion to his point of view is shown in two events: Cooke's attendance at the Hillsborough demonstration of 1834, and the failure of the Belfast Voluntary Church Association, formed, with slightly ambiguous support from Paul, to promote the principle of Disestablishment.

The 1834 Hillsborough demonstration was held to protest against encroachments on the Church of Ireland interest and especially against the proposal that tithes that had been withheld in the tithe war should be paid out of the church's own endowments, saved as the result of the suppression of eight bishoprics and two archbishoprics by the Irish Church Temporalities Act of 1833. Cooke attended the demonstration hesitantly, knowing that he would encounter strong Presbyterian opposition but arguing that, though he could not support the distinguishing doctrines of the Church of England, he could defend its right to its own property. At the demonstration he announced what was to be the major policy of the rest of his life — the policy of 'Protestant union', a sinking of sectarian divisions among Protestants in the face of the common Catholic threat. Only nine other Presbyterian ministers attended the demonstration, three of them Seceders. Cooke was not censured at the following meeting of the Synod of Ulster, but nor did his policy of Protestant union attract very much support. Six years later the Synod unanimously endorsed the pamphlet *The Plea of Presbytery* — a fierce attack on the Established Churches of England and Ireland which still, however, fell short of demanding Disestablishment.[118]

The Irish Church Temporalities Act was a traumatic event in English church history. The great objection to Catholic Emancipation had been that parliament was the effective sovereign body of the Established Church. Catholic M.P.s were required to sign a declaration that they would not use their position to subvert the church establishment (O'Connell reconciled this with his conscience by distinguishing, as Cooke did, between the Established Church itself and the property of the Established Church). With the Irish Church Temporalities Act, a parliament acting under substantial Catholic and Nonconformist pressure had exercised its sovereignty to engineer a radical transformation of the Church of Ireland's structure — 'ten mitres blown away with one puff of the British parliament', as John Paul put it. The old Presbyterian arguments against Erastianism seemed to be abundantly confirmed. The church had no independent authority of its own to resist the will of a parliament which was no longer confined to its own laity. The absurdity of the church's claim to an independent authority conferred by God and transmitted through the apostolic succession was exposed. Ten apostolic successions had been wiped out by, to use Cooke's language, an alliance of papists and infidels. The act caused much soul-searching in Anglican circles and provided a major stimulus to the rise of the Tractarian movement, whose central concern was the nature and independent authority of the Christian Church. It also gave great encouragement to the Voluntaryist and Free Church movements in Scotland and England, arguing that only by breaking its connection with the state could the church be free to order its own affairs. Even Cooke, arguing against the Voluntaries in the Belfast Voluntary Debate of 1836, could not resist a sneer at the Convocations of the Churches of Ireland and England 'bottled up like a preserved commodity in the pocket of the Prime Minister'.[119]

The assault on the Church of Ireland was, in contrast, welcomed by Paul. In 1835 the Eastern Presbytery of the Reformed Presbyterian Synod published a *Causes of Fasting and Thanksgiving* which gave as a cause of thanksgiving the tithe war and almost the whole programme of the Whigs in the reformed parliament, especially the assault on the Church of Ireland. The pamphlet was written in a spirit of what we might call 'revolutionary optimism', arguing in terms strongly reminiscent of the United Irish period that Catholics fighting the oppressions of a Protestant church would necessarily become liberals:

> The position in which they at present stand, fighting the battles of civil and religious liberty, is certainly well calculated to eradicate persecuting principles and to innoculate them with principles of liberality and charity. We cannot but admire both the wisdom and goodness of God in putting them into such a position at the very time that he is putting the sacred oracles into their hands, and that these holy scriptures are making rapid progress among them. (p. 31)

I suggested earlier that Paul was the nineteenth-century figure who came closest to the spirit of the United Irishmen. In 1819 he published an attack on the principle of Non-Subscription entitled *Creeds and Confessions Defended*, in which he reconciled the traditional Covenanting opposition to toleration with an insistence on freedom of religious expression and thought. He uses the same arguments as James McKinney in *A View of the Rights of God and Man*, including one (that the magistrate should not be conceded a right to tolerate because it implies a right to persecute) that is found in Tom Paine's *Rights of Man* (pp 107-8). His revolutionary optimism as to the transformation to be expected in the nature of Irish Catholicism was based on his view, shared by some of the United Irishmen, that the millennium was imminent. It did not imply any affection for Roman Catholicism in itself. The major objection raised by the *Causes of Fasting and Thanksgiving* to tithes was that the oppression of Catholics by Protestants rendered their conversion impossible: 'A Popish ascendancy is prophesied by the enemies of civil and religious liberty; and they themselves are doing everything in their power to fulfil their own predictions.' (p. 10) Again he is echoing McKinney (whose *View of the Rights of God and Man* was republished in *The Covenanter* at Paul's suggestion in 1831):

> It is a piece, perhaps of the most shameless effrontery that has ever been practised, when the despots of the earth pretend to sigh and sob at the growth of infidelity, while their own wretched and abominable principles have been the true cause of at least nine-tenths of all the evil which at present threatens the interest of Immanuel upon earth. . . . The roaring lion of infidelity, with all its yelping whelps, is not so offensive to the ears of a pious, honest-hearted Christian, as the melancholy croakings of these devouring ravens. (p. 246)

(We may remark here in parenthesis that millenarianism amongst the Ulster Presbyterians in this period was almost entirely optimistic in tone and liberal in spirit. In the 1790s and in Paul's writing it was a means by which liberals leaped over the problem of Catholic power. By contrast, the millenarianism which was becoming fashionable in Anglican circles in the late 1820s, and which influenced the emergence of the Plymouth Brethren and the Catholic Apostolic Church, tended to be pessimistic and politically conservative.)[120]

As a result of Paul's *Causes*, the *Christian Liberator*, for which Paul wrote anonymously, was launched, and the Belfast Voluntary Church Association followed shortly after on the initiative of a Congregationalist minister, the Rev. James Carlile, not to be confused with his Presbyterian namesake. The *Liberator* and the Association were, however, short-lived, and Carlile was soon complaining about the lack of support from the mainstream Belfast Liberals, though it should be noted that the Voluntary cause was supported by the *Northern Whig*, which published a series of articles under the pseudonym 'Q.E.D.' by another Congregationalist minister, the Rev. James Godkin, who was to be both a lifelong opponent of the Church of Ireland and a Repealer. The ministers who supported the Association belonged to the fringes of

Nonconformist churches not in receipt of *regium donum*, which, of course, was also threatened by the Disestablishment principle.[121]

Paul himself was in trouble with his own Synod. He had been the dominant intellectual force among the Covenanters in the 1820s, but in the 1830s he was challenged by the Rev. Thomas Holmes Houston, editor of *The Covenanter*, arguing for the traditional Reformed Presbyterian ideal of a covenanted state, whose magistracy would have the right to punish heresy. In 1839 Paul and the Eastern Presbytery seceded from the Synod. Paul had difficulty in arguing unrestrainedly for Voluntaryism, given the quite indisputable commitment of the Reformed Presbyterian tradition to the covenanted state. He was not present at the Belfast Voluntary debate of 1836, when Cooke stood against the Scottish Voluntary leader, John Ritchie. His absence is greatly to be deplored, since a direct conflict between Paul and Cooke would have been a delight for those of us with a taste for polemical theology.[122]

Neither Cooke's Protestant union nor Paul's (or, more accurately, the Congregationalist James Carlile's) Voluntaryism became central planks of Presbyterian policy. The failure of the Seceders to adopt Voluntaryism was perhaps surprising, since the Seceders were the principal promoters of Voluntaryism in Scotland. Undoubtedly their receipt of *regium donum* had much to do with it, as Paul continually emphasised. But the underlying fear of Catholic ascendancy made for a cautious approach. Also, now that the Synod of Ulster was unequivocally orthodox in its theology, there was little reason to agitate differences between the two bodies, who were so similarly situated. In 1840 they combined to form the General Assembly of the Presbyterian Church in Ireland.

Almost all Paul's writings of the 1830s and 1840s were devoted to defending the right to free expression of religious opinions. It was a battle one might have thought had been won everywhere except in the ideals of the Reformed Presbyterian and Roman Catholic Churches, but Paul was able to push the issue into virtual Voluntaryism by treating the requirement to pay for the upkeep of a church of which one was not a member as a form of persecution. The basic

issue of the right of a magistrate to punish heresy did, however, become an issue in the Synod of Ulster when, in 1836,
it introduced unqualified subscription to the Westminster
Confession of Faith. This enabled it to reopen ministerial
communion with the Church of Scotland, but the Westminster
Confession contained, in Chapter 23, an acknowledgment of
a duty to suppress heresy. Objections to Chapter 23 had been
one of the main reasons for the Pacific Act of 1720, allowing
ministers to explain their objections to particular passages.
Cooke himself had declared in 1826 that he could not subscribe to it. He was now an enthusiastic supporter of unqualified subscription despite his being engaged, in alliance
with the English Nonconformists of Exeter Hall, in a campaign to expose the persecuting principles of a theological
textbook by a Roman Catholic writer, Peter Dens, then in
use in Maynooth. Unqualified subscription was agreed, but
not without fierce opposition, partly an instinctive reaction
against the loss of one of the distinguishing peculiarities of
the Ulster Presbyterian tradition. Among the pamphlets
attacking Cooke and unqualified subscription were two by
James MacKnight: *The Dens Theology Humbug* and *Persecution Sanctioned by the Westminster Confession of Faith*.
MacKnight, editor of the *Belfast News-Letter*, had given great
prominence to the disputes in the Reformed Presbyterian
Synod, and his pamphlets were deeply influenced by Paul.
This was not his first dispute with Cooke: he had already
fallen out with him on the question of the National Education
System.[123]

2. *Control of Primary Education*

To understand the National Education System we must go
back to what was said in the previous chapter about the
Evangelical proselytising agencies and their interest in popular
education. Catholic Ireland, especially at popular level, was
outside British society. It had no grounds for loyalty to, or
identification with, such a fundamentally Protestant culture.
In the eighteenth century there had been some loyalty to
Jacobitism, which was a British political tradition. But Jacobitism had ceased to be politically viable after 1745, and

residual Jacobitism tended to merge with a nostalgia for a lost Gaelic society, which in turn was alien and hostile to the existing political structure.

Education, and especially education in the English language, was widely seen as the key to incorporating this disaffected mass into the circle of British society. It was also seen by Catholics themselves as the only possible means of social advance. A determined renunciation of the Gaelic language was one of the most notable features of Irish social history, especially in Munster, in the nineteenth century.[124]

The 'hedge schools' had been evidence of the people's desire to improve themselves. The opportunity was seen and the task taken up by the Evangelical societies with their greater resources. But this interest in the well-being of the Catholic poor occurred too late to be of any real benefit to the Anglican ascendancy, since they no longer had the advantage of legal restrictions on the practice and spread of the Roman Catholic religion. From the start they recognised that their proselytising role had to be exercised with tact. They placed great hopes in the principle of education through the Bible 'without note or comment' and conceded the right of parents to withdraw their children from any specifically denominational teaching.

The problem was recognised by the government, which had still not accepted any responsibility for the education of the poor in Great Britain. In 1816 the newly formed Society for Educating the Poor in Ireland, better known as the Kildare Place Society, received a generous government grant, the first grant ever given by the British parliament for popular education. Parliament aimed to enlist the support of the Catholic Church, and a condition of the grant was that the education provided would be non-sectarian, though it was still based on the Bible, which was still thought to be a non-sectarian textbook.

In 1818, however, the principle of the free popular availability of the Bible was condemned in a letter to the Irish bishops from Cardinal Fontana of the Sacred Congregation de Propaganda Fide in Rome, and the issue was taken up, notably by the newly appointed Professor of Dogmatic Theology in Maynooth College, John MacHale, in his *Letters of Hierophilos*. Catholic support for the Kildare Place Society was withdrawn, and O'Connell, among others, resigned from the Society's board after disputes over the use of the Bible.[125]

The parliamentary commission of inquiry into Irish education held in 1825, to which, as we have seen, Henry Cooke gave evidence, was held as a result and eventually led to the National Education System, introduced by the Whig Chief Secretary, Edward Stanley, shortly before the Reform Act. Stanley, interestingly enough, was shortly afterwards to secede from the Whigs in protest against the proposal to alienate the endowments of the Church of Ireland in 1834, the same issue that prompted the Hillsborough demonstration. As Earl of Derby he was later to become leader of the Conservative Party.[126]

Under the National Education System a board was directly appointed by the government to subsidise schools, which were to observe certain clearly defined rules and be subject to the board's inspection. The aim of the rules was to ensure that the education provided was non-sectarian, and that the system would operate uniformly throughout Ireland irrespective of religious distinctions. It may be seen as the most ambitious attempt ever made to create a unified Irish national culture. More realistically, however, it was an attempt to provide a popular education for Irish Catholics without directly subsidising either Roman Catholicism itself or anti-Catholic proselytism. From a Protestant point of view, its chief distinguishing feature was the exclusion of the Bible from normal school hours.

The government was expecting of the Irish churches a much greater degree of secularisation than it would have dreamed of demanding of the churches in Great Britain. At the same time as the National Education System was established in Ireland, the first grants were given for popular education in England, Wales and Scotland. In England and Wales they were given to the National Society for Promoting the Education of the Poor in the Principles of the Established Church and to the British and Foreign Schools Society, which had become effectively the educational society for the Dissenters. These were voluntary bodies independent of the government, and there was no question of the government imposing restrictions on the teaching of religion. Quarrels between the Dissenters and the Established Church prevented the government from making direct provision for schools in areas not served by the voluntary societies until Forster's Education Act of 1870. Schoolmasters in Scotland had to be approved by the presbyteries and had to subscribe to the Westminster Confession. They were not relieved of this obligation until 1861, and even then the 1861 act required that they should 'conform faithfully to the Bible and Shorter Catechism in the teaching of schools'.[127]

The churches in Ireland were both privileged by the generosity and universality of the grant for education, and discriminated against by the restrictions put on it. The grievance felt by the Church of Ireland was especially great. Anglicans had committed themselves to the aim of popular education largely in the hope of converting Catholics. They had accepted the need for some restraint — to concentrate on simple Bible teaching without emphasising denominational peculiarities, and to excuse pupils from religious lessons on request. Now they were being asked to restrict the use of the Bible, to facilitate Catholic priests in providing religious instruction, and to take the initiative in excluding Catholic children from their own religious classes. More seriously still, their status as the national church was being effectively denied by the government and, especially in conjunction with the Irish Church Temporalities Act and the assault on tithes and church rates, was made to look ridiculous. They accordingly withdrew from the system and established their own Church Education Society, which received no government aid.

The Roman Catholic Church equally had reason to feel aggrieved. They were unquestionably the church of the great majority in Ireland, and they too were subjected to humiliating restrictions in promoting their own religious teaching. The system was quite clearly designed to educate Catholics with the co-operation of the church but without directly supporting it. As such it was opposed by John MacHale after he became Archbishop of Tuam in 1834. He kept the schools out of his archdiocese in the west of Ireland, to the great loss of his parishioners. By contrast, the Catholic Archbishop of Dublin, Daniel Murray, recognised that the system provided a great opportunity for Catholic education and was the best that could be obtained from a Protestant government. A virtual denominational system could be established in large areas of Ireland where the Protestant population was minimal. The subsequent history of the scheme consisted of its conversion into a straightforwardly and uninhibitedly denominational system, especially under the influence of Paul Cullen, who became Archbishop of Dublin in 1852 and who, as the influential Rector of the Irish College in Rome, had supported MacHale in the 1830s.

The Presbyterians shared the sense of grievance of the Church of Ireland, but were in a weaker position because they had not attended to the business of providing popular education themselves. As the historian James Seaton Reid commented during the Synod's debates on the subject, they 'had never come out of the mass of people to establish schools for themselves' (*Northern Whig*, 3 July 1834).

Nor had they shown any great interest in converting the mass of the Catholic population. James Carlile, the minister of Mary's Abbey in Dublin, whom we have seen as a supporter of the Belfast Academical Institution and of the principle of Non-Subscription in the early stages of the Arian Controversy, was an exception. He had been assistant to Benjamin McDowell, who had conducted a long, isolated battle with the Synod for a more evangelical approach, and he had been an early member of the Dublin-based, and largely Congregationalist, Irish Evangelical Society. Carlile accepted a place on the National Board and defended the system vigorously in the Synod, arguing that through the use of 'Scripture extracts' which he had prepared, and which had been approved by Archbishop Murray, Roman Catholic pupils would at least be introduced to the Bible.[128]

The introduction of the National Education System coincided with the new energy and self-confidence given to the Synod by the Arian Controversy. They now knew what they were — a body dedicated to the preservation and promotion of a distinct set of theological beliefs. The sytem was based on the non-sectarian ideal of 'common Christianity' from which they had recently freed themselves, but it also provided the means of engaging in the new and obviously important field of popular education. The Synod was almost equally divided on the issue. In the debates in 1834 a small majority of ministers supported the system, but were defeated through the votes of elders. Nevertheless, those ministers who had already attached schools to the board refused to withdraw them. The board's opponents, led by Cooke, attempted to establish their own schools without government aid. In 1839 modifications were made to the board's rules which enabled the Synod formally to approve the system. Catholic priests were no longer given *ex officio* rights of visitation; teachers were not obliged to exclude Catholic pupils who wished to attend religious instruction; restrictions on the use of the Bible in normal school hours were less severe.[129]

This was undoubtedly a step away from the non-sectarian 'national' principles on which the system was established. But the system's non-sectarianism was unrealistic for the conditions of the nineteenth century. 'Common Christianity' might have been a possible ideal for the eighteenth century, when culture and political thought were confined to a narrow circle. With the advance of democracy in the nineteenth century and the intellectual turmoil that accompanied it, the suppression of important differences of religious principle was not possible. It was not possible in Great Britain and it was less so in Ireland. The non-sectarianism of the Belfast Academical Institution was based on the fiction that it was not a Presbyterian seminary. The non-sectarianism of the National Education System was based on the fiction that it had been introduced for the benefit of an Irish population rather than an Irish Catholic population. The fiction was maintained because it would have been politically impossible for Westminster to directly subsidise the Roman Catholic Church on the scale that would have been necessary. The logical alternatives facing the government were to subsidise the denominations, including the Catholic Church, to provide their own education, or to insist that Ireland was part of a Protestant United Kingdom and to subsidise only a Protestant provision for education — whether confined to the Church of Ireland or including the Dissenters. With the refusal to pursue the latter course, the eventual settling of the National Education System into the former course was almost inevitable.

3. *Control of Higher Education*

The same difficulties were soon to be seen at work again in the 1840s, in the question of the provision of university education in Ireland. In England university education outside the ancient universities of Oxford and Cambridge had been provided on private initiative and subsequently subsidised by the government. University College, London, which initially excluded religious education, had been followed by the explicitly Anglican King's College, London, and Durham University. To apply the same principle to Catholic Ireland, however, would again be to directly subsidise the Roman Catholic Church, or at least its religious orders as teaching bodies. This was impossible, not because of Irish Protestant opposition, which by itself was marginal in parliament, but because of British public opinion. A substantial section of British public opinion could tolerate attacks on the Church of Ireland, because the establishment principle was itself being questioned, but direct subsidy of Roman Catholicism was a different matter. Once again the fiction of the need to promote a non-sectarian Irish national culture had to be resorted to. And once again the Presbyterians derived benefits from a government generosity they would not have received were it not for the need to respond to distinctly Irish Catholic needs; and they were compelled to agree to restrictions on religious education which derived not from government suspicion of themselves but from the need to impose restrictions on Catholic religious education while maintaining the appearance of even-handedness in order to secure the support, or at least the tolerance, of the Roman Catholic Church. In this case, however, Cooke appeared on the more 'liberal', pro-government side. One reason among several was that, although the proposal for the Queen's Colleges was taken up and implemented by the Whig ministry of Lord John Russell, it was introduced by the Tory ministry of Sir Robert Peel.

In contrast with popular education, university education was a field in which the Ulster Presbyterians had already taken the initiative with the Belfast Academical Institution. The Institution had initially received government support, then lost it and maintained itself through the early 1820s.

As a result of the government education inquiry, the grant was restored and a medical faculty was added to the arts and theological faculties in 1832. It was still, however, principally a seminary for the training of Presbyterian ministers, though, apart from the distinct theological faculty, it was still outside the control of the Synod. The government, in restoring the grant, had proposed giving the Synod a veto on the appointment of professors, but the Synod had settled for an undertaking from the Institution's boards that its recommendations would be taken into account.

Cooke had failed to stir the Synod in the matter of the appointment of Bruce and Hincks, but he had more success in the case of John Ferrie, Professor of Moral Philosophy, in the 1830s.[130]

On the face of it, the case against Ferrie might appear less strong than the case against Bruce and Hincks. Ferrie was not a Unitarian, and he had, as a Scottish professor, subscribed the Westminster Confession. There was, however, an early bias against him, since he had been appointed in 1829, at the end of the Arian Controversy, over the head of the Synod's nominee, the Rev. James Carlile. Carlile, as we have seen, had supported the Non-Subscribers in 1826, but he had turned against them when their Arianism was avowed. It was widely felt that he had been rejected by the boards, in which Unitarian influence was strong, in a fit of pique directed both against himself and against the Synod.

Cooke had accused Ferrie in 1829 of being an Arian. Throughout the 1830s there was a series of attacks on his orthodoxy, in which the Secession and Reformed Synods also took part. Now that the Synod of Ulster was itself an orthodox sect rather than a 'broad church' the latitudinarianism of the Belfast Academical Institution was becoming increasingly galling. It withdrew its pupils from Ferrie's classes and appointed its own moral philosophy professors — Cooke and William Molyneaux, who was, interestingly enough, an opponent of Cooke's on the questions of the National Education System and of unqualified subscription. In 1838 the Synod withdrew altogether from the Institution's theological faculty in protest against the appointment of Henry Montgomery and John Scott Porter as theology professors for the Remonstrant Synod and the Presbytery of Antrim respectively.

Implicit in this was the demand for a distinct orthodox Presbyterian college — either as a complete university or as a seminary for Presbyterian ministers. In 1844, in a mood of spirited Presbyterian sectarian pride — which was causing Cooke anxiety because it was also directed against the Church of Ireland — the proposal for a complete college was taken up. Government aid was to be sought, but if it was not obtained, the Presbyterian community would provide a college out of its own resources.

This mood of Presbyterian pride and militancy had been affected by a series of events in the late 1830s and early 1840s. There had been a controversy with the Church of Ireland on the question of the validity of marriages between Anglicans and Presbyterians solemnised by Presbyterian clergymen. The points of principle which distinguished the two churches had been agitated in a pamphlet war between the curate of Londonderry, the Rev. Archibald Boyd, and four Presbyterian ministers, whose *Plea of Presbytery* was endorsed by the Synod as a whole in 1840. The union of the Synod of Ulster and the Secession Synod in the General Assembly in the same year was a great accession of strength, which brought in what was traditionally the more militant and sectarian section of Presbyterian opinion. In 1842 the *Banner of Ulster* was founded as a new paper to argue for a distinct Presbyterian politics in opposition to the Conservatives in whom Cooke had put his trust. In 1843 this need for a distinct Presbyterian politics seemed to be confirmed when the government's refusal to end the system of lay patronage in the Church of Scotland resulted in the secession of the Free Church, led by Church of Scotland ministers who believed in the establishment principle but who were prepared to organise on a voluntary basis rather than submit to government dictation. The Free Church was enthusiastically supported by the Irish General Assembly, and in the same year a motion was passed calling for 'measures for securing a more adequate representation of the principles and interests of Presbyterianism in the legislature of the country'. The motion was proposed by John Brown of Aghadowey and seconded by Richard Dill of

Ussher's Quay, Dublin. Brown and Dill, especially the latter, were to be leaders of the campaign for a complete Presbyterian college. Cooke was so strongly opposed to the motion that he refused to attend the General Assembly for the next four years until 1847, when the measure was repealed. These events, however, were merely a prelude to one of the century's most determined efforts to establish a distinct Presbyterian radical politics based on the question of tenant right. In 1844 orthodox hostility to Peel seemed abundantly justified with the Dissenters' Chapels Act, when Unitarian properties were defended against the decision in favour of the orthodox given by the courts in the Lady Hewley Bequest Case in 1842.[131]

An appeal for funds for the new college was launched, but negotiations with the government quickly (and largely under Cooke's influence) became negotiations over the new proposals being put forward for the Queen's Colleges. The possibility that was opened up was for a non-sectarian university directly responsible to the government but, owing to its situation in Ulster, with a distinct Presbyterian flavour, together with a Presbyterian seminary supported by a generous government grant, directly responsible to the Synod. It was certainly a practical proposal, but it lacked the inspiring appeal of a complete Presbyterian college. The education of ministers would be freed from the 'common Christianity' of the Queen's Colleges, but lay university education would still be in the hands of a government whose first concern in Ireland was with the problems posed by the Catholic interest. A complete Presbyterian college was the logical culmination of the Arian Controversy, of the struggle with the Belfast Academical Institution, of the struggle over the National Education System, of the pamphlet war with the Church of Ireland, and of the support for the Free Church of Scotland.

An account of the attempt to establish a complete Presbyterian college was published by Richard Dill in 1856 under the title *Prelatico-Presbyterianism*. Dill was deeply embittered by the opposition he encountered from what he describes as a small faction of Belfast ministers led by Cooke, manoeuvering behind his back and using the weapons of innuendo and slander. Through his bitterness, however, one can still feel his excitement at the freedom a complete college would give the

Ulster Presbyterians to develop themselves as a distinct religious community, firmly grounded in their own principles and able to defy the government, the Catholics and the Church of Ireland. The spirit bears a resemblance to the spirit of Drennan in the early days of the Belfast Academical Institution, and of John Henry Newman, also writing in the 1850s, as first Rector of the Catholic University in Dublin. It is the spirit of the Free Church of Scotland, of the voluntary association of civil society defying government patronage.[132]

In the event both sides won. Queen's College, Belfast, was established, together with Assembly's College for the education of ministers. But a complete Presbyterian college was also established in Londonderry through the bequest of Dill's parishioner, Mrs Martha Magee. The Belfast faction fought with Dill, as a trustee of the Magee bequest, a long battle in the Court of Chancery to apply the Magee bequest to Assembly's College. The Master of Chancery, William Brooke (a direct ancestor of the present writer), found in favour of Dill and, in the course of his judgment, indicated a personal enthusiasm for the opportunities offered to the Ulster Presbyterians by the prospect of a complete college. Brooke was subsequently influential in the reorganisation of the Church of Ireland after Disestablishment and played a role in giving it something of a democratic and Presbyterian character.[133]

Queen's Colleges were also established in Cork and Galway, in both of which, especially Galway, they could be expected to be effectively Catholic colleges from which, as in the case of the effectively Presbyterian Belfast college, religious instruction was to be excluded. The Roman Catholic Church had the same difficulty in accepting this principle as the Presbyterians. The bishops were almost evenly divided. O'Connell's opposition to the proposal led to the famous controversy with Thomas Davis and the Young Ireland movement.

The alliance between Young Ireland and the government on this issue is instructive. Both had set themselves the aim of creating a unified Irish nation, the government within the United Kingdom, Young Ireland outside it. Both saw education as an essential means of achieving this aim. Both saw the religious differences in Ireland as a major obstacle to achieving it. Davis, inspired by the racial theories of German romanticism, looked for a popularly based national ideal which would transcend these differences. O'Connell, paying lip-service to the need to transcend religious differences, grounded himself in the strength of militant Catholicism, which was about to assert itself after his death with redoubled force under the leadership of Paul Cullen.

Cullen secured the Irish Catholic Church's condemnation of the Queen's Colleges at the Synod of Thurles in 1850. The older generation of Irish bishops who were prepared, like Daniel Murray, to accept them as the best prospect for Catholic advance under a Protestant government, were replaced as they died with Cullen's supporters. A complete, self-financed Catholic university was established in Dublin, initially under the direction of John Henry Newman, whose ambition to mould a new, liberal and independent-minded Irish Catholic gentry was quickly brought to an end by Cullen. The great guiding principle of government policy that a unified Ireland could be established by inhibiting religious ideals and commitments was to appear ever more hopeless.[134]

From Presbyterian to Protestant

1. *Individual Salvation and Social Organisation*

There is a contradiction at the heart of Presbyterianism between its role as a means of social organisation and its Calvinist doctrine which stresses the inability of man to contribute anything to the process of his own salvation. The great social function of religion is to provide sanctions, incentives and reminders of a higher reality in order to encourage good citizenship. That is not a cynical point of view. For any society good citizenship is important, and for most human societies religion has been the only possible means of promoting it. Hence the incalculable importance of church/state relations as a subject for historical study.

Calvinism, however, is singularly inappropriate for this very important function. In stressing man's powerlessness in relation to God, in distinguishing between the elect and the non-elect and resting the distinction on the quite arbitrary decree of God, it offers no sanctions or incentives for good behaviour — and in its rejection of symbolism and ritual it offers few reminders of a higher reality. Where it is established as the religion of a state or even, as in the case of the Ulster Presbyterians, a whole society within the state, it quickly becomes 'Arminian' in outlook, finding some argument by which human beings can be said to contribute to the work of their own salvation. This occurred first in Arminius' own homeland, the United Provinces; in Geneva after the death of Calvin's successor, Beza; and in England, where Arminianism was formally adopted in the 1630s. It occurred in the life of Martin Luther, who was a 'Calvinist' while he was a dissenter from the Roman Catholic Church, but who became effectively 'Arminian' when his teaching became the state religion of Saxony. It was the work of the Stuarts to bring about the same process in Scotland, and when the Church of Scotland was stabilised in the eighteenth century it effectively signalled its conversion to Arminianism by condemning *The Marrow of Modern Divinity*'s 'anti-nomianism'. Antinomianism is the view that the saved Christian is not obliged to observe the moral law. Half of *The Marrow of Modern Divinity* is devoted to an attack on that proposition. What the Established Church of Scotland was condemning was the proposition that observance of the moral law is not a means of salvation. That is the doctrine of Calvinism, as expressed in the Church of Scotland's own Westminster Confession.

The revival of orthodox Calvinism in the early nineteenth century was therefore implicitly subversive of the church's role as a means of social organisation. This is a great apparent paradox of the nineteenth century — that the revival of an intense interest in and concern for religion, often conducted in an evangelising spirit, aiming to incorporate sections of the society that were outside the ambit of the church, actually facilitated the process of secularisation. In the Catholic countries of Europe secularisation occurred through a battle between the church recognised by the state and the consciously and determinedly secular forces of republicanism, socialism and communism. In Britain it occurred mainly through battles among the religious sects themselves, including divisions within the state church. The process had largely taken place by the second half of the nineteenth century. Thus British socialism never had to engage in battle with the church, and this is one reason why the dogmatic secularist world-view of Marxism — a total world-view, able to counter at every point the total world-view of Christianity — seems so alien to it.

I have argued that the Ulster Presbyterians were a distinct political society, and that in relation to that society the Synod of Ulster played something of the role of a national church. It is with the Presbyterians as a distinct political society that this book is chiefly concerned. I have tried to describe how this anomalous, almost unique, society arose. I am now to try the more difficult task of describing how, in the nineteenth century, it declined. Of course, the Presbyterian Church continues to exist and even to thrive. But the distinct political society no longer exists. There is a distinct Ulster *Protestant* political society, but not a distinct Ulster *Presbyterian* political society. The paradox — and I would argue that it is a paradox that is typical of British history in the nineteenth century — is that the decline of the society complemented the flourishing of the church.

2. *Secularisation in Britain and Ireland*

The term 'secularisation' is complicated in Britain by the comparative weakness of self-conscious secularist forces. To an Evangelical the eighteenth century will appear more secular, more 'destitute of vital godliness' than the nineteenth century. But in the eighteenth century the church was an arm of the state. It was still the means by which the nation was united in a common structure, with common values, loyalties and beliefs. It was the principal vehicle of social communication. This was the case even if only a small proportion of the total population actually went to church. Attendance at church was still a distinguishing mark of 'civilised' society, even if religion was not taken too seriously. What was taught in church was important to the well-being of the state.

I have suggested that at the beginning of the nineteenth century the rise of religious earnestness and 'vital godliness' was at least partly prompted by the recognition of just how fragile civilised society was, and how wide was the gulf between the civilised society that went to church and the massive population that didn't. Hence the emphasis on popular education and the need for an exciting religious doctrine that would capture the imagination of an un-religious people — an Evangelical endeavour that had been pioneered by the Methodists, especially in Wales.

These were not needs that were particularly felt among the Ulster Presbyterians, who were a small, self-contained society defined by their participation in the organisation and discipline of their church. They were felt more strongly within the Church of Ireland, supposedly the national church, with responsibility for a large, unassimilated Catholic population.

The rise of Evangelical Calvinism had a divisive effect on the national churches of England, Scotland and Wales. It had already in the eighteenth century produced the Methodist division in England and the Seceder and Relief divisions in Scotland. In the nineteenth century it produced Evangelical branches of the Churches of England and Ireland which, even if they did not formally separate from the church, behaved like separate sects, with their own journals and organisations; it also precipitated similar developments in the High Church section, even forcing the mainstream latitudinarian 'Broad Church' into behaving like a sect. In Scotland the rise of Evangelical Calvinism produced yet another divison with the Disruption of 1843 and the departure of the Free Church of Scotland.[135]

Among the Ulster Presbyterians, by contrast, it appeared as if the whole Synod had adopted Evangelical Calvinism in the 1820s; and this facilitated reunion with the Church of Scotland in 1836 and with the Seceders in 1840, three years before the Church of Scotland split. But I have argued that the Synod's conversion was not due to an already existing Evangelical Calvinist impetus. In the 1820s the issue was simply the doctrine of the Trinity. Cooke's achievement was to press the latitudinarians into declaring their disbelief in the doctrine of the Trinity, which was regarded by all the mainstream churches as an essential doctrine of Christianity. Although this was not the result of Evangelical pressure on the Synod, it helped to generate a new Evangelical outlook in the 1830s, to which it seemed that most of the old Presbyterian political society was now committed. There was, or appeared to be, no equivalent of the moderate wing of the Church of Scotland, which continued to dominate the Established Church of Scotland after the Disruption of 1843, or the latitudinarian centre which was still numerically the strongest part of the Churches of England and Ireland. The main division evident in the 1830s and 1840s was a political one between those who tended towards Cooke's policy of 'Protestant union' with the Church of Ireland against Catholic

Ireland, and those who tended towards Paul's and MacKnight's attempts to develop a distinctly Presbyterian opposition to the Church of Ireland in alliance with the Whig government. Both sides regarded themselves as Evangelical Calvinist.

What was happening, though it was not yet evident, was that the Ulster Presbyterians were ceasing to be a distinct political society and were instead becoming a sect within a wider British political society. Hence the ease with which they combined with what had been their own sectarian fringe — the Seceders.

It was more evident to Cooke than to Paul and MacKnight, and was implicit in Cooke's policy of Protestant union, his connections with the orthodox and anti-Catholic Exeter Hall, and his opposition to the attempt to establish a distinctly Presbyterian political movement in the 1840s. Cooke was in the anomalous position of a Presbyterian wishing to preserve an episcopal national church. The argument of the defenders of church establishments was that the nation required a unifying spiritual life. A national church was a necessary support to national morality. Thomas Chalmers, the champion of the Church of Scotland, argued in a great debate with the Scottish Congregationalist Ralph Wardlaw in London in 1839 that because men were inherently sinful they could not be trusted to organise and support the church, or churches, on their own initiative. The state was obliged to provide for religion. If the state failed to do so, the natural human tendency to sin and sensuality would result in the decadence and dissolution of political society.

Wardlaw, by contrast, put his faith in God and God's power to convert sinners, arguing that the church or churches would be stronger if they were freed from the necessarily Erastian and Arminian hand of the state, which could certainly build and support churches but which would be more interested in its own self-preservation than in the work of winning souls to Christ. Four years later Chalmers was to experience the conflict between the Evangelical desire to save souls that he shared with Wardlaw and the state's desire to maintain social control of the church, and he resolved his personal dilemma by leaving the Established Church and joining the Free Church.[136]

Cooke, who had employed arguments similar to Chalmers's in the 1836 Belfast voluntary church debate, used what influence he had to prevent the Disruption of the Church of Scotland, and he was somewhat half-hearted in the support he gave, with the rest of the Irish General Assembly, to the Free Church. He was certainly strongly opposed to the Assembly's desire to emulate the spirit of the Free Church in opposition to the government, of which the call for a complete Presbyterian college and the opposition to the Queen's Colleges was a part. The public recognition of Protestantism, even if it was an Episcopalian Protestantism, and even if it was not a wholly Calvinist Protestantism, was the surest preservative against the natural tendency of mankind to sin.

The state in which Cooke had put his trust was, however, withdrawing from its earlier commitment to the establishment principle. Following Catholic Emancipation in 1829 and the Reform Act in 1832, parliament was no longer an Anglican club. In the eighteenth century commitment to the establishment principle had been fundamental to parliament. The division between Whigs and Tories had turned on the nature of the Established Church and the attitude to be taken to Dissent, not on the establishment principle itself. Now disestablishment, on the essentially religious grounds argued by Wardlaw, was a substantial force in British society in England and Scotland, mainly associated with the inherently disruptive forces of Evangelical Calvinism. The Churches of England and Scotland were still strong enough to resist outright disestablishment, but the Church of Ireland was vulnerable, especially given the strength of the Irish Catholic caucus of M.P.s in parliament in the 1830s and 1840s.

The Irish Church Temporalities Act of 1833 had been a formal recognition by the state that the Church of Ireland was not the spiritual voice of the Irish people. It had aimed to cut the Church of Ireland down to a size corresponding more closely to its actual membership rather than to its claim to be the organising spiritual authority of the whole society.

The National Education System likewise had been based on the recognition that Ireland was not Protestant. The Protestant representatives on the board, Carlile and the

Archbishop of Dublin, Richard Whately, had seen it as a possible vehicle for proselytism — 'common Christianity' being a step towards Protestantism. But theirs was very much a minority position which was not sustained in practice. While the state continued to operate the system through individual ministers of religion, it had taken a position above and separate from the churches, requiring the schools to conform to its rules, which aimed to foster a national loyalty above denominational differences. In practice its refusal to support Protestantism as such, especially the Church of Ireland, meant that the system favoured the numerically stronger Catholic Church.[137]

The same principle was applied in the Colleges Bill, and if the Queen's Colleges had been introduced in the 1830s, there can be little doubt that they would have received the support of the majority of Catholic bishops. The colleges originated in a plan formulated by Peel, who had risen to power as a strong supporter of the establishment principle. He had been M.P. for Oxford University and continued to support its efforts to maintain itself as an Anglican preserve. Yet the state's control over the Irish colleges was explicitly used to restrict the influence of the churches over the colleges, described by the then M.P. for Oxford University, Sir Robert Inglis, as 'a gigantic scheme of Godless education'. The state was adopting as its own the non-sectarian principles of University College, London, which had been founded on a private initiative and which had resulted in the explicitly Anglican King's College, London, and Durham College in reaction against it. Again, the motive behind the Irish colleges was to provide a higher education for Catholics without endowing Catholicism. This time, however, the Roman Catholic Church felt in a strong enough position to be able to take offence at the proposal, while the proportionately weaker Protestant churches supported it.[138]

That the state should promote a religious outlook to which the Presbyterians were hostile was, of course, nothing new, and the promotion of non-sectarianism could be seen as an improvement over the promotion of Anglicanism. What was new was that the Presbyterians were being drawn into this state structure and were thus, at the very fundamental level of education obliged to accept a moral discipline which was other than the discipline provided by their own community. Queen's College, Belfast, continued to be Presbyterian in character. Its first President, Pooley Shuldam Henry, was a Presbyterian minister, and he was succeeded by Josias Porter, Cooke's son-in-law and biographer. The restrictions on the promotion of religion were not unlike those of the Belfast Academical Institution. But its establishment, regulations and future were in the hands of the government — precisely the situation that Drennan and the founders of the Academical Institution had sought to avoid.

3. *Radical Sectarianism Fights Back*

In politics, the 1832 reform was crucial. Previously the Presbyterians had been virtually unable to participate in politics at the parliamentary level, apart from the period of the 1780s and 1790s when it had seemed that they could achieve a reform by main force and even assume a dominant place in Irish society. The possibilities opened up by the 1832 reform were more modest, but from that point on the British parliament and its disputes became the focus of a lively political interest. The Conservatives, as the principal bulwark against O'Connell and Repeal, were at an advantage. James Emerson Tennent, in a speech replying to O'Connell in 1834, explained why Irish Protestants were forced to become Conservatives: it was because the only possible political choice was between Repeal and Conservatism. Thus Cooke found it easy to transcend the narrow boundaries of the Ulster Presbyterian community to ally with Anglican landlords and become part of the wider British Conservative network.[139]

His opponents in the Belfast Reform Society were equally anxious to immerse themselves in wider politics, but they were tainted with Arianism, and their natural allies, both local Catholics and British Whigs, were identified with O'Connell. In 1837 they had more success with an impeccably orthodox Presbyterian candidate, James Gibson, an elder in the Third Belfast congregation (Rosemary Street), who had opposed Cooke over the National Education System, unqualified subscription and support for the Church of Ireland, but who also supported the attack on Unitarian properties and was unequivocally opposed to O'Connell, using the arguments of Paul and MacKnight that a liberal attitude to Catholics was the best programme for undermining Catholicism. Gibson was elected, though his election was overthrown on a technicality; nevertheless, his adoption by the Reform Society facilitated the emergence of a distinct O'Connellite and pro-Repeal Catholic party in Belfast, identified with Charles Gavan Duffy and his paper, *The Vindicator*.[140]

Ironically, the Whig tradition was being forced back into a closer identification with distinct Presbyterian interests. This renewed emphasis seemed to triumph when in 1844 the General Assembly resolved to press for the representation of Presbyterian interests in parliament, but in the event it came to nothing largely because of the dispute over the Queen's Colleges, the main political issue with which they were almost immediately faced. New possibilities, however, opened up with the tenant-right agitation of 1850.

The question of tenant right had been raised as early as 1835 by William Sharman Crawford, whom we encountered as one of the Belfast Reform Society's candidates in the 1832 election. Crawford had, in a manner of speaking, accepted the logic of James Emerson Tennent's view that the only possible choice was between Conservatism and O'Connell. He had been elected as the O'Connellite candidate for Dundalk in 1835. He was, however, unhappy about Repeal, though taking the view that some form of domestic legislature would be desirable for Ireland, and only agreed to stand for O'Connell on condition that Repeal would not be agitated. He soon became dissatisfied with O'Connell as a social reformer, believing for one thing that he could have achieved the complete abolition of tithes (instead of their mere 'commutation' — to be paid by the landlord and therefore, ultimately, through rent).[141]

Crawford raised the issue of tenant right in response to the warfare which was the permanent state of the landholding system over large areas in the south of Ireland. Agrarian outrage was the means by which the southern peasantry, long before the days of the Tenant League or Land League, preserved the 'three Fs' — fair rent, fixity of tenure and free sale. What was being preserved, however, was an enormous population living at subsistence level. Over large areas of the country the production of an agricultural surplus for sale was virtually impossible.

It was the common view of economists, including (or even especially) Whigs and Radicals, that these areas were over-populated and that the problem could only be resolved by a massive reduction in the numbers living off the land, a policy rendered impossible by the vicious reprisals which followed any attempt to implement it. Crawford argued, by contrast, that the land could support a large population at a level higher than subsistence, and he cited Ulster, which also had a large rural population, as a model. In Ulster, however, the problem had been alleviated by the presence of a widespread rural industry — the linen industry. The combination of weaving and small farming allowed for greater flexibility, in that the industry could act as a safeguard against fluctuations in agriculture, and agriculture could act as a safeguard against fluctuations in the linen market. The Ulster tenants had therefore been in a stronger position in relation to their landlords and had not had to fight for their interest in the land on a perpetual basis since the Steelboy and Oakboy revolts of the second half of the eighteenth century.[142]

This desirable state of affairs was under threat from industrialisation, but the process of industrialisation was slower in the linen industry than in the cotton industry, and Ulster did not develop a large-scale engineering industry until the second half of the nineteenth century. For the development of radical politics in the first half of the nineteenth century, this was a misfortune. In England radical politics could be based on industrial as against agricultural interests, while in Ulster it was based largely on the farmer/weaver, a class doomed to extinction. Crawford, who was, with Michael Davitt, one of the very few genuinely radical thinkers in Irish political history, supported the Chartists in the 1830s and formed a close alliance with Bright and Cobden; but his social policies for Ireland were, and had to be, based on principles very different from their confident commitment to free trade.[143]

Crawford argued that the rights that had been recognised

in Ulster should be extended to the whole country, where they were at present being achieved only by a state of continual warfare. They were to be established both in Ulster and elsewhere by law. This flew in the face of the commitment of Liberals and Radicals to the principle of minimal government involvement in private contracts. The old Radical Joseph Hume described Crawford's proposals as 'communism . . . a principle which implied spoliation and would lead to the robbery of all property'.[144]

Crawford received little support from the O'Connellites and broke with them in 1837 over what he saw as their slavish dependence on the Whigs. He declined to stand again in the 1837 election. His opposition to O'Connell was confirmed in 1839 when O'Connell returned to the Repeal agitation.

In 1840 Crawford became secretary to the newly formed Ulster Constitutional Association, which can be seen as a continuation of the Belfast Reform Society, opposed to the reliance on Presbyterian sectarian interests which characterised the politics of James MacKnight. It included the Unitarian Henry Montgomery and the Roman Catholic Archbishop William Crolly as well as the aristocrat Lord Charlemont. It opposed O'Connell's demand for Repeal and boycotted the 'reform dinner' held in Belfast in his honour by the militant Repealers associated with Gavan Duffy and *The Vindicator* (this was the occasion of Cooke's famous challenge to a public debate with O'Connell). One of the principles of the Ulster Constitutional Association was:

> to obtain for Ireland an equalisation of all rights, franchises and benefits with Britain, and the closest possible assimilation of the laws and institutions of both countries, to the end that by complete incorporation, the system of imperial legislation may be rendered permanently beneficial to the interests of the United Kingdom.[145]

The eventual fate of this political tradition still needs to be researched, though some useful ideas have been put forward by Peter Gibbon in his *Origins of Ulster Unionism* (pp 87-111). Gibbon describes its failure to take a hold in Belfast. Its successes were in rural constituencies and were largely dependent on Catholic support. In the 1880 election it secured one-third of the seats in Ulster, but in 1885, it was wiped out by the Home Rule Party. I would suggest that it fell victim to the Catholic Church's policy of alliance with British Liberalism, developed largely by the Archbishop of Dublin, Paul Cullen, following O'Connell's earlier policy of an alliance with the Whigs. Unlike O'Connell, Cullen effectively abandoned Repeal. He emphasised the distinct interests of his church, especially in education, but did not insist on the development of a distinct Catholic political party. The British Liberals were happy to secure this Irish support and to make the concessions necessary to maintaining it, without inquiring too closely into the nature of the social development they were facilitating in Ireland. The result in Ulster was that Liberalism had a non-sectarian Protestant leadership and a sectarian Catholic electoral base without much in the way of a permanent bond of loyalty between the two. Nevertheless, unlike the more spectacular agitations of the tenant-right movement or of the later independent breakaways from Conservatism, it did maintain an organisational continuum which lasted from 1830 to 1886, and it might have contributed to a breaking down of cross-denominational barriers if Repeal had not reasserted itself, after Cullen's death, with the rise of the Parnellite Home Rule Party.[146]

Crawford in 1841 became M.P. for the English town of Rochdale, making it clear that he would continue to take a close interest in Irish affairs. He continued his battle for tenant right throughout the 1840s, until in 1850, in the wake of the Famine, a centrally organised, nation-wide Tenant League with a clear programme of demands emerged for the first time.

The Famine provides a horrible illustration of the gap between the needs of English and southern Irish politics, especially radical politics. The year 1845, which saw the beginning of the Famine, also saw a triumph for the English radical industrial interest with Peel's conversion to the repeal of the Corn Laws. The 1840s, as well as being the decade of the Famine in Ireland, were the 'hungry forties' in Britain, where the hunger was felt by the urban working class. In these circumstances, the radical demand for free trade and an end to protection of the price of corn was successful. In Ireland the problem lay in the countryside, with the failure of the single crop that had supported a vast rural population. For the radical Young Ireland group, which was now organised separately from O'Connell following the controversy over the Queen's Colleges, the continued export of corn, in accordance with the principle of free trade, was scandalous. They argued that massive government intervention was necessary to mobilise all the food-producing resources of Ireland to feed its own population. In these circumstances, Crawford too became a supporter of the demand for repeal of the Union and the institution of a powerful separate Irish government.[147]

The Famine, while it lasted, enormously weakened the southern peasantry in relation to their landlords, who were pressed by the imminence of bankruptcy to take advantage of that weakness. The view was, of course, expressed that the depopulation caused by the Famine, preferably achieved through emigration rather than through starvation, would greatly ease Ireland's endemic agrarian problem. Brutal as that argument was, there was a great deal of truth in it. The eventual resolution of the agrarian problem through peasant proprietorship in the Conservative and Unionist government's Land Act of 1903 would not have been so successful in the conditions before the Famine.

The forced evictions and the inability of the population to resist them raised the question of a legal provision for tenant right in a stark form. Gavan Duffy, who had left Belfast and *The Vindicator* to edit the Young Ireland paper, *The Nation*, in Dublin, formed an alliance with his old friend and political enemy in Belfast, James MacKnight, now editing the Presbyterian paper, the *Banner of Ulster*, to form what Duffy was later to call 'the League of North and South'.

The alliance between MacKnight and Duffy was remarkable. Duffy had made himself intensely unpopular among northern Presbyterians through his editorship of *The Vindicator*. His paper *The Nation* had struck a chord among some Irish Anglicans, but, despite the involvement of John Mitchel, son of one of the first members of the Remonstrant Synod, its romantic evocation of an Irish past had no charm for the Presbyterians. Mitchel had only recently been imprisoned for his association with the 1848 rebellion, which could only appear quixotic and absurd in Presbyterian eyes.

But tenant right was under attack in Ulster, where the position of the tenant farmer was now eroded by the industrialisation of the linen industry, and MacKnight shared Crawford's desire to see it given legal status. The demand connected with no substantial interest in British politics, and Ulster's influence in parliament was too weak, despite the fact that Crawford's arguments were beginning to appeal even to Conservative M.P.s, for it to make much impact unless it was linked with a wider Irish agitation. The prospect of such an alliance was now more feasible, since, with the failure of the 1848 rising, the death of O'Connell and the immediately pressing problem of the aftermath of the Famine, the cause of national separation had collapsed. There was also, briefly, a kindlier feeling between Catholics and Protestants, because, however much the government could be castigated for the slowness of its response, and however much proselytism might have been practised, the fact remained that Protestant Ireland, including the Presbyterians, had put an enormous effort into famine relief.[148]

The period of the Tenant League was short. It lasted only three years. Its electoral successes were confined to the south. Crawford himself failed to secure a seat for Co. Down in the 1852 election. Nevertheless, it was a brief moment in which an Irish national political movement combining the influence of Roman Catholic priests and Ulster Presbyterian ministers was possible. The ministers in question were mostly very young and influenced by the abrasive tone pioneered by John Paul and adopted in current Presbyterian polemic against the Church of Ireland in *The Plea of Presbytery*, the *Banner of Ulster* and the *Derry Standard*.

The immediate problem was resolved, especially in Ulster by an agricultural revival in the countryside, which restored the landlords' ability to recognise tenant right. The Tenant League itself, according to Duffy, failed through the rising influence of Archbishop Cullen and his Catholic Defence Association, formed in response to Protestant agitation against the establishment in 1850 of a Roman Catholic hierarchy in England. Cullen regarded Duffy as a dangerous revolutionary in the mould of Mazzini, who was causing considerable problems for the pope at the time in Italy. Under Cullen's influence there was little chance of the priests supporting any movement with which Duffy was associated, and, as Duffy was to remark in *My Life in Two Hemispheres*, 'Elections could no more be won without the help of the local priests than Charles Edward could have raised the Scottish Highlanders without the help of their chiefs.' (Vol. II, p. 97) The Presbyterian ministers involved had been too young to have played a particularly authoritative role, and older ministers who might have sympathised, such as Alexander Goudy of Strabane, one of the authors of *The Plea of Presbytery*, could not bring themselves to share a political platform with Roman Catholic priests.[149]

It was therefore a short-lived movement, but, taken in conjunction with the later land agitations in Ulster which were almost continuous, even despite the threat of Home Rule, for the last thirty years of the century, it is important as illustrating that the Ulster Protestant tenant farmers did not take the deferential attitude to the aristocracy that has often — quite ludicrously — been ascribed to them. They were certainly less deferential than their English counterparts, largely because they had a stronger independent base, of which the Presbyterian Church, with its tradition of self-organisation independent of the establishment, formed a part.

There is, however, something very unsatisfactory about this rural radicalism. Crawford had had severe doubts about the demand for 'fixity of tenure', which, in Ireland as a whole, was calculated to preserve a *status quo* that was itself intolerable and had given rise to the potato famine. He wished to tie the rights of tenants not to the mere occupation but to the improvement of the land. The problem with farmers as a basis for radical agitation is that it is quite possible to live off the land with little or even no involvement in a wider market and therefore with a wider society. Davitt recognised the problem when he called not for peasant proprietorship but for land nationalisation. He recognised that society at large had an interest in obtaining food from the farmer which was not necessarily identical with the interests of the farmer himself. The establishment of peasant proprietorship in 1903, followed by an independent state in which farmers were the predominant social interest in the absence of a substantial industrial sector, has resulted in a conservative and inefficient agricultural economy in the Republic of Ireland.[150]

4. *The 1859 Revival*

The 1850s, which began with the involvement of Presbyterians in the tenant-right campaign, ended with their involvement in the 1859 Revival. To understand this we must return to our consideration of the Evangelical movement.

I have suggested that the attack on the Arians in the 1820s was not the result of pressures towards Evangelicalism experienced within the Ulster Presbyterian community itself. Presbyterians continued to behave as a distinct political community, though one which had been defeated and demoralised. They then recovered some self-confidence through the assertion of orthodoxy in the face of a threat from heresy. In so doing they took a step towards being a sect within society rather than a whole society in themselves, and they acted in concert with the Evangelical movement in Britain at large, especially in their support for the Free Church of Scotland. They shared the typically Evangelical interests in social improvements and missionary work. But they did not develop an Evangelical wing of their own — a group of people who felt that they had undergone a special experience of conversion and who recognised each other as especially earnest in their religious commitment.

The principal differences that developed among them were political and, in the years before the tenant-right movement, turned largely on the same issues with which they had been preoccupied in the eighteenth and early nineteenth centuries — the right of the civil magistrate to punish heresy, relations with the Established Church and with Roman Catholics, and the injustice of classified *regium donum*, together with the new, externally imposed issue of popular education, all considered in the light of a new desire to secure doctrinal orthodoxy. In these political concerns they were increasingly forced to think in terms of the interest of a wider British society rather than of their own distinct community. They were being drawn into the evolving British political party system —

Conservative, Liberal and Radical — with the position of the 'Liberals' complicated by the use being made of British Liberalism by the Irish Catholic interest, and the position of the 'Radicals' complicated by the fact that their rurally based demands did not correspond to the urban radicalism of their British equivalents. As in the rest of Britain in the nineteenth century, the state, aided by the progressively widening franchise, was replacing the church as the major instrument of social cohesion (the major exceptions being Catholic Ireland and parts of the north of Scotland remote from the centre of the state, where the influence of the Free Church was strongest).

The lack of a specialist Evangelical wing in the early nineteenth century is a tribute to the continued effectiveness of Presbyterianism in ensuring social cohesion. The spectacular outburst of the 1859 Revival indicates the extent to which that central organising principle had been undermined. In the eighteenth century to be a Presbyterian was to be a member of a self-organising community. By the 1850s to be a Presbyterian was to be a person with particular religious views.

It is easy to see why some ministers would have wanted a revival in 1859. Their community was slipping out of their grasp. The system of discipline through 'kirk sessions', which had been the principal characteristic of seventeenth- and eighteenth-century Presbyterianism, supported by orthodox and latitudinarian alike, had long been unworkable. The secular law had eclipsed the discipline of the church as the means by which moral behaviour and mutual responsibility were enforced. The only basis for the church's authority was now nakedly what it had always been ultimately — the subjective and entirely voluntary faith of its members. These members were themselves undergoing the trauma of the conversion of the linen industry from a rurally based cottage industry to large-scale factory production.[151]

The 1859 Revival was a planned event. The periodical literature of Ulster Presbyterianism in the period preceding it shows an increased interest in the possibility of individual conversion experiences which, as I have argued before, had not previously been part of the Scottish Presbyterian tradition.

There was   a special interest in the American experience. William Gibson, author of the standard account of the Revival, *The Year of Grace*, toured America in 1858 to study the revival that was taking place there. The General Assembly prayed for a revival at its annual meeting the same year. They may have been surprised and even alarmed by their success, perhaps considering it to be out of all proportion to their own efforts, but this merely indicates that their desire for a revival met a corresponding desperate need felt by their congregations. Mere membership of a self-organising community, or even a doctrinally pure church, was no longer sufficient.[152]

The intensity of the religious feeling, and the physical afflictions that accompanied it, need not surprise us too much. If it was miraculous, it was a miracle that is a permanent part of Pentecostalist worship. The Pentecostalists believe in the power of the Holy Ghost to overpower the mind and break its independence. A highly charged atmosphere is created through powerful preaching, and those disposed to enter into the spirit of the occasion are duly afflicted. A similar cathartic purging of the emotions is achieved in our own times in rock concerts. I am not suggesting that the Pentecostalist experience is not a religious experience, or that such emotional outlets are not necessary and desirable and may be better if they occur in the context of a system of religious values rather than on the basis of pure sensuality or gestalt therapy. I am only suggesting that it is a normal part of human life that such experiences can be had if there is a disposition to have them.

The desire to experience God personally is such a natural desire that we may reasonably ask why such Pentecostalism is not a permanent central part of Western Christian worship, especially since it has strong Biblical support in the references to the 'baptism of fire' in the Acts of the Apostles. The answer lies partly in the difficulty in believing that it really is the work of the Holy Spirit, when human technique has such a large part to play; yet without a conviction that there is a divine origin for the experience, it has no more value than the rock concert.

The attempt to distinguish the human and divine parts of the work forms a large part of the literature of revivalism. It was a perpetual preoccupation of the theorist of the American Great Awakening, Jonathan Edwards. The ministers involved in the Ulster Revival were also concerned to distinguish between those who were genuinely stricken and genuinely repentant and those who were merely participating in the general mood. One of the Revival's supporters was the Rev. James McCosh, a Scottish minister who was in Belfast as the Professor of Logic and Metaphysics at the Queen's College, a post he had gained partly through the influence of William Gibson. His book *The Scottish Philosophy* is still highly regarded as a summary account of the Scottish literature on the nature of the mind. He also wrote extensively, attempting to develop a natural theology on the basis of modern science. He eventually became Professor of Philosophy and President of Princeton, playing an important part in reorganising it after the American Civil War and guiding it to university status. A number of revivals took place among the students under his guidance.[153]

In a paper entitled *The Ulster Revival and Its Physiological Accidents* (1859) McCosh argued that the 'physiological accidents' had not been as spectacular as was pretended and that they were not evidence of divine intervention. The fear of God's wrath, he suggested, would produce the same physical agitation as any other great fear, but 'feelings which contemplate the good . . . have no tendency to agitate or prostrate the body' (p. 5). Visions, blindness, deafness and mesmeric sleep were and remained unhealthy and should be discouraged: 'Nothing, in my humble opinion, is so much fitted to grieve the Spirit, as to find persons gazing at the weakness of man as if it were the power of God.' (p. 14)

The Ulster Presbyterians had no Pentecostalist theory to sustain such physical manifestations as a permanent part of their worship, and they did not again attempt anything so ambitious as the 1859 Revival. Nonetheless, the Revival had a permanent effect. It broke the Presbyterian monopoly of Protestantism outside the Established Church. It provided an opening for churches organised on Congregational lines — Baptists and Plymouth Brethren. It saw the growth of the Gospel Hall, which is such a typical part of religious life in Northern Ireland today. As such it was another substantial step towards religion becoming a subjective personal commitment rather than the organising principle of a unified community.

5. *Part of a Wider Culture*

The controversial literature of the eighteenth and early nineteenth centuries can be seen as something resembling a national culture — the community absorbedly interested in its own ideas. The Presbyterian ministers who engaged in it came close to Coleridge's ideal of a 'clerisy' — the intellectual centre of their society. It was a culture whose very coherence was based on its divisions — a continual running argument conducted by ministers firmly connected with their own communities through the corporate life encouraged by the Presbyterian system of sessions, presbyteries and synods. Although the argument turned on matters of theology, it was principally theology in its bearings on politics (particularly on the great question of the right of the civil magistrate to punish heresy), and it had a distinct political function in maintaining the character of the community.

The absorption of this community into the wider British national community was part of the whole development of British society, but the contrast with Catholic Ireland indicates that the process was by no means inevitable. To have resisted it the society would have had to have maintained a profound hostility to the Church of Ireland. *The Plea of Presbytery*, the *Banner of Ulster*, the resolution in favour of a distinct Presbyterian politics and the proposal for a complete Presbyterian college all indicated that this was still a possibility as late as the 1840s. But however reluctant Presbyterians may have been to accept Cooke's arguments for Protestant union, there was a logic in it which could not be resisted. That logic was grounded in the steady advance of Catholic Ireland. The marriage controversy of the late 1830s was the last major threat posed to the Presbyterians from the Church of Ireland, and it was resolved in the early 1840s. The sectarian enthusiasm of the 1840s has the appearance of a last effort to preserve a community whose absorption was nearly inevitable.

The establishment of the Queen's College in Belfast created a new intellectual centre at once more diverse than the Presbyterian ministers and less well grounded in the community. The Belfast Academical Institution had not had the same effect. Despite its non-sectarian intentions, it was first and foremost a Presbyterian seminary, and it was created by and responsible to a mainly Presbyterian community. Queen's College, by contrast, was created by and responsible to a non-Presbyterian government. Theology was excluded under its constitution and catered for by the separate Assembly's College, a process that had been prefigured when the Presbyterian theology faculty dissociated itself from the Academical Institution. John Henry Newman in his essays on university education is eloquent on the effects of separating religious and non-religious education. He argues that the absence of religion from a university curriculum necessarily creates a dynamic towards secularist habits of thought. The argument is basic to the Roman Catholic Church's rejection of the kind of education endorsed by the Ulster Presbyterians in the 1840s.[154]

The establishment of Assembly's College itself can be seen as a blow to the popular controversial writing of the previous 150 years. That writing had flourished in the absence of such a college, at a time when ministers were trained in Glasgow, which was too remote to have a permanent influence on them, and where the Irish ministers were not regarded as academically very distinguished. Their intellectual life was formed not by their university education but by their relations with each other and with their community. With Assembly's College, theology became a specialist academic subject, and the controversies which preoccupied the ministers were now international in scope. A culture of specialist books replaced a culture of popular pamphlets.

Assembly's College acquired a reputation for strict orthodoxy. It was modelled on, and maintained connections with, Princeton in America. It had a revivalist character, and it may be no coincidence that the 1859 Revival occurred six years after it opened. William Gibson, the theorist of the Revival, was its first Professor of Moral Philosophy, and Robert Watts, who became Professor of Systematic Theology in 1866 after working in Princeton, was a supporter of the revivalist campaigns of Moody and Sankey and a strong opponent of the 'higher criticism', which set itself the task of investigating how the Bible had been compiled by the methods of ordinary historical inquiry. The college was briefly used until Watts's death in 1895 by the Free Presbyterian Church of Scotland, which had withdrawn from the Free Church after it had adopted a declaratory act in 1892 rejecting 'the foreordination of men to death irrespective of their own sin'.

But the intellectual influence of the Ulster Presbyterian ministers had been at its greatest at a time when there had been very great, openly agitated disagreements among them. The strict Calvinist orthodoxy of Assembly's College in the second half of the nineteenth century was not a determining feature in the intellectual life of the wider community, which was being formed by the whole range of influences operating in British culture in this period through books, periodicals and newspapers. The 'higher criticism' itself entered the college in the person of Thomas Walker in 1888, and in 1926 the failure to arraign the Professor of Biblical Criticism, Ernest Davey, for heresy resulted in the departure of the Irish Evangelical Church (now called the Evangelical Presbyterian Church) on the principles which had been promoted thirty years earlier by Watts.[155]

The triumph of Calvinist orthodoxy in the 1830s, then, did not result in a community characterised by Calvinist orthodoxy (if that is a proper term for a religious tendency in which revivalism has an important part to play). On the contrary, it was symptomatic of a decline in the church's importance as an organisational and intellectual centre to the society. Its place was being taken by the Queen's College as an intellectual centre, the factories as a social centre, and the political parties as the connection between the populace and the state. Revivalism and the growth of the Town Mission can be seen as the attempt of ministers to regain territory they were losing. Before 1850 the main emphasis of missionary work had been to gain converts from Roman Catholicism. After 1850 the futility of this venture became increasingly apparent, and the main emphasis moved to recovering Protestant support.

We have seen that revivalism was not an idea intrinsic to Ulster Presbyterian thinking, whether latitudinarian or orthodox. It used techniques which had been pioneered in areas of England, Wales and Scotland, where the national church was weak, and in America, where there was no national church, and where the principle of Voluntaryism, requiring the churches to compete for a free market of congregations, was established in practice in Pennsylvania, and where the old 'visible saints' of Congregationalist New England were having difficulty reproducing themselves in succeeding generations. It had been resisted by the Church of Scotland and by the Synod of Ulster in the confidence of their strength. Its effect was not to restore the church as the organising centre of the political community, but to multiply the sects and to reinforce the nature of religion as a specialist interest.

Conclusion:
The Ulster Protestants

1. *Exclusion from British Political Development*

By the end of the nineteenth century the established Churches of England and Scotland could no longer be described as central to the way in which their societies were organised and defined. The state, which had long been the dominant partner in the church/state relationship, especially in England, now stood alone as the unifying centre of the nation. The churches had become what Locke in his *First Letter on Toleration* had said they ought to be — voluntary societies gathered together for the purpose of worshipping God. The role of the established church as the means by which society was organised and unified at parish level throughout the country was now superseded by the political parties.

The decline in the importance of the Church of England broadly coincides with the rise in the importance and representative nature of the parties through the extension of the electoral franchise. Instead of being a little Anglican or Dissenter, every English child alive was either a little Liberal or else a little Conservative. The parties, rather than the church, form the connection between the people and the state. If only a minority of people are actively involved in the work of the parties, the same could be said of the Established Church in its heyday in the eighteenth century. The parties are organised at constituency level in every part of Great Britain so that whatever local interests particular M.P.s might represent, they are each involved in a national movement with national ideals, and at each election the wider population which is not involved in the actual organisation of the parties can choose between them. The churches rank with trade unions and certain great business enterprises as private societies dispersed throughout the nation, but only the political parties can claim to provide the nation-wide basis for the state.[156]

This puts Northern Ireland in a peculiar position in relation to the British state, since the national parties are not organised there. Consequently Northern Ireland is excluded from the means by which the British nation is organised and unified. Although it has many British institutions such as the B.B.C. and the main British-based unions, it is excluded from the national life of the United Kingdom.

The origins of this exclusion go back to 1886 and the need to submerge the religious and political differences among the Ulster Protestants in the Unionist Party to resist the demand of Catholic Ireland for national separation from the United Kingdom. Possibilities of political differentiation could be seen in the Unionist bloc in the popularity of T. W. Russell in his demand for the compulsory buying out of the landlords, which was achieved in 1903; in the Presbyterian Unionist Voters' Association; in the Ulster Liberal Association and the Independent Orange Order; and, most importantly, in the organisation of the trade unions, of the Independent Labour Party and of the Labour Representation Committee, forerunner of the Labour Party, which held a conference in Belfast in 1907. None of these, however, with the obvious exception of the unions, could secure a substantial or permanent political base so long as Home Rule was a real possibility. Between 1886 and 1920, the period in which British Liberalism gave way to British Labour, politics in Ulster froze into the confrontation between Unionist and Nationalist.[157]

The Unionist Party was, of course, a mass-based party which fulfilled at least one of the historical purposes of the British political parties — to override religious differences (in this case, as principally in the case of the British parties, the differences among Protestants) in favour of a great national secular cause. But this political unity was not based on social ideals. The Unionist Party was allied to the British Conservative Party because the Conservatives were also committed to the Union. Conservatism had been strongly based in Ulster before 1886, largely because of the Catholic Church's policy of alliance with the Liberals. It was, of course, identified with the landlord interest, but the party which finally expropriated the Irish landlords in 1903 with the acquiescence of the Ulster Unionist M.P.s and the enthusiastic support of much of the Ulster Unionist population, could not be described as a party committed to Irish landlordism. Despite the formal connection, the Unionist Party was a separate party with its own discipline and its own very different historical development which has placed it, at the time of writing, in a position of outright antagonism to the Conservative Party (exactly one hundred years after the Ulster Liberals found themselves in a position of outright antagonism to the British Liberal Party).

Irish nationalism did not perform the role of subsuming the church interest into a political interest. There was the possibility of such a development in Young Ireland, in its ideal vision of a 'romantic Ireland' (a fabricated concept which proved attractive to certain elements in the southern Protestant ascendancy), in the frictions between the church and the Fenian movement, and in the political skill, popularity and personal integrity of Parnell. But they came to nothing, and when Catholic Ireland achieved its independence in 1921 there was nothing in the political society that could confront the church. Writers such as W. B. Yeats, George Russell and Lennox Robinson, who had developed an impressive secular literature, quickly found themselves to be marginal to the society they thought they had helped to form. The boundaries between church and state were set by the church, which maintained and strengthened its control over education, health and public welfare services, areas which in the United Kingdom were being taken over by the state.[158]

The need for a distinct Unionist movement in Ulster should have ended with partition. With Northern Ireland securely established as part of the United Kingdom state, it should have been possible to develop differences based on the politics of that state, differences that could ultimately have subsumed even the Unionist/Nationalist, Protestant/Catholic division, great as that was in 1920. That this development failed to occur is entirely the responsibility of Westminster and its political parties. A separate parliament and state apparatus was imposed on Northern Ireland against the advice of the Ulster Unionist leaders, especially Carson, and the British political parties boycotted the new sub-state they had brought into existence.

Of the four constituent parts of the United Kingdom, Northern Ireland was the one least suitable for a separate parliament, precisely because it contains a large minority which had developed as part — in some respects a leading part — of Catholic Ireland. This minority, like the new southern state, has maintained an organisational and ideological cohesion through the Catholic Church, which has continued to control its own schools. Within a separate Northern Ireland, this minority was sufficiently large to pose a permanent threat to the integrity of the state. Within the United Kingdom parliament, Catholics and Protestants in Northern Ireland would have been insignificant minorities, each forced to find allies within the wider framework of British politics. The structure of the British state would not have been endangered by their quarrel. As it was, the stability of Northern Ireland could only be maintained by the continued solidarity of the Ulster Protestants in the Unionist bloc. A permanent majority held state power over a permanent minority; the minority, for its part, was committed not merely to the defence of its material interests and cultural identity but to the overthrow of the state. The situation was bound to create an unhealthy preoccupation with keeping its power on the one side, and unlimited scope for the development of a sense of grievance on the other.

The nation which supported the new state was the Ulster Protestant nation. The use of the term 'Protestant' suggests not a nation but a religious community. That religious communities are nowadays not seen as a proper basis for nations is a modern, nineteenth-century phenomenon — a product of the abandonment of national churches. Yet even in the nineteenth and twentieth centuries it is an untenable assumption. Poland is unquestionably a Catholic nation, in conflict with its own non-Catholic state. Israel is unquestionably a Jewish nation. Pakistan and all the Arab states, with the unappealing exception of the Lebanon, are unquestionably Islamic. The Irish nation which wished to separate from the United Kingdom is unquestionably Roman Catholic.

But 'Protestantism' is not a religion. There is no such thing as 'the Protestant Church' (except in the popular use of the term to refer solely to the Church of Ireland). The use of the term 'Protestantism' in itself implies at least a reconciliation of the interests of different churches. A Protestant state for a Protestant people is a state that is not identified with the interests of any one particular church.

We have seen that the differences between the churches that go to make this common 'Protestantism' have been very great. In the seventeenth century they led to wars. When alliances were formed against the common Catholic enemy, they were alliances of the same kind as the alliances between the political parties in our own day in time of war — a temporary suspension of the struggle for supremacy. In the eighteenth century, I have suggested, the Presbyterians virtually formed a nation in their own right, but in the nineteenth century this distinct 'nationhood' of the Ulster Presbyterians began to break down and the great political divisions of British politics began to develop in the difficult circumstances created by the threat from Catholic Ireland. The process of political differentiation was unavoidably arrested by the Home Rule crisis between 1886 and 1920 and was then avoidably aborted by the British government policy of excluding Northern Ireland from British politics — a policy that has prevailed to the present day. That Northern Ireland continued to develop as if it was part of the British state, despite its separate state apparatus, is almost entirely due to the remarkable political skill of the leaders of the Ulster Unionist Party, James Craig (Lord Craigavon) and Basil Brooke (Lord Brookeborough — who was not related to the present writer).

The Government of Ireland Act of 1920 aimed to establish two Home Rule parliaments in Ireland, and it embodied the hope that in time their common 'Irishness' would prevail and the two could be united. In the event the common Irishness, which was much stronger in 1920 than it is today, proved to be less substantial a force than the Catholicism of one and identification of the other with the increasingly secular society of the United Kingdom. Catholic Ireland consolidated its independence from the United Kingdom, while Protestant Ulster managed to constitute itself part of an economic unit with the rest of the United Kingdom, thus sharing in the benefits of the increasing socialist redistribution of wealth, while still being excluded from the political process by which it was achieved. Stormont, originally expected to operate within a budget based on a calculation of taxation raised from within Northern Ireland, pursued a policy of 'step-by-step' development with the rest of the United Kingdom, replicating British legislation — including socialist legislation — with the financial support of the United Kingdom as a whole.

2. *Church, State and Education in Northern Ireland*

The difference between the two Irish states became apparent very shortly after they were established. The Northern Ireland government was soon engaged in a church/state confrontation which would have been unthinkable for the Cumann na nGaedheal government in the South.

This confrontation turned on the question of control of education. The Unionists had been attempting since 1907 to rationalise the Irish education system by bringing the three education sectors — national (primary), intermediate and technical — under the control of a government ministry; and to consolidate small schools under the control of local government bodies, along similar lines to the Conservative government's act of 1902, which established local education authorities in Great Britain. They were thus fully committed to the principle of lay control over education, and this was not seriously questioned by the Protestant churches. In the eyes of the Roman Catholic Church, however, it was a fundamentally 'Protestant' principle.

The new Unionist government soon set about a radical reorganisation of the education system. A Ministry of Education was established and the schools divided into three classes. The first class was to be fully funded by the state and fully controlled by the local authorities. The second class was to have half its costs paid by the state and was to be run by a management committee consisting of four representatives of the independent sponsoring body (usually one of the churches) and two representatives of the state. The third was to be wholly denominational and was to receive no state aid for capital or running costs, except for heating and lighting. The state was to pay teachers' salaries in all three classes.

The controversy between the Protestant churches and the government turned on the first class. The Minister of Education, Lord Londonderry, insisted on a fully secularist approach. Religious instruction was to be wholly excluded from school hours; no account was to be taken of the religious views of teachers; and the churches were not to be represented on the school management committees. He took his stand on the Government of Ireland Act, which had provided that no government support was to be given to any religious denomination. The Westminster political parties believed that by such a fiat they had done their duty by the cause of non-sectarianism in Northern Ireland and could then wash their hands of the matter. What the English aristocrat Lord Londonderry was demanding was a much higher degree of secularisation than obtained at the time in Great Britain.

D. H. Akenson, whose *Education and Enmity* is the basis for the present account, describes William Corkey, the Presbyterian minister who led the opposition to the Londonderry proposals, as 'in educational matters the Henry Cooke of the twentieth century' (p. 75), and he shows the same inability to understand Corkey's position as he shows in his account (in *The Irish Education Experiment*) of Presbyterian opposition to the National Education System in the 1830s. To propose that there should be lay control of the schools and that there should be restrictions on religious education was one thing; to propose that all consideration of religion should be purposefully excluded from the schools was quite another. Londonderry's proposals were unreasonable, and they were defeated. What is surprising is the degree of support they received. The government at first supported them, as did the union which represented the Protestant teachers, the Ulster Teachers' Union, a body which consistently opposed clerical involvement in educational affairs.

Akenson defends the Londonderry proposals and expresses indignation at their failure on the grounds that, since there was no question of the Roman Catholic Church handing its schools over to the local authorities (even to those under Roman Catholic control), the government, in permitting Bible instruction and minority church representation on the boards of management, was effectively endowing Protestantism. But the same terms were available to the Roman Catholic Church and would certainly have been modified further had the church been prepared to take part in the negotiations. Akenson is arguing that because the Roman Catholic Church refused to have anything to do with the system, the government should have discriminated against the Protestant churches and excluded religion altogether. In other words, it should have committed itself to a position of dogmatic secularism.

Dogmatic secularism, however, has never been a substantial force in British political development. Secularism has advanced in Britain through the need to reach compromises among the different religious denominations. Dogmatic secularism could only have been justified in schools in Northern Ireland if it had been a means of incorporating Catholics into the system, which clearly it was not. Had the Roman Catholic Church been prepared to consider any possibility of lay control, the system would have been modified to allow more, not less, of a specifically denominational influence. As it was, the Roman Catholic Church, with a small handful of exceptions, refused even to consider placing its schools in the second class, which allowed for majority clerical control but required a minority state representation on the boards of management. Under such circumstances the government would have been behaving in an outrageously dictatorial manner had it not based its education system on compromises among the Protestant population who had accepted the principle of lay control of schools. This population included ministers of different denominations as well as teachers, who were not themselves dogmatic secularists but who believed, like many parents, that laymen were as well able to provide for the religious interests of their pupils as the clergy.

We may thus correctly describe the state education sector in Northern Ireland as 'Protestant' as long as we remember that 'Protestantism' (as opposed to Anglicanism, Presbyterianism, Methodism, etc.) is itself pluralist, and that whatever privileges are accorded to the Protestant churches have always been equally available to the Roman Catholic Church.

After the Second World War education in Northern Ireland was reorganised with the introduction of compulsory secondary education, and the government introduced a new system of state support providing 65 per cent funding of the running costs of all voluntary (non-state) schools, primary and secondary. It is surprising that Akenson, who opposes any religious instruction in state schools on the basis of the Government of Ireland Act, does not regard this funding of denominational schools, which allowed no state representation whatsoever, as excessively generous. It aroused strong Protestant and, in the person of the socialist Harry Midgley, secularist opposition which, together with other discontents, led to the forced resignation of the Minister of Education, Colonel Hall-Thompson. But the legislation was already in place and was implemented by Midgley himself as his successor. More recently the Roman Catholic Church has accepted the principle of minority state representation on its boards of management — an acceptance which could have secured 50 per cent of the running costs of its schools at any time between 1924 and 1947. Catholic schools now receive all their running costs and 85 per cent of their capital costs.[159]

3. The Challenge from Catholic Ireland

Northern Ireland exists on the interface between Catholic Ireland and secular Britain — two societies which at least until recently were developing in opposite directions. Since the Second Vatican Council the adventure of constructing a Catholic state in the Republic has lost some of its lustre, but before Vatican II it was the principal determining characteristic of the new state. The contrast between Catholic Ireland and secular Britain is a telling illustration of the difference between the church as a means of organising the community and the churches as private worshipping societies.

In England and Scotland, of course, there are still, formally, national churches, while in Ireland church and state are formally separate. But however important the Churches of England and Scotland may be in the lives of individuals, they have little influence on the nature of society as a whole. By contrast, the Irish Catholic Church has a large measure of control in the field of education, medical ethics and social welfare, though this influence has declined more sharply in the past twenty years in the last of these than in the other two. Thus when we consider the formal separation of church and state we have to bear in mind that much that is the responsibility of the state in Britain is the responsibility of the church, financially supported by the state, in the Republic of Ireland.

Such a degree of church influence over everyday life would have been impossible in Protestant Britain even when the national church was at its most powerful. Protestantism knows only church officers and laity: it has no equivalent of the Roman Catholic religious orders. The most it can require is that laymen placed in influential positions subscribe to its doctrines. But it cannot guarantee the level of permanent commitment to its cause that can be expected of men and women who voluntarily accept the discipline of membership of an order. And in Catholic Ireland most of the schools and many of the hospitals are controlled by the religious orders.[160]

Irish Catholicism, as we know it today, is still a relatively raw, recent phenomenon. In the nineteenth century it lost its connection with the old Gaelic and English aristocracies, the tradition of the Confederation of Kilkenny and of eighteenth-century Jacobitism, and emerged as effectively a new, popularly based church. Archbishop MacHale, one of the pioneers of the development, saw it as a 'democratic' and 'national' church, but in fact the break with the aristocratic tradition facilitated its development as one of the most 'Roman' of Roman Catholic churches. The reassertion of papal claims which characterised Rome in the nineteenth century met little opposition from any well-established local church tradition. The dissensions, the chief of which was between Cullen and Fenianism, were over politics, without theological implications, and were largely resolved when Croke of Cashel and Walsh of Dublin succeeded to Cullen and brought about a marriage between the Catholic Church and the (largely Fenian-inspired) Land League.

The absence of theological controversy is a major distinguishing feature of Irish Catholicism in relation to Catholicism in the rest of Europe. Whatever quarrels there may have been between different orders or sections of the church, they did not take their stand on great theological principles. It also sharply distinguishes Irish Catholicism from Ulster Presbyterianism, which, at least until the second half of the nineteenth century, delighted in controversy.

The Ulster Protestants were surrounded by the development of Catholic Ireland, and it greatly distorted their own social and political development. Yet they never developed an adequate critique of it. The best hostile accounts of the rise of Catholic Ireland are those of M. J. F. McCarthy, a former Catholic and Parnellite writing at the turn of the century; Paul Blanshard, an American liberal secularist writing in the 1950s; and Brendan Clifford, a Cork-born communist writing at the present day. The period mainly covered by the present book shows the Ulster Presbyterians as a society with an intense and lively interest in ideas and controversy. Their inability to articulate the position in which they have found themselves in the present century requires some explanation.

A partial explanation may lie in the peculiar relationship with the rest of the United Kingdom outlined at the beginning of this chapter. Northern Ireland and its Protestant inhabitants were a part of the British state which yet had no part in the politics of the British state. Northern Ireland legislation followed British legislation without sharing in the political struggles which produced it. Socialist legislation was enacted without the development of socialist politics. A similar process could be seen at work in the cultural and intellectual spheres.

We have already seen that in schools and universities a much higher degree of non-sectarianism was required by government policy in Ireland than anywhere else in the United Kingdom, and that this was not a product of pressures from, and did not correspond to, the subjective needs of the society itself. It was successfully overcome by Catholic Ireland, which was able to develop freely after 1921. Protestant Ulster, by contrast, continued to follow a British development which was being determined by social and intellectual pressures from which the Ulster Protestants were isolated. From the mid-nineteenth century onwards British society was increasingly able to absorb its Catholic minority, which in turn was increasingly willing to be absorbed. Tractarianism had seemed to be the importation of a subversive and foreign ideology into the Church of England and had provoked a fierce anti-Catholic reaction, climaxing in the 'papal aggression' crisis of the 1850s. In the long run, however, it can be seen as having facilitated the emergence of a Roman Catholic Church free to develop its own nature, unlike the highly constrained Catholicism of the eighteenth century, but clearly not a threat to the integrity of the state, which was no longer tied to the integrity of the national church.

The values which had developed in Great Britain were also adopted in Ulster Protestant culture, where they were not sustained by the same social development, and where they were not entirely appropriate to the political circumstances. In Northern Ireland the Roman Catholic Church was not content with the role of a private worshipping society in an essentially secular state. It had, in its own eyes, been artificially cut off from a country where the relations between church and state were more nearly perfect than anywhere else in Europe, with the possible but doubtful exception of Franco's Spain and Salazar's Portugal (the doubt arises because of the Spanish and Portuguese tradition of national churches, in which the church acquires its importance as an arm of the state, not as an independent power in its own right). The great achievement of the Roman Catholic Church in Northern Ireland was to realise something approaching the freedom to develop that was achieved in the Republic. The result was that a large segment of the society was effectively removed from what limited political life there was in Northern Ireland. Northern Catholics may be compared in this respect to the Ulster Presbyterians of the eighteenth century, though without their wealth of internal controversy.

In pursuing this work the Roman Catholic Church had a positive aim — the advancement of its own religious and social ideas, and the achievement of an autonomous united Ireland. But there was no similarly clearcut objective which could be pursued by the Ulster Protestants, isolated from the cut-and-thrust of the various and contradictory ideals of the United Kingdom. Ulster Conservatism had not shared in the intellectual development of British Conservatism. It had continued to be preoccupied with a Catholic threat which had ceased to be felt in mainstream British Conservatism (though not in areas such as Liverpool and Glasgow, where there was a sizeable Irish Catholic population). 'Those foul Ulster Conservatives', as they were characterised by Randolph Churchill, were Conservatives who had been unmoved by Disraeli's vision of a national Toryism recovering its pre-Reformation Catholic and Jacobite traditions. Their strength lay in the local need for a defensive front against Catholicism, but this in turn put them out of sympathy with British culture. The Ulster Liberals, by contrast, were more in tune with British culture, but proportionately out of touch with local needs. Socialism, in this respect, has inherited the mantle of the Liberals.

Under concerted ideological and, occasionally, military attack from Catholic Ireland, the Ulster Protestant intellectuals have been unable to launch an effective intellectual counter-offensive because they are part of a culture that regards anti-Catholicism as obsolete. Ironically, those who are most British in their reflexes are those who are most vulnerable to nationalist influence. The problem was personified at the end of the nineteenth century in the Presbyterian minister J. B. Armour of Ballymoney who became a Home Ruler, not because he belonged to a tradition of Irish patriotism but because he was Gladstone's most faithful Ulster disciple. Those able to use the language of British politics, in which a liberal approach to religious matters is taken for granted, are reluctant to think seriously about their own political situation, lest their thoughts should be illiberal. Protestant Fundamentalists have no such problem, hence their effectiveness in local politics; but they are ineffective in relation to British politics because they are unable to use its language.

4. *The Rise of Ian Paisley*

I shall finish with some comments on this Fundamentalist Protestantism which is now most usually associated with the name of the Rev. Ian Paisley. It is frequently asserted that Dr Paisley belongs to a substantial tradition of Ulster Presbyterian preachers. The names of Henry Cooke, Hugh Hanna and W. P. Nicholson are usually invoked. To trace the tradition back beyond Cooke would be a little embarrassing, since we would have to mention Thomas Ledlie Birch, Sinclare Kelburn and William Stavely, the Calvinist political preachers of the United Irishmen.

Paisley's style of preaching is enthusiastic, designed to provoke an immediate spiritual experience on the part of his listeners. He preaches the 'new birth' — a positive subjective awareness of having been converted, cleansed and saved. This was not a part of the Ulster Presbyterian tradition before the 1859 Revival. As we have seen, it belonged to an English and American rather than to a Scottish religious tradition — the tradition of the English 'gathered churches', the American Great Awakening and the early days of English Methodism. It is difficult to reconcile it with the Scottish Presbyterian emphasis on the church as a means of organising society. It is inherently divisive, distinguishing between those who have had the special experience and those who have not.

Cooke and Hanna both supported the 1859 Revival, but its methods did not become part of the permanent practice of Ulster Presbyterianism. There was a further, less spectacular revivalist outburst in the 1870s, but this was promoted by the visits of Moody and Sankey from outside the Presbyterian ambit.

Hanna is given a place in the 'tradition' because, like Cooke, he supported British Conservatism, preached against the Roman Catholic Church, and supported the Church of Ireland. His fame was based on an incident when, while he was preaching an outdoor sermon in 1857, his listeners were attacked by a Catholic mob. The incident was part of a rising tide of militancy on both sides as, on the one side, Catholic organisation and self-confidence were tightened under the leadership of Paul Cullen, while, on the other, the Protestant churches attempted to incorporate and mobilise the enthusiasm of the rapidly developing industrial working class.[161]

Nicholson, who led a revivalist movement in the 1920s, was American and not a Presbyterian. Paisley certainly belongs to his preaching tradition, but, in contrast to Paisley, Nicholson made a point of eschewing politics.

Although the Presbyterians did not incorporate this revivalism into their own practice, it became a permanent part of Ulster Protestant practice through the rise of the Gospel Hall and the smaller denominations such as the Baptists and Plymouth Brethren. Paisley's father was a Baptist, and he himself has close connections with the American Bob Jones, a man much respected in Fundamentalist circles, who gave him his honorary doctorate.

Paisley, then, belongs to a tradition which, although it overlaps with the Presbyterian tradition, is independent from it. It consists of people who could be described as specialists in faith — who are not content with simply attending church on a Sunday or with an intellectual assent to the doctrines of Christianity, but who require a direct personal religious experience and who have developed techniques for cultivating this experience.

This kind of religion developed in America in the spirit of free enterprise. The Voluntaries, opposed to state support for religion, frequently appealed to the arguments of the political economists, the theorists of liberal capitalism. The people should be free to choose their own pastor and should pay for his upkeep. They choose the pastor on the basis of his ability to move them and to engage their enthusiasm. It thus encourages a powerful form of preaching, developed in competition among preachers and sharpened by the need to maintain support, which can easily be lost.

Paisley's particular success in Northern Ireland can be explained as a product of the inability of the Northern Ireland government and the main churches to counter the attack of militant Catholic nationalism with a convincing ideological offensive of their own. The policy of replicating British developments without being able to share in the British political process, and in particular without involvement in the British political parties, has left the Ulster Protestants in an ideologically weak position. The nation on which Northern Ireland is based is the Ulster Protestant nation; yet Ulster Protestantism, like British Protestantism, has accepted the view that religion is a private affair. The common denominator of Protestantism is anti-Catholicism; but to take a stand on anti-Catholicism is to be classified, and in many cases to classify oneself, as a bigot, especially when the nationalists represent themselves as being not Catholic but 'Irish', a term that apparently has no sectarian connotations, despite the very obviously Catholic nature of the Irish Republic.

In these circumstances, a militant, unapologetically anti-Catholic Fundamentalist Protestantism is very attractive. The progressive — that is, the British — development of the Ulster Protestants has been cut off by the British themselves. The community is forced back on its own resources. A return to the church as a principal means of social organisation would be a very natural development, but the mainstream churches, who have long lost their role as leaders of public opinion, are in no position to act as organising centres to the society; while the Unionist politicians who, through no fault of their own, have not engaged in the real political conflicts which determined the shape of the society in which they live, lack a vocation for and competence in political struggle.

In these circumstances, the pugnacious preacher, possessed of a radiantly self-confident world-view, and who has built up his own church and his own political party out of nothing, flourishes; and though even Paisley does not aspire to anything like the level of clerical control that is enjoyed by the Roman Catholic Church in Ireland (the very nature of evangelical enthusiastic religion precludes it), the world stands appalled at the 'bigotry' of the Ulster Protestant population.

Henry Grattan once declared in the Irish House of Commons, in a speech attacking the penal code, that 'When men begin to differ upon principles of religion it is because they have no other great object to engage their attention.' 'Bigotry' is not overcome by pious exhortations but through the development of political organisations which can transcend the organisation of society into distinct religious communities. If Northern Ireland continues to be suspended in a limbo between Catholic Ireland and secular Britain, if it continues to be excluded from the wider politics of the British state, then 'bigotry' will have a very long future before it.[162]

Notes

The notes should be read in conjunction with the bibliography.

Chapter 1: *Clearing the Ground* (pp 1-13)
1. For a general account of the Reformation in different parts of Europe I strongly recommend Lindsay, *History of the Reformation*.
2. The 'sanctification of matter' in Roman Catholicism is defended in Newman, *Essay on the Development of Christian Doctrine*, pp 377-82. For the interaction between the principles of painting and religious sensibilities see Gleizes, *La Peinture et ses Lois*, and the ongoing discussion in my own journal, *Cubism*.
3. Luther's view on the 'power of the keys' in 'To the Christian Nobility of the German Nation' in Luther, *Works*, XLIV, 134-5. For his encouraging a variety of forms of church organisation see Lindsay, *History of the Reformation*, I, 404.
4. Calvin, *Theological Treatises*, especially the 'Articles concerning the Organisation of the Church and of Worship at Geneva' (1537) and the 'Draft Ecclesiastical Ordinances'. See also Calvin, *Institutes of the Christian Religion*, especially Book IV. Calvin's career in Parker, *John Calvin*.
5. Account of the Scottish Reformation from Calderwood, *History of the Kirk of Scotland*; Donaldson, *Scottish Reformation*; Froude, *History of England*; Kirk, 'The Polities of the Best Reformed Kirks'; Kirk (ed.), *The Second Book of Discipline*, Introduction; Knox, *History of the Reformation in Scotland*; McCrie, *Life of John Knox*; McCrie, *Life of Andrew Melville*; Mathieson, *Politics and Religion*; Spottiswoode, *History of the Church of Scotland*. For the dispute as to whether or not the church was committed to the principle of hierarchy see the opposing views of Calderwood and Spottiswoode in the seventeenth century and Kirk and Donaldson in the twentieth century. For the French discipline see Bondriot and Hesse (ed.), *Confession de Foy*.
6. The Two Kingdoms in Kirk (ed.), *The Second Book of Discipline*, especially pp 166-72.

7. The theory of absolute monarchy can be found in Bodin, *Six Books of the Commonwealth*, and James VI and I, *Basilicon Doron*. Hotman's opposing view in *Francogallia*. See also Smith, 'François Hotman'.

8. 'The Discovery of the True Causes' in Davies, *Works*, II, 1-162. For a further elaboration of Davies's views on Ireland see Brooke, 'Sir John Davies and the Origin of Irish Politics'. The case of the United Provinces is discussed in Froude, *History of England*, XII, ch. 68, and in Geyl, *Revolt of the Netherlands*, especially p. 139.

9. Davies on the Irish parliament in 'The Speaker's Second Speech in the Higher House', *Works*, III, 234.

10. For good, readable accounts of the Elizabethan subjection of the O'Neills see Falls, *Birth of Ulster*, and O'Faolain, *The Great O'Neill*. For the MacDonnells see Hill, *The MacDonnells of Antrim*, and Perceval-Maxwell, *Scottish Migration to Ulster*. James on the Highlands and Islands in *Basilicon Doron*, p. 71.

Chapter 2: *The Birth of Ulster Presbyterianism* (pp 14-42)

11. English sixteenth-century Presbyterianism in Frere and Douglas (ed.), *Puritan Manifestoes*; Pearson, *Church and State*; Pearson, *Thomas Cartwright*; Sykes, *Church of England*; Travers, *A Full and Plain Declaration*.

12. Account of Andrew Knox in Perceval-Maxwell, *Scottish Migration to Ulster*, especially pp 257-61.

13. Settlement of Presbyterian ministers in Ulster and Sixmilewater Revival in Reid, *History of the Presbyterian Church in Ireland*, I; Blair, *Memoirs*; Livingstone, 'A Brief Historical Relation of the Life of Mr John Livingstone' in Tweedie (ed.), *Select Biographies*; Adair, *True Narrative*; Livingstone on physical manifestations, p. 146; Blair on Glendinning, pp 72-4, and on his relations with Hamilton, p. 66.

14. For Elizabeth's alleged Catholic sympathies see Froude, *History of England*, XII, 7, 489.

15. Bonnard, *Thomas Eraste*.

16. The Dutch Calvinist and Arminian disputes in Geyl, *Revolt of the Netherlands*, especially pp 205-15, and Geyl, *The Netherlands in the Seventeenth Century*, I, especially pp 42-82.

17. Froude on the twin sources of the bishops' authority in *History of England*, XII, 499-500; James's warning to Charles in Trevor-Roper, *Archbishop Laud*, p. 57.

18. For the conciliar movement in the Roman Catholic Church see Tierney, *Foundations of the Conciliar Theory*.

19. Ussher and the theory of episcopal authority in Knox, *James Ussher*, pp 122-45.

20. General account of the Scottish Covenanters taken from, e.g., Mathieson, *Politics and Religion*; Makey, *Church of the Covenant*.

21. Blair quoted in Makey, *Church of the Covenant*, p. 60.

22. Text of National Covenant in Free Church of Scotland, *Subordinate Standards*.

23. This interpretation of the Confederation of Kilkenny is suggested in Clifford, *Veto Controversy*, pp 174-80, and in turn derived from O'Connor, *Letters of Columbanus*, especially *Columbanus ad Hibernos No. 2.* For a spirited and entertaining if fanciful, defence of Owen Roe O'Neill see O'Cahan, *Owen Roe O'Neill*. General accounts of the period in Ulster in Reid, *Presbyterian Church*; Adair, *True Narrative*; Stevenson, *Scottish Covenanters and Irish Confederates*.

24. For the raising of the Scottish army see especially Stevenson, *Scottish Covenanters and Irish Confederates*. Presbytery of the Route in Reid, *Presbyterian Church*, 1, 494-6; Adair, *True Narrative* pp 127-41, for disputes over ministers' rights to exercise jurisdiction.

25. Brooke, 'On the Arrogance of the Ulster Presbyterians'; *A Necessary Representation* in Milton, *Complete Prose Works*, III, 296; Adair, *True Narrative*, pp 154-5.

26. Dispute between Cartwright and Browne in Pearson, *Thomas Cartwright*, pp 211-21. See also Skeats and Miall, *History of the Free Churches of England*, pp 18-21. For a near contemporary account of the Puritan settlement in America see Mather, *The Great Works of Christ in America*. For Edwards's *Treatise concerning Religious Affections* see his *Works*, I. For American influence in England see Shaw, *History of the English Church*, p. 127.

27. General account of Westminster Assembly from Shaw, *History of the English Church*; Dering on the Independents, p. 101; Baillie on the usual attendance, p. 60.

28. Owen arguing as a Presbyterian in *The Duty of Pastors and People Distinguished* (1643) and as an Independent in *Of Schism: The True Nature of It Discovered and Considered* (1657), both in *Works*, XIII. Owen's development is described in Toon, *God's Statesman*. Milton as a Presbyterian in *Of Reformation in England and the Causes that Hitherto Have Hindered It* (1641) in *Prose Writings*, and rejecting Presbyterianism in the poem 'On the New Forcers of Conscience under the Long Parliament'.

29. Milton, *Observations upon the Articles of Peace with the Irish Rebels, on the Letter of Ormond to Col. Jones, and the Representation of the Presbytery at Belfast* (1649) in *Complete Prose Works*, III, 300. Bangor Declaration in Tisdall, *A Sample of True-Blue Presbyterian Loyalty*, p. 25.

30. Text of the Commonwealth Engagements in Reid, *Presbyterian Church*, II, 151.

31. General account of the Cromwellian settlement in Ireland in Barnard, *Cromwellian Ireland*; reference to Ireland as 'a white paper', p. 14.

32. Adair on debate with Independents, *True Narrative*, pp 186-91, and on the power of presbyteries, pp 213-14.
33. General account of Protestors and Resolutioners under the Cromwellian settlement in Dow, *Cromwellian Scotland*; Burnet, *History of His Own Time*; Livingstone, 'Brief Historical Relation' in Tweedie (ed.), *Select Biographies*. Cowan's account, *Scottish Covenanters*, p. 32.
34. Account of the Act of Bangor in Adair, *True Narrative*, pp 208-15.

Chapter 3: *A Church without Patrons* (pp 43-62)
35. For Baxter's objections to English Episcopalianism see his *Autobiography*, pp 180-5; Adair on his relations with the English Presbyterians in *True Narrative*, pp 241-3.
36. General accounts of the post-Restoration settlement of the Church of Scotland in Burnet, *History of His Own Time*, and Cowan, *Scottish Covenanters*. An excellent fictional account in Scott, *Old Mortality*. There is also a large Scottish literature of Covenanting tales, essential reading for anyone with an interest in the ideals of Presbyterianism; a recent example is Purves, *Fair Sunshine*.
37. Figure for Scottish ejections in Cowan, *Scottish Covenanters*, pp 52-3. Baxter on English ejections, *Autobiography*, p. 175.
38. Bramhall in defence of Erastus against the Presbyterians in 'A Fair Warning to take heed of the Scottish Discipline as being of all others most injurious to the Civil Magistrate, most oppressive to the Subject, most pernicious to both' in Bramhall, *Works*, III, 242.
39. General account of English Presbyterianism after the Restoration in Baxter, *Autobiography*; Nuttall, *Richard Baxter*; Bolam et al., *English Presbyterians*.
40. Attempt to form organised dissenting church in 1676 and 1677 in Cowan, *Scottish Covenanters*, p. 86; General Correspondence of Praying Societies, ibid., p. 110.
41. Rules for ordination in Reid, *Presbyterian Church*, II, 567-70.
42. Adair, *True Narrative*, pp 257-60; for David Houston see Loughridge, *The Covenanters in Ireland*, pp 11-13.
43. General account of the Glorious Revolution in Macaulay, *History of England*. Macaulay, who remains the model on whom all historians should base themselves, especially for his ability to think about how the past has created present realities, also gives full accounts of events in Scotland and Ireland.
44. Bodin, *Six Books of the Commonwealth*, p. 32; James VI and I, *Basilicon Doron*, pp 57-9.
45. The question of comprehension as against toleration is discussed at length in Burnet, *History of His Own Time*, especially in Book II; for Charles II and James as Duke of York favouring toleration see, e.g., p. 325. Burnet himself favoured comprehension and

claims credit for much of the thinking behind the Scottish Indulgences. See also account in Every, *High Church Party*.

46. See, e.g., Willman, 'The Origins of "Whig" and "Tory"'. I am taking the term 'totalitarian' to suggest the dispersion throughout society of a 'total' world-view such as Roman Catholicism or Marxism. It is part of the argument of the present book that, whatever totalitarian ambitions particular churches might have, 'Protestantism' is inherently unsuitable as a totalitarian ideology. Hobbes's attempt to work out scientific principles for politics could be described as 'totalitarian', but he was by temperament a heretic and freethinker, as is apparent from the religious views expressed in *Leviathan*, whose heretical tendencies were attacked by Bramhall. Although prepared to subject his will to human authority, he opposed any suggestion that he should subject his reason or faith to human authority (pp 409-10). His whole concern was with the material interest of the subject, not with any great idea which may transcend those interests.

47. General accounts of Restoration settlement in Scotland in Cowan, *Scottish Covenanters*; Burnet, *History of His Own Time*; Macaulay, *History of England*; Story (ed.), *Church of Scotland*, IV; Drummond and Bulloch, *Scottish Church*. Bishop of Edinburgh in Cowan, *Scottish Covenanters*, p. 137.

48. General account of Irish events in Macaulay, *History of England*, and in Simms, *Jacobite Ireland, 1685-91*. A contemporary account in King, *State of the Protestants*.

49. Innocent XI's relations with Louis XIV in Macaulay, *History of England*, I, 553-4 (Jansenist controversy) and II, 40-1 (affair of the Roman embassy); death of Innocent and continuation of his policy by Alexander VIII, ibid., pp 548-9.

50. See note 36 above. For general accounts of the Church of Scotland's legal position see Church of Scotland, *Abridgement of Acts of Assemblies*, and Lyall, *Of Presbyters and Kings*.

Chapter 4: *Free to Develop* (pp 63-92)

51. Holmes, *Our Irish Presbyterian Heritage*, p. 48 speculates that the Presbyterians in 1641 and 1688-9 could have allied with the Irish Catholics. I can't understand how the thought can even have occurred to him.

52. Account of Boyse in Brown, *Irish Presbyterian Theology*, and in *D.N.B.*

53. Swift, *Letter concerning the Sacramental Test*. For an account of Swift which also describes the politics of the period see Murry, *Jonathan Swift*.

54. The settlement of the Church of England after the Revolution is discussed in Macaulay, *History of England*, pp 792-9; Skeats and Miall, *History of the Free Churches of England*, pp 120-222; Every, *High Church Party*. Swift's 'Ode to Dr Sancroft' is quoted and discussed in Murry, *Jonathan Swift*, pp 31-2.

55. General account of Sacheverell case and accession of Harley and St John in Morley, *Walpole*, pp 14-40; Hoadly's career in *D.N.B.*

56. Account of Convocation of Canterbury and its relations with Hoadly in Every, *High Church Party*, and, very usefully, Newman, 'The Convocation of the Province of Canterbury' in *Historical Sketches*, III.

57. The case of Thomas Emlyn is discussed in Allen, 'The Principle of Non-Subscription', and Brown, *Irish Presbyterian Theology*, which also gives a detailed account of his theological views. See also Brown, 'A Theological Interpretation of the First Subscription Controversy' in Barkley et al., *Challenge and Conflict*.

58. General accounts of Salter's Hall Controversy and the spread of Arian and Socinian ideas in Bolam et al., *English Presbyterians*, and Skeats and Miall, *History of the Free Churches of England*, especially pp 236-50. See also Bruce, 'Progress of Non-Subscription'. Bolam et al., *English Presbyterians*, p. 161 for Hoadly on Salter's Hall, and p. 132 for Calamy on Church of Scotland.

59. Abernethy's career in *D.N.B.* and in Brown, *Irish Presbyterian Theology*. His sermon, *Religious Obedience Founded on Personal Persuasion*, may be found in Abernethy, *Scarce and Valuable Tracts and Sermons*.

60. General accounts of dispute in works cited in note 57 above, as well as Reid, *Presbyterian Church*, III. Contemporary account in Presbytery of Antrim, *Narrative of the Proceedings of Seven General Synods*. See also Gordon, *Historic Memorials of the First Presbyterian Church*, and Millin, *History of the Second Congregation*. Moore, *History of the First Presbyterian Church* is more interesting on the material problems of the church than on theological or political problems.

61. Case of Alexander Colville in Reid, *Presbyterian Church*, III, 191-4.

Chapter 5: *The New Dissenters* (pp 93-111)

62. For a discussion of Scottish influence see Allen, 'Scottish Ecclesiastical Influence upon Irish Presbyterianism'.

63. Account of John Cameron in Brown, *Irish Presbyterian Theology*, and in Armstrong, *Calvinism and the Amyraut Heresy*. For a general account of Scottish seventeenth-century theology see Macleod, *Scottish Theology*, and for Rutherford see Rutherford, *Letters*, and the biographical introduction by Andrew Bonar.

64. Account of High Calvinism in seventeenth-century England in Toon, *Emergence of Hyper-Calvinism*.

65. General accounts of the Church of Scotland in the early eighteenth century in Drummond and Bulloch, *Scottish Church*; Burleigh, *Church History of Scotland*; and especially McKerrow, *History of the Secession Church*. Boston's difficulty in finding a heritor in Boston, *Human Nature*, Introduction, p. 11.

66. Account of Wesley in Southey, *Life of John Wesley*, and of

Methodism in general in Stevens, *History of Methodism*. For the Great Awakening in America see Edwards, *Works*; Tracy, *The Great Awakening*; Lodge, 'The Crisis of the Churches in the Middle Colonies'.

67. Whitfield's encounter with the Seceders in McKerrow, *History of the Secession Church*, pp 156-65. Whitefield in America in Tracy, *The Great Awakening*, and Whitefield, *Journals*.

68 Account of early American Presbyterianism in Hodge, *Constitional History*; see also Barkley, *Francis Makemie*.

69. Tennent's attack on the unconverted ministry in Hodge, *Constitutional History*, p. 199. Account of the Log College in Alexander, *Log College*.

70. Hutchinson's *Compendious View*, quoted and discussed in Struthers, *Relief Church*, pp 294-320.

71. The divisions of the Presbyteries of Armagh and Bangor are discussed in Allen, 'Principle of Non-Subscription', and McMillan, 'Subscription Controversy'. The variety of practice in subscribing to the Westminster Confession is discussed in Barkley, *The Westminster Formularies*.

72. 'The Presbyterian Ministers of the Northern Association in Ireland' in Reid, *Presbyterian Church*, III, 322.

73. General accounts of the Seceders in McKerrow, *History of the Secession Church*, and Stewart, *The Seceders in Ireland*. Text of the Burgesses' Oath in Stewart, p. 51.

74. For the New Light / Old Light split among the Scottish Seceders see McCrie, *Church of Scotland*, pp 70-83. For the impact of the Evangelical Society of Ulster see Brooke, 'Controversies in Ulster Presbyterianism'. My statement that the Ulster Seceders had a preference for the New Light position is based on observations in Rev. John Tennent to Dr Robert Tennent, 16 June 1802, P.R.O.N.I., Tennent MSS, D1748/B/211/35.

75. Account of the Reformed Presbyterians in the eighteenth century in Hutchinson, *Reformed Presbyterian Church in Scotland*.

Chapter 6: *Political Ambitions* (pp 112-136)

76. Considering the romantic appeal of the subject, it is surprising that there is no straightforward history of the Volunteer and United Irish period in Ulster. Joy, *Historical Collections* remains after over 150 years the most useful account, though a start has been made in Stewart, 'Transformation of Presbyterian Radicalism'. For the general, all-Ireland politics of the period, I have made extensive use of Froude, *The English in Ireland*. There is an account of the Volunteers in Smyth, 'The Volunteer Movement in Ulster'. Elliott, *Partners in Revolution* is mainly concerned with the negotiations in France. For a more detailed account of the ideas peculiar to the Presbyterians see Brooke, 'Controversies in Ulster Presbyteriansism'.

77. Paine's arguments in *Common Sense*. General account of back-

ground in Pole, *Foundations of American Independence*.
78. Petition for a union in Froude, *The English in Ireland*, I, 317-38.
79. 1783 election in *Historical Account of the Late Election*, which is hostile to the Presbyterians; both elections, but especially that of 1790, in Dickson, *Narrative of the Confinement and Exile*, pp 15-22. Seceders' opposition to reform in Birch, *Physicians Languishing under Disease*. Hillsborough's complaint in Earl of Hillsborough to Lord Nottingham, 1 Mar. 1784, P.R.O.N.I., Pelham MSS, T755/2, pp 59-60. Hope's views in *Memoirs of Jemmy Hope*, pp 11-12. 1790 election also in Hyde, *Rise of Castlereagh*, pp 55-6.
80. Rousseau, *The Social Contract and Discourses*.
81. Other examples of Volunteer sermons include Delap, *An Inquiry Whether, and How Far, Magistracy is of a Divine Appointment*, and Alexander, *The Advantages of a General Knowledge of the Use of Arms*.
82. For English radicalism in the late eighteenth century see Thompson, *Making of the English Working Class*; Brown, *The French Revolution in English History*; Guttridge, *English Whiggism and the American Revolution*; Mitchell, 'The Association Movement of 1792-3'; Ginter, 'The Loyalist Association Movement of 1792-3 and British Public Opinion'. For relations between the English and Irish revolutionaries see Elliott, 'The "Despard Conspiracy" Reconsidered'.
83. Arguments on the admission of Catholics to the franchise in McDowell, *Irish Public Opinion, 1750-1800*.
84. For an account of the nature of Gaelic culture in the eighteenth century see Clifford, *Connolly: The Polish Aspect*, pp 111-41.
85. Drennan defending the United Irish oath against criticisms, *Belfast News-Letter*, Feb.-Mar. 1792, quoted in Joy and Bruce, *Belfast Politics*, p. 51.
86. For a very readable account of the French Revolution see Hibbert, *French Revolution*. The *Northern Star* welcoming the Civil Constitution in Clifford, *Veto Controversy*, p. 145. Burgher Synod in Stewart, *Seceders in Ireland*, pp 182-4.
87. Discussion of differences between English and Irish Catholic Committees and their declaration in Clifford, *Veto Controversy*, pp 94-112.
88. Belfast town debate in Joy and Bruce, *Belfast Politics*. It is also discussed in Stewart, 'Transformation of Presbyterian Radicalism', and in Brooke, 'Controversies in Ulster Presbyterianism'.
89. Birch, *Obligations upon Christians*, p. 31. For fuller accounts of the millenarianism of the United Irishmen see British and Irish Communist Organisation, *Birth of Ulster Unionism*, pp 57-61; Brooke, 'Controversies in Ulster Presbyterianism', pp 26-35; Miller, 'Presbyterianism and "Modernisation" in Ulster', pp 80-3.
90. Tone, *Argument on Behalf of the Catholics*, p. 28.
91. Killen on New Light involvement in Reid, *Presbyterian Church*,

III, 397. Account of Stavely, including briefly his relations with Orr, in Ferguson, *Brief Biographical Sketches*. The Tennent story is still waiting to be unravelled from the Tennent MSS. There is a much fuller discussion of the interaction between theological and political views in Brooke, 'Controversies in Ulster Presbyterianism', and Miller, 'Presbyterianism and "Modernisation" in Ulster'; both conclude that supporters of the radical agitation of the time were as likely to be Calvinist as Non-Subscribing.

92. For the continued dislike of Castlereagh see Barkley, 'The Arian Schism in Ireland, 1830'. For a defence of Castlereagh see Clifford, *Veto Controversy*, pp 73-6.

93. For the negotiations surrounding the Union see Hyde, *Rise of Castlereagh*, and Castlereagh, *Memoirs and Correspondence*.

94. Knox's defence of the *regium donum* in Castlereagh, *Memoirs and Correspondence*, pp 216-22 and 252-62. There is a more detailed account of these negotiations in Brooke, 'Controversies in Ulster Presbyterianism', pp 77-109.

95. For the Seceders' acceptance of the grant see Stewart, *Seceders in Ireland*, pp 113-21; a contemporary account in Bryce, *Narrative of the Proceedings of the Associate (Antiburgher) Synods*.

Chapter 7: *Retrenchment and Reorientation* (pp 137-153)

96. Drennan attacking the Act of Union in *Drennan Letters* and in *Belfast Monthly Magazine*, I, 2 (1808), p. 153. For the Spanish war and revolution see ibid. pp 70-2; for 'Don Cervallos' see Clive, *Scotch Reviewers*, p. 110, and New, *Life of Henry Brougham to 1830*, pp 46-9.

97. Drennan attacking *regium donum* in *Drennan Letters* (letters to Samuel McTier, 27 Feb. 1792 (no. 326), and 31 Jan. 1793 (no. 381), and to Mrs McTier, 9 Aug. 1800 (no. 865), and 19 Oct. 1800 (no. 876)). Drennan against the Veto in *Belfast Monthly Magazine*, I, 2 (1808), p. 154, and I, 5 (1808), p. 395.

98. Scale of Manchester College in Davis, *History of Manchester College*, especially pp 60-70. First staff of University College, London, in Bellot, *University College, London*, pp 37-9.

99. For the breach between the Church of Scotland and the Synod of Ulster see *Records of the General Synod of Ulster*, III (June 1814, June 1815, June 1816).

100. General accounts of Castlereagh in Hyde, *Rise of Castlereagh* (for early life), and Clifford, *Veto Controversy*.

101. General accounts of the negotiations surrounding the Belfast Academical Institution in Brooke, 'Controversies in Ulster Presbyterianism'; Fisher and Robb, *Royal Belfast Academical Institution Centenary Volume*, and Jamieson, *History of the Royal Belfast Academical Institution*. The main MS source for the present account is in P.R.O.N.I., Royal Belfast Academical Institution MSS, SCH 524. For Lord Moira's connection with the agitations of the 1780s and 1790s see Froude, *The English in Ireland*, III, 315-17, 354-6.

102. Case of John Knowles in P.R.O.N.I., Royal Belfast Academical Institution MSS, SCH 524/3A/2, p. 106 (7 May 1816).

103. Barnet on the different attitudes of the Seceders and Synod of Ulster in Parliamentary Papers, *Fourth Report of the Commissioners of the Irish Education Inquiry*, 1826-7, XIII (Minutes of Evidence), pp 120-1.

104. Text of Lord John Russell's letter to the Bishop of Durham, 1850, on the Catholic hierarchy, and extracts from Gladstone's *The Vatican Decrees in their Bearing on Civil Allegiance* (1874) in Norman, *Anti-Catholicism in Victorian England*. Discussion in Clifford, *Rise of Papal Power*. Accounts of the Free Church movement in Skeats and Miall, *History of the Free Churches of England*, and Thompson, 'The Liberation Society'. The best attempt to argue the case that the controversy was politically motivated is Barkley, 'The Arian Schism in Ireland, 1830', but see also Jamieson, 'The Influence of Henry Cooke'. It is merely stated as a fact in Boyd, *Holy War in Belfast*, and de Paor, *Divided Ulster*.

105. Cooke's relations with Peel in Holmes, *Henry Cooke*, pp 117-18, 151-60; the *regium donum* issue, ibid., pp 117-18.

106. There is a discussion of the Royal Cork Institute in *Belfast Monthly Magazine*, I, 3 (1808) pp 167-70.

107. Accounts of Arianism in the fourth century in Stanley, *Lectures on the History of the Eastern Church*; Newman, *The Arians of the Fourth Century*; Rainy, *Ancient Catholic Church*. For the High Arianism of Bruce and Montgomery see Brooke, 'Controversies in Ulster Presbyterianism', pp 158-9. Montgomery and 'Arian prayers' in Crozier, *Life of Henry Montgomery*, p. 986.

108. Paul's *Refutation of Arianism* can be found in Paul, *Works*.

109. There are general accounts of the Arian Controversy in Brooke, 'Controversies in Ulster Presbyterianism'; Barkley, 'The Arian Schism in Ireland, 1830'; Holmes, *Henry Cooke*; Crozier, *Life of Henry Montgomery*; Porter, *Life and Times of Henry Cooke*. Contemporary accounts in *Northern Whig*, *Belfast News-Letter* and *Christian Moderator*.

110. Carlile's moderatorial sermon in *Christian Moderator*, I (1826), p. 144.

111. Brougham and the anti-slavery and popular education movements in New, *Life of Henry Brougham to 1830*. See also Brooke, 'The Schoolmaster Is Abroad'.

112. There is an excellent account of the origins of the Evangelical movement in the Church of Ireland in Whelan, 'New Lights and Old Enemies'. For Evangelicalism in Britain, and especially its interest in social welfare, see Bradley, *The Call to Seriousness*.

113. The involvement of the Synod of Ulster and Seceders in missionary work before 1820 is discussed in Brooke, 'Controversies in Ulster Presbyterianism', pp 51-65. My main sources for the Synod's relations with the Hibernian Bible Society are *Records of the General Synod of Ulster*, 1807-11, and *Ulster Register*, 18

Apr. 1817; and, for the Seceders, the Minutes of the Secession Synod in P.R.O.N.I., Stewart MSS, D1759/1F/2, June 1819, July 1820, and *Report of the Missions of the Presbyterian Synod of Ireland*. See also Rodgers, 'Presbyterian Missionary Activity'.

114. The need for Unitarians to form a separate organisation in *Christian Moderator*, II (1827), pp 382-3. For an English Unitarian minister arguing the same view in a sermon preached in Belfast see Hutton, *The Duty and Benefits of Co-operation among the Friends of Scriptural Christianity*.

Chapter 8: *Parliamentary Politics* (pp 154-174)

115. Account of the Dissenters and the Test and Corporation Acts in Manning, *Protestant Dissenting Deputies*, pp 217-52; problem posed by Catholic Emancipation, ibid., pp 225-6. Cooke's support for Catholic Emancipation in Parliamentary Papers, *Minutes of Evidence on the State of Ireland*, 1825, IX, pp 206-21, 268-71, and *Third Report from the Select Committee on the State of Ireland*, 1825, VIII, pp 341-80.

116. The fullest account of the 1832 election in Belfast is Slater, 'Belfast Politics, 1798-1868'. See also Kennedy, 'Sharman Crawford', pp 42-52, and Brooke, 'Controversies in Ulster Presbyterianism', pp 186-9. Edgar's comment in John Edgar to R. J. Tennent, 20 Dec. 1832, P.R.O.N.I., Tennent MSS, D1748/C/ 180/2. Conversion of Belfast Society to Belfast Conservative Society in Parliamentary Papers, *Minutes of Evidence taken before the Select Committee of the House of Lords Appointed to Inquire into the Progress and Operation of the New Plan of Education in Ireland*, 1837, VIII, pp 1170-2, 1355-6.

117. William Smith and Unitarian controversies in Manning, *Protestant Dissenting Deputies*, especially pp 52-93.

118. Cooke at Hillsborough in Brooke, 'Controversies in Ulster Presbyterianism', pp 211-18, and Holmes, *Henry Cooke*, pp 113-17. An account of the meeting in the *Ulster Guardian*, 31 Sept. 1834, gives the names of the other Presbyterian ministers present.

119. Impact of Irish Church Temporalities Act in England in Gwynn, *The Second Spring, 1818-1852*, p. 49, and Halévy, *History of the English People, 1830-41*, pp 142-6, 174-9. Paul on the 'ten mitres' in Eastern Presbytery, *Causes of Fasting and Thanksgiving*, p. 5. Cooke on Convocation in *Voluntaries in Belfast*, p. 38.

120. For the Plymouth Brethren and Catholic Apostolic Church see respectively Coad, *History of the Brethren Movement*, and Dallimore, *Life of Edward Irving*. Discussion of British millenarianism and its opposition to 'progress' in Sandeen, *Roots of Fundamentalism*, pp 4-41.

121. There is a brief account of the Congregationalist James Carlile in Archibald, *A Century of Congregationalism*. Carlile on lack of support from Belfast Liberals in Carlile to Tennent 28 July 1837, P.R.O.N.I., Tennent MSS, D1748/C94/10.

122. The dispute among the Reformed Presbyterians is discussed in Brooke, 'Controversies in Ulster Presbyterianism', pp 220-30, 236-40, and in Loughridge, *Covenanters in Ireland*, pp 66-7. Belfast Voluntary debate in *Voluntaries in Belfast*, and Ritchie, *Reply to Rev. Dr Henry Cooke*.

123. The dispute on unqualified subscription in Brooke, 'Controversies in Ulster Presbyterianism', pp 243-53. My main source was *Northern Whig*, 15 Aug. 1836. For the connection between MacKnight (or MacNeight, as he was then known) and Paul see Houston, *The Covenanter's Narrative and Plea*, p. 35.

124. Considering that it is probably the single most important development in Irish cultural history in the nineteenth century, the change in language has received surprisingly little attention. One study is Wall, 'Decline of the Irish Language'. The difference between Munster and Connaught is observed in Clifford, *Connolly: The Polish Aspect*, especially pp 132-41. The importance of the issue is appreciated in Larkin, 'Devotional Revolution in Ireland'.

125. The Catholic agitation against the use of the Bible in the Kildare Place Society in Whelan, 'Old Lights and New Enemies', pp 137-40. Akenson, *Irish Education Experiment*, pp 89-90, ignores the letter from Propaganda and ascribes the disruption to the managers' decision to fund the proselytising bodies ('the petty proselytisers', as he calls them) in 1820, although he has already shown that O'Connell started his agitation in 1819.

126. Despite reservations mainly caused by his habit of following the views of the administrative establishment, Akenson, *Irish Education Experiment* remains the classic study of the National Education System.

127. General account of the controversies surrounding English schools in Best, 'Religious Difficulties of National Education in England', and Manning, *Protestant Dissenting Deputies*, pp 334-67. For Scotland see Drummond and Bulloch, *Church in Victorian Scotland*, especially pp 84-107; 1861 act quoted p. 90.

128. Career of the Presbyterian James Carlile in Rodgers, 'James Carlile'. Akenson, *Irish Education Experiment*, p. 165 manages to suggest that his role was sinister because he represented the Synod's view to the Commissioners and the Commissioners' views to the Synod. He would have been acting more suspiciously had he merely told each body what it wanted to hear.

129. The Synod's disputes on the National Education System in Brooke, 'Controversies in Ulster Presbyterianism', pp 190-202. My main contemporary source was *Northern Whig*, 3, 4 Aug., 18, 22 Dec. 1834, 15 Sept. 1836. There is a very useful account in Holmes, *Henry Cooke*, pp 93-112, 135-9.

130. Ferrie case in Holmes, *Henry Cooke*, pp 68-73, 125-7, and Rodgers, 'James Carlile', pp 104-29.

131. The best account of this rise in Presbyterian sectarian militancy is in Holmes, *Henry Cooke*, pp 150-60; resolution in favour of

Presbyterian politics, ibid., p. 157. See also Killen, *Reminiscences of a Long Life*, especially pp 68-9, 81-7; Croskery and Witherow, *Life of A. P. Goudy*, especially pp 72-107.

132. Newman, *On the Scope and Nature of University Education*.

133. Dill, *Prelatico-Presbyterianism* gives sizeable quotes (favouring his viewpoint) from documents throughout the controversy, including the Chancery case. For alternative views see Killen, *Reminiscences of a Long Life*, pp 128-45; Croskery and Witherow, *Life of A. P. Goudy*, pp 109-32; Morgan, *Recollections of My Life and Times*, pp 59-65. See also Allen, *Presbyterian College, Belfast*, especially pp 55-96; Moody and Beckett, *Queen's, Belfast*, pp 1-38.

134. General accounts of the negotiations over the colleges in Moody and Beckett, *Queen's, Belfast*, pp 1-38, and Kerr, *Peel, Priests and Politics*, pp 290-351. The dispute between O'Connell and Young Ireland in Gwynn, *Young Ireland and 1848*, pp 40-8, and Gwynn, *O'Connell, Davis and the Colleges Bill*. See also Duffy, *My Life in Two Hemispheres*, pp 106-14. Cullen and Newman in Bowen, *Paul Cardinal Cullen*, pp 150-3.

Chapter 9: *From Presbyterian to Protestant* (pp 175-197)

135. The standard history of the Church of England in this period is Chadwick, *The Victorian Church*. For a summary account of the divisions in Anglicanism and for the development of the 'Broad Church' see Crowther, *Church Embattled*, and for the thinking of the Evangelicals see Toon, *Evangelical Theology, 1833-1856*.

136. Chalmers in Hanna, *Memoirs of the Life and Writings of Thomas Chalmers*; Wardlaw in Alexander, *Memoirs of the Life and Writings of Ralph Wardlaw*, and for his argument against Chalmers on the Voluntary principle, Wardlaw, *National Church Establishments Examined*.

137. Whately's views are discussed in Akenson, *Irish Education Experiment*, and Akenson, *A Protestant in Purgatory*. See also Fitzpatrick, *Memoirs of Richard Whately*, II, 170-1, 245.

138. Sir Robert Inglis, *Hansard*, lxxx, 377-80 (9 May 1845).

139. J. E. Tennent, *Hansard*, xxii, 1288-1333 (24 Apr 1834) — on need to ally with the Conservatives, 1326.

140. Account of 1837 election in Slater, 'Belfast Politics'.

141. There is an excellent account of Crawford's career and policies in Kennedy, 'Sharman Crawford'. See also British and Irish Communist Organisation, *Birth of Ulster Unionism*, pp 14-18.

142. For a brief survey of early nineteenth-century thinking on the land question see Steele, *Irish Land and British Politics*, especially ch. 1. The advantages of Ulster in British and Irish Communist Organisation, *Economics of Partition*.

143. Industrialisation in Ulster in Gribbon, *History of Water Power in Ulster*, and Coe, *Engineering Industry of the North of Ireland*. The cotton and linen industries in Crawford, *Domestic Industry in Ireland*.

144. Joseph Hume, *Hansard*, cxlix, 1088 (14 Apr. 1858), quoted in Steele, *Irish Land and British Politics*, p. 36.

145. Ulster Constitutional Association in Kennedy, 'Sharman Crawford', pp 155-61. Quotation taken from *Northern Whig*, 23 July 1840. For O'Connell's visit to Belfast see *The Repealer Repulsed*, and for the same event from the point of view of the organisers, Duffy, *My Life in Two Hemispheres*, I, 47-52. There are extracts from *The Repealer Repulsed* and from *The Vindicator* in British and Irish Communist Organisation, *Ulster As It Is*.

146. For the electoral fate of the Ulster Liberals see Bew and Wright, 'Agrarian Opposition in Ulster Politics', and Walker, 'The Land Question and Elections in Ulster, 1868-86'. Cullen's politics in Norman, *Catholic Church and Ireland in the Age of Rebellion*, and Bowen, *Paul Cardinal Cullen*.

147. The agitation against the Corn Laws in Trevelyan, *Life of John Bright*, pp 64-153. Contrast with Irish interests in Gwynn, *Young Ireland and 1848*, pp 54-6, 67-9. Gwynn is interestingly sceptical about Mitchel's views (expressed in, e.g., *Jail Journal*, pp xxxiii-xxxiv) that Ireland was self-sufficient in grain.

148. General account of tenant-right agitation in Bew and Wright, 'Agrarian Opposition in Ulster Politics'; Duffy, *My Life in Two Hemispheres*, II, 29-106; Duffy, *League of North and South*; Kennedy, 'Sharman Crawford', pp 362-482. Presbyterian reaction to the famine in Killen, *Memoir of John Edgar*, pp 193-251. For an account of Irish Protestant reactions to the Famine see Bowen, *Souperism: Myth or Reality?*

149. Goudy's refusal to co-operate with priests in Croskery and Witherow, *Life of A. P. Goudy*, p. 144.

150. Crawford insisting on relating rights to improvements in Kennedy, 'Sharman Crawford', pp 381-2; Davitt and the case for nationalisation of land in Clifford, 'Davitt on Land Tax'. Discussion of the state of present-day Irish agriculture in relation to the political triumph of the farming class in Clifford, *Socialism and the Farmer*.

151. Very little work has been done on the important question of the moral discipline exercised by the sessions, though there is an abundance of material in the surviving session books. A preliminary survey of the Presbyterian Church in Ireland MSS in the Public Record Office of Northern Ireland suggests to me that discipline, still administered in the late eighteenth century, collapsed about the turn of the century. This is not to say that people started to sin for the first time, but that they no longer felt obliged to report their sins to the session. This would confirm my view that there was a collapse in morale in the wake of the failure of the political agitation ot the late eighteenth century, but a comparison should be made with Scotland. For modern theories on the Revival see Gibbon, *Origins of Ulster Unionism*, pp 44-65, and Miller, 'Presbyterianism and "Modernisation" in Ulster'.

152. Prayer for revival in *Minutes of the General Assembly of the*

Presbyterian Church in Ireland, p. 655 (Londonderry, July 1858).

153. Career of James McCosh in Sloane (ed.), *Life of James McCosh*.
154. Newman, *On the Scope and Nature of University Education*.
155. Allen, *Presbyterian College, Belfast*. Watts is discussed briefly in Brooke, 'Religion and Secular Thought, 1800-75'. For the Free Presbyterian Church of Scotland and the reasons for its separating from the Free Church of Scotland see Free Presbyterian Church, *History of the Free Presbyterian Church of Scotland, 1893-1970*, especially pp 70-95. For the Davey heresy trial see Fulton, *J. Ernest Davey*, and Grier, *Origin and Witness of the Irish Evangelical Church*.

Conclusion: *The Ulster Protestants* (pp 198-214)

156. General accounts of the various attempts to form political movements in Ulster Protestantism independent of mainstream Unionism in Bew, 'Politics and the Rise of the Skilled Working Man'; McMinn, 'James Brown Armour'; Patterson, *Class Conflict and Sectarianism*; Carr, *Belfast Labour Movement*, and Campaign for Labour Representation, *Forgotten Conference of the Labour Party in Belfast, 1907*.
157. The importance of Northern Ireland's exclusion from the British party system is cogently argued in Clifford, *Parliamentary Sovereignty and Northern Ireland*.
158. The marginalisation of the writers of the 'Irish literary renaissance' in the Irish Free State is discussed in Clifford, 'The Irish Academy of Letters'.
159. Account of Midgley in Walker, *Politics of Frustration*. For an account of education under Stormont from a Roman Catholic viewpoint see Dallat et al., *Aspects of Catholic Education*.
160. For educational policy in the Republic see Akenson, *A Mirror to Kathleen's Face*. The question of religious influence on hospitals is discussed in Clifford, 'Religion and Hospitals', and social welfare in Clifford, *Poor Law in Ireland*. The best accounts of Catholic Ireland before the Second Vatican Council are still, from a liberal viewpoint, Blanshard, *The Irish and Catholic Power*, and, from a Catholic viewpoint, Blanchard, *The Church in Contemporary Ireland*.
161. There is an account of Hanna in Barkley, *St Enoch's Congregation, 1872-1972*.
162. Grattan in the Irish parliament, 20 Feb. 1782, in Grattan, *Selected Speeches*.

Bibliography

Books, pamphlets, articles, theses and manuscripts referred to in the text and notes.

Abernethy, John, *Scarce and Valuable Tracts and Sermons*, London 1751

Adair, Patrick, *A True Narrative of the Rise and Progress of the Presbyterian Church in Ireland*, Belfast 1866

Akenson, Donald H., *Education and Enmity: The Control of Schooling in Northern Ireland, 1920-50*, Newton Abbot (David & Charles) 1973

—— *The Irish Education Experiment*, London (Routledge & Kegan Paul) 1970

—— *A Mirror to Kathleen's Face: Education in Independent Ireland, 1922-1960*, Montreal/London (McGill/Queen's University Press) 1975

—— *A Protestant in Purgatory: Richard Whately*, Hamden, Conn. (Archon) 1981

Alexander, Andrew, *The Advantages of a General Knowledge of the Use of Arms: A Sermon preached before the Strabane, Finwater and Urney Volunteers and the Strabane Rangers*, Strabane 1779

Alexander, Archibald, *The Log College: Biographical Sketches of William Tennent and his Students, together with an Account of the Revivals under their Ministries*, London (Banner of Truth) 1968

Alexander, William Lindsay, *Memoirs of the Life and Writings of Ralph Wardlaw, D.D.*, Edinburgh 1856

Allen, Robert, *The Presbyterian College, Belfast, 1853-1953*, Belfast (Mullan) 1954

—— 'The Principle of Non-Subscription to Creeds and Confessions of Faith, as Exemplified in Irish Presbyterian History' (Ph.D. thesis, Queen's University of Belfast, 1944)

—— 'Scottish Ecclesiastical Influence upon Irish Presbyterianism, from the Non-Subscription Controversy to the Union of the Synods' (M.A. thesis, Queen's University of Belfast, 1940)

Archibald, James, *A Century of Congregationalism: The Story of Donegall St Church*, Belfast 1901

Armstrong, Brian G., *Calvinism and the Amyraut Heresy: Protestant Scholasticism and Humanism in Seventeenth-Century France*, Madison/Milwaukee/London (University of Wisconsin Press) 1969

Barkley, J. M., 'The Arian Schism in Ireland, 1830' in Derek Baker (ed.), *Studies in Church History*, IX, Cambridge (Cambridge University Press) 1972

—— *Francis Makemie of Ramelton – Father of American Presbyterianism*, Belfast (Presbyterian Historical Society of Ireland) 1981

—— *St Enoch's Congregation, 1872-1972*, Belfast 1972

—— *The Westminster Formularies in Irish Presbyterianism, being the Carey Lectures, 1954-1956*, Belfast 1956

—— et al., *Challenge and Conflict: Essays in Irish Presbyterian History and Doctrine*, Antrim (W. & G. Baird) 1981

Barnard, T. C., *Cromwellian Ireland: English Government and Reform in Ireland, 1649-1660*, London (Oxford University Press) 1975

Baxter, Richard, *The Autobiography of Richard Baxter, being the 'Reliquiae Baxterianae' abridged from the folio (1696)*, London (Dent) 1925

Beckett, J. C., *Protestant Dissent in Ireland, 1687-1780*, London 1948

—— *see also* Moody, T. W.

Belfast Presbytery, *A Necessary Representation of the Present Evils and Eminent Dangers to Religion, Laws and Liberties*, Belfast 1649, *see* Milton, *Complete Prose Works*

Bellot, H. Hale, *University College, London, 1826-1926*, London 1929

Best, G. F. A., 'The Religious Difficulties of National Education in England, 1800-70', *Cambridge Historical Journal*, XII, 2 (1956)

Bew, Paul, 'Politics and the Rise of the Skilled Working Man' in J. C. Beckett et al., *Belfast: The Making of the City*, Belfast (Appletree) 1983

—— and Wright, Frank, 'The Agrarian Opposition in Ulster Politics, 1848-87' in Samuel Clark and James S. Donnelly, jr (ed.), *Irish Peasants: Violence and Political Unrest, 1780-1914*, Madison (University of Wisconsin) 1983

Birch, Thomas Ledlie, *The Obligations upon Christians and especially Ministers to be Exemplary in their Lives, particularly at this important period when the prophecies are seemingly to be fulfilled in the fall of Anti-Christ as an introduction to the flowing in of Jew and Gentile to the Christian Church*, Belfast 1794

—— *Physicians Languishing under Disease: An Address to the Seceder or Associate Synod of Ireland*, Belfast 1796

Blair, Robert, *Memoirs*, ed. William Row, Belfast 1844

Blanchard, Jean, *The Church in Contemporary Ireland*, Dublin (Clonmore & Reynolds) 1963

Blanshard, Paul, *The Irish and Catholic Power: An American Interpretation*, London (Verschoyle) 1954

Bodin, Jean, *Six Books of the Commonwealth*, Oxford (Blackwell) n.d.

Bolam, C. G., Goring J., Short, H. L., and Thomas, R., *The English Presbyterians*, London (George Allen & Unwin) 1968

Bonar, Andrew, *see* Rutherford, Samuel

Bondriot, Wilhelm, and Hesse, Theodor (ed.), *Confession de Foy et Discipline Ecclesiastique*, Munich 1938

Bonnard, Auguste, *Thomas Eraste (1524-1583) et la Discipline Ecclesiastique*, Lausanne 1894

Boston, Thomas, *Human Nature in Its Fourfold State, of Primitive Integrity, Entire Depravity, Begun Recovery and Consummate Happiness or Misery*, London (Banner of Truth) 1964

Bowen, Desmond, *Paul Cardinal Cullen and the Shaping of Modern Irish Catholicism*, Dublin (Gill & Macmillan) 1983

—— *Souperism: Myth or Reality?*, Cork (Mercier Press) 1971

Boyd, Andrew, *Holy War in Belfast*, New York (Black Cat Evergreen) 1972

Boyse, Joseph, *Remarks on a Late Discourse of William, Lord Bishop of Derry, concerning the Inventions of Men in the Worship of God*, London 1694

Bradley, Ian, *The Call to Seriousness*, London (Jonathan Cape) 1976

Bramhall, John, Bishop of Derry, *Works*, 5 vols, Oxford 1844

British and Irish Communist Organisation, *The Birth of Ulster Unionism*, Belfast (Athol Books) 1984

—— *The Economics of Partition*, Belfast (B+ICO) 1972

—— *Ulster As It Is*, Belfast (B+ICO) 1973

—— *see also* Brooke, Peter; Clifford, Angela; Clifford, Brendan; Hope, James; Joy, Henry, and Bruce, William; Tone, Theobald Wolfe

Brooke, Peter, 'Controversies in Ulster Presbyterianism' (Ph.D. thesis, University of Cambridge, 1981)

—— 'On the Arrogance of the Ulster Presbyterians', *Church and State*, 14 (summer 1984)

—— 'Religion and Secular Thought, 1800-75' in J. C. Beckett et al., *Belfast: The Making of the City*, Belfast (Appletree) 1983

—— 'The Schoolmaster Is Abroad', *Irish Communist*, 227 (Jan. 1985)

—— 'Sir John Davies and the Origin of Irish Politics', *Irish Communist*, 237 (Nov. 1985)

Brown, A. W. Godfrey, 'Irish Presbyterian Theology in the Early Eighteenth Century' (Ph.D. thesis, Queen's University of Belfast, 1977)

Brown, Philip, *The French Revolution in English History*, London 1965

Browne, Robert, *A Treatise of Reformation without Tarrying for Any* (1582) in Albert Peel and Leland Carlson (ed.), *The Writings of Robert Harrison and Robert Browne*, London (George Allen & Unwin) 1953

Bruce, Michael, *The Rattling of the Dry Bones, or a Sermon Preached in the Night Time at Chapel Yard in the Parish of Carluke, Clydesdale, May 1672*, n.p., n.d. (available in British Library)

—— *Six Dreadful Alarms in Order to the Right Improving of the Gospel*, n.p., n.d. (available in British Library)

[Bruce, William], 'The Progress of Non-Subscription', *Christian Moderator* (1826-7)

——— *Sermons on the Study of the Bible and on the Doctrines of Christianity as Taught by Our Lord Jesus Christ*, London/Belfast 1826

——— *see also* Joy, Henry

Bryce, James, *A Narrative of the Proceedings of the Associate (Antiburgher) Synods in Ireland and Scotland in the Affair of the Royal Bounty*, Belfast 1816

Bulloch, James, *see* Drummond, Andrew L.

Bunyan, John, *Grace Abounding to the Chief of Sinners*, Chicago (Moody Press) 1959

Burleigh, J. H. S., *A Church History of Scotland*, Oxford (Oxford University Press) 1960

Burnet, Gilbert, Bishop of Salisbury, *History of His Own Time*, Oxford 1833

Calderwood, David, *The History of the Kirk of Scotland*, 8 vols, Edinburgh 1842-9

Calvin, John, *Institutes of the Christian Religion*, 2 vols, Philadelphia (Westminster Press) 1977

——— *Institution of the Christian Religion (1536)*, Atlanta (John Knox Press) 1975

——— *Theological Treatises*, transl. J. K. S. Reid, Philadelphia (Westminster Press) 1951

Cameron, J. K. (ed.), *The First Book of Discipline*, Edinburgh (St Andrew's Press) 1972

Cameron, John, *see* Philander, Theophilus

Campaign for Labour Representation, *The Forgotten Conference of the Labour Party in Belfast, 1907*, Belfast (CLR) 1983

Campbell, William, *A Vindication of the Principles and Character of the Presbyterians of Ireland addressed to the Bishop of Cloyne in Answer to his Book entitled 'The Present State of the Church of Ireland'*, Belfast 1787

Carr, Alan, *The Belfast Labour Movement*, Pt 1: *1885-93*, Belfast (Athol Books) 1974

Castlereagh, Robert Stewart, Viscount, *Memoirs and Correspondence*, 4 vols, London 1848-9

Chadwick, Owen, *The Victorian Church*, Pt 1, London (A. & C. Black) 1968

Church of Scotland, *Abridgement of Acts of Assemblies*, Edinburgh 1821

Clifford, Angela, 'The Irish Academy of Letters', *Church and State*, 17 (spring 1985); 19 (autumn 1985)

——— *Poor Law in Ireland, with an Account of the Belfast Outdoor Relief Dispute, 1932, and the Development of the British Welfare State, and Social Welfare in the Republic*, Belfast (Athol Books) 1983

[———], 'Religion and Hospitals', *Church and State*, 14 (summer 1984)

Clifford, Brendan, *Connolly: The Polish Aspect*, Belfast (Athol Books) 1985

[——], 'Davitt on Land Tax', *Irish Communist*, 224 (Oct. 1984)

—— *Parliamentary Sovereignty and Northern Ireland: A Review of the Party System in the British Constitution, with relation to the Anglo-Irish Agreement*, Belfast (Athol Books) 1985

[——], *The Rise of Papal Power*, Belfast (Athol Books/Church and State*) 1974

[——], *Socialism and the Farmer: A View of the Agricultural Economy of the Republic*, Cork (Labour Comment) 1984

—— *The Veto Controversy*, Belfast (Athol Books) 1985

Clive, John, *Scotch Reviewers: The Edinburgh Review, 1802-1815*, London (Faber & Faber) 1957

Coad, Roy, *A History of the Brethren Movement*, Exeter (Paternoster Press) 1976

Coe, William, *The Engineering Industry of the North of Ireland*, Newton Abbot (David & Charles) 1969

Cooke, Henry, see *The Repealer Repulsed* and *The Voluntaries in Belfast*

Cowan, Ian, *The Scottish Covenanters, 1660-88*, London (Gollancz) 1976

Crawford, W. H., *Domestic Industry in Ireland: The Experience of the Linen Industry*, Dublin (Gill & Macmillan) 1972

Croskery, Thomas, and Witherow, Thomas, *Life of the Rev A. P. Goudy, D.D.*, Dublin 1887

Crowther, M. A., *Church Embattled: Religious Controversy in Mid-Victorian England*, Newton Abbot (David & Charles) 1970

Crozier, J. L., *Life of the Rev. Henry Montgomery, LL.D.*, London 1875

Dallat, M., et al., *Aspects of Catholic Education: papers read at a conference organised by the Guild of Catholic Teachers, Diocese of Down and Connor*, Belfast (St Jospeh's College) 1970

Dallimore, Arnold, *The Life of Edward Irving*, Edinburgh (Banner of Truth) 1983

Davies, Sir John, *Works*, 3 vols, ed. Alexander B. Grosart, Fuller Worthies' Library, London 1876

Davis, V. P., *A History of Manchester College*, London (George Allen & Unwin) 1932

[Defoe, Daniel], *The Parallel, or Persecution of Protestants the Shortest Way to Prevent the Growth of Popery in Ireland*, Dublin 1705

[——], *The Shortest Way with the Dissenters, or Proposals for the Establishment of the Church*, London 1702

Delap, Hugh, *An Inquiry Whether, and How Far, Magistracy is of a Divine Appointment, and of the Subjection due thereunto: A Sermon preached . . . before the Omagh and Cappagh Volunteers, published at their request*, Strabane 1779

Denham, James, *see* Killen, W. D.

de Paor, Liam, *Divided Ulster*, Harmondsworth (Penguin) 1971

Dickson, William Steel, *A Narrative of the Confinement and Exile of William Steel Dickson, D.D.*, Dublin 1812

—— *Three Sermons on the Subject of Scripture Politics*, Belfast 1793

Dictionary of National Biography, London 1908-9

Dill, Richard, *Prelatico-Presbyterianism*, Dublin 1856

Donaldson, Gordon, *The Scottish Reformation*, Cambridge (Cambridge University Press) 1960

Douglas, C. E., *see* Frere, W. H.

Dow, F., *Cromwellian Scotland, 1651-1660*, Edinburgh (John Donald) 1979

Drennan, William, *The Drennan Letters*, ed. D. A. Chart, Belfast (HMSO) 1931

—— *Letters of Orellana, an Irish Helot, to the Seven Northern Counties Not Represented in the National Assembly of Delegates held at Dublin in October 1784*, Belfast 1785

Drummond, Andrew L., and Bulloch, James, *The Church in Victorian Scotland, 1843-74*, Edinburgh (St Andrew Press) 1975

—— *The Scottish Church, 1688-1843*, Edinburgh (St Andrew Press) 1973

Duffy, Charles Gavan, *My Life in Two Hemispheres*, 2 vols in 1, Shannon (Irish University Press) 1968

Eastern Presbytery of the Reformed Presbyterian Synod of Ireland, *Causes of Fasting and Thanksgiving*, Belfast 1835

Edwards, Jonathan, *Works*, 2 vols, Edinburgh (Banner of Truth) 1979

Elliott, Marianne, 'The "Despard Conspiracy" Reconsidered', *Past and Present*, 75 (May 1977)

—— *Partners in Revolution: The United Irishmen and France*, New Haven/London (Yale University Press) 1982

Every, George, *The High Church Party, 1688-1718*, London (SPCK) 1956

Falls, Cyril, *The Birth of Ulster*, London (Methuen) 1936

Ferguson, Samuel, *Brief Biographical Sketches of Some Irish Covenanting Ministers who Laboured during the Latter Half of the Eighteenth Century*, Londonderry 1897

First Book of Discipline, *see* Cameron, J. K.

Fisher, Edward, *The Marrow of Modern Divinity*, Swengel (Reiner Publications) 1978

Fisher, Joseph R., and Robb, John H., *Royal Belfast Academical Institution Centenary Volume*, Belfast 1913

Fitzpatrick, William John, *Memoirs of Richard Whately, Archbishop of Dublin*, 2 vols, London 1864

Free Church of Scotland, *The Subordinate Standards and other authoritative documents of the Free Church of Scotland*, Edinburgh 1880

Free Presbyterian Church of Scotland, *History of the Free Presbyterian Church of Scotland, 1893-1970*, Inverness (Free Presbyterian Church) n.d.

Frere, W. H., and Douglas, C. E. (ed.), *Puritan Manifestoes*, London (SPCK) 1954

Froude, James Anthony, *The English in Ireland in the Eighteenth Century*, 3 vols, London/Bombay (Longman, Green & Co.) 1906

—— *History of England from the Fall of Wolsey to the Defeat of the Spanish Armada*, 12 vols, London 1870

Fulton, Austin, *J. Ernest Davey*, Belfast (Presbyterian Church in Ireland) 1970

General Assembly, *Minutes of the General Assembly of the Presbyterian Church in Ireland, 1840-70*, 3 vols, Belfast

—— *see also* Synod of Ulster

Geyl, Pieter, *The Netherlands in the Seventeenth Century*, 2 vols London (Ernest Benn) 1961

—— *The Revolt of the Netherlands, 1555-1609*, London (Ernest Benn) 1966

Gibbon, Peter, *The Origins of Ulster Unionism: The Formation of Popular Protestant Politics and Ideology in Nineteenth-Century Ireland*, Manchester (Manchester University Press) 1975

Gibson, William, *The Year of Grace*, Belfast 1860

Ginter, Donald E., 'The Loyalist Association Movement of 1792-3 and British Public Opinion', *Historical Journal*, IX, 2 (1966)

Gleizes, Albert, *La Peinture et ses Lois ce qui devait partir du Cubisme* Paris 1924

Gordon, Alexander, *Historic Memorials of the First Presbyterian Church*, Belfast 1887

Goring, J., *see* Bolam, C. G.

Goudy, Alexander, *see* Killen, W. D.

Grattan, Henry, *Selected Speeches*, Dublin 1845

Gribbon, H. D., *A History of Water Power in Ulster*, Newton Abbot (David & Charles) 1969

Grier, W. J., *The Origin and Witness of the Irish Evangelical Church* Belfast (Evangelical Book Shop) 1945

Guttridge, G. H., *English Whiggism and the American Revolution* Berkeley/Los Angeles 1963

Gwynn, Denis, *O'Connell, Davis and the Colleges Bill*, Cork (Cork University Press) 1948

—— *The Second Spring, 1818-1852*, London (Burns Oates) 1942

—— *Young Ireland and 1848*, Cork (Cork University Press) 1949

Halévy, Élie, *History of the English People, 1830-41*, London 1927

Haliday, Samuel, *Reasons against the Imposition of Subscription* Belfast 1724

Hanna, William, *Memoirs of the Life and Writings of Thomas Chalmers D.D., LL.D*, Edinburgh/London 1851

Hesse, Theodor, *see* Bondriot, Wilhelm

Hibbert, Christopher, *The French Revolution*, Harmondsworth (Penguin) 1980

Hill, George, *The MacDonnells of Antrim*, facsimile of 1873 edition Belfast (Glens of Antrim Historical Society) 1976

An Historical Account of the Late Election of the Knights of the Shire for the Co. of Down, n.p., 1784

Hoadly, Benjamin, *The Nature of the Kingdom or Church of Christ A Sermon preached before the King at the Royal Chapel at St*

James's on Sunday, March 31, 1717, London 1717

—— *A Preservative against the Principles and Practice of the Non-jurors both in Church and State*, Dublin 1716

Hobbes, Thomas, *Leviathan*, Harmondsworth (Penguin) 1968

Hodge, Charles, *The Constitutional History of the Presbyterian Church in the United States of America*, Philadelphia 1851

Holmes, R. F. G., *Henry Cooke*, Belfast/Ottowa (Christian Journals) 1981

—— *Our Irish Presbyterian Heritage*, [Belfast] (Presbyterian Church in Ireland) 1985

Hooker, Richard, *Of the Laws of Ecclesiastical Polity*, 2 vols, London (Everyman) 1969

Hope, James, *The Memoirs of Jemmy Hope: An Autobiography of a Working-Class United Irishman*, Belfast (Athol Books) 1973

Hotman, François, *Francogallia*, Cambridge (Cambridge University Press) 1972

Houston, Thomas Holmes, *The Covenanter's Narrative and Plea, Exhibiting the Error, Schism, Radicalism and Slander of Dr Paul and other Separatists from the Reformed Presbyterian Church*, Belfast 1841

Hutchinson, M., *The Reformed Presbyterian Church in Scotland*, Edinburgh/Glasgow 1893

Hutton, Hugh, *The Duty and Benefits of Co-operation among the Friends of Scriptural Christianity*, London 1827

Hyde, H. Montgomery, *The Rise of Castlereagh*, London (Macmillan) 1933

James VI and I, *Basilicon Doron*, 2 vols, Edinburgh/London (Scottish Text Society) 1944-50

James, William, *Homesius Enervatus: A Letter addressed to Mr John Holmes, Minister at Glendermond*, Londonderry 1772

Jamieson, John L., *History of the Royal Belfast Academical Institution, 1810-1960*, Belfast 1959

—— 'The Influence of the Rev. Henry Cooke on the Political Life of Ulster' (M.A. thesis, Queen's University of Belfast, 1950)

Joy, Henry, *Historical Collections relative to the Town of Belfast from the Earliest Period to the Union with Great Britain*, Belfast 1817

—— and Bruce, William, *Belfast Politics*, Belfast (Athol Books) 1974

Kearney, Richard (ed.), *The Irish Mind: Exploring Intellectual Traditions*, Dublin (Wolfhound) 1985

Kennedy, Brian A., 'Sharman Crawford, 1780-1881' (D. Litt. thesis, Queen's University of Belfast, 1953)

Kennedy, Gilbert, *A Defence of the Principles and Conduct of the Reverend General Synod of Ulster, being an Answer to a Pamphlet published by the Rev. Mr Samuel Haliday, containing his Reasons against the Imposition of Subscription unto the Westminster Confession, or any such Humane Tests of Orthodoxy*, Belfast 1724

Kerr, Donal, *Peel, Priests and Politics*, Oxford (Clarendon Press) 1984

Killen, W. D., *History of the Presbyterian Church in Ireland*, *see* Reid, James Seaton

——— *Memoir of John Edgar, D.D., LL.D.*, Belfast/London/Edinburgh 1867

——— *Reminiscences of a Long Life*, London (Hodder & Stoughton) 1901

——— McClure, William, Denham, James, and Goudy, Alexander, *The Plea of Presbytery on behalf of the Ordination, Government, Discipline and Worship of the Christian Church, as opposed to the Unscriptural Character and Claims of Prelacy*, Belfast 1841

King, William, *A Discourse concerning the Inventions of Men in the Worship of God*, Northants 1840

[———], *The State of the Protestants of Ireland under the late King James's Government*, London 1692

Kirk, James, 'The Polities of the Best Reformed Kirks', *Scottish Historical Review*, 29 (1980)

——— (ed.), *The Second Book of Discipline*, Edinburgh (St Andrew Press) 1980

Kirkpatrick, James, *An Historical Essay upon the Loyalty of Presbyterians in Great Britain and Ireland from the Reformation to this Present Year, 1713*, [Belfast] 1713

Knox, John, *The History of the Reformation of Religion in Scotland*, London 1905

Knox, R. Buick, *James Ussher, Archbishop of Armagh*, Cardiff University of Wales Press) 1967

Larkin, Emmet, 'The Devotional Revolution in Ireland, 1850-75', *American Historical Review*, LXXVII (1972)

Law, William, *The Bishop of Bangor's Late Sermon and his Letter to Dr Snape in Defence of it Answered*, Dublin 1717

Lindsay, Thomas M., *A History of the Reformation*, 2 vols, Edinburgh 1906

Locke, John, *Letters on Toleration*, Bombay 1867

Lodge, Martin E., 'The Crisis of the Churches in the Middle Colonies, 1720-50', *Pennsylvania Magazine*, 95 (1971)

Loughridge, Adam, *The Covenanters in Ireland*, Belfast (Cameron Press) 1984

Luther, Martin, *Works*, 55 vols, Philadelphia (Fortress Press) 1958-67

Lyall, Francis, *Of Presbyters and Kings: Church and State in the Law of Scotland*, Aberdeen (Aberdeen University Press) 1980

Macaulay, Thomas Babington, *History of England*, 2 vols, London 1909

[McBride, John], *A Sample of Jet-Black Prelatic Calumny*, Glasgow 1713

McCarthy, M. J. F., *Priests and People in Ireland*, Dublin/London 1902

McClure, William, *see* Killen, W. D.

McConnell, James and S. G., and Stewart, David, *Fasti of the Irish Presbyterian Church, 1613-1840*, Belfast n.d.

McCosh, James, *The Scottish Philosophy from Hutcheson to Hamilton*, Edinburgh 1874

——— *The Ulster Revival and Its Physiological Accidents: a paper read*

before the Evangelical Alliance, Sept 22, 1859, Belfast 1859
—— *see also* Sloane, W. M.
McCrie, C. G., *The Church of Scotland, Her Divisions and Her Reunions*, Edinburgh 1901
McCrie, Thomas, *The Life of Andrew Melville*, Edinburgh 1926
—— *The Life of John Knox*, Glasgow (Free Presbyterian Publications) 1976
McDowell, R. B., *Irish Public Opinion, 1750-1800*, London (Faber & Faber) 1944
McKerrow, John, *History of the Secession Church*, Edinburgh 1848
McKinney, James, 'A View of the Rights of God and Man', reprinted in *The Covenanter*, I (1831)
—— *see also* Reformed Presbytery of Ireland
[MacKnight, James], *The Dens Theology Humbug: A Letter to those Ministers and Members of the Church of Scotland who have lent themselves to the Dens Theology Humbug, by a member of the General Synod of Ulster*, Edinburgh 1836
[——], *Persecution Sanctioned by the Westminster Confession: A Letter to the Synod of Ulster showing the Doctrines of Intolerance to which the late Vote of Unqualified Subscription has committed them*, Belfast 1836
Macleod, John, *Scottish Theology*, Edinburgh (Banner of Truth) 1974
McMillan, William, 'The Subscription Controversy in Irish Presbyterianism . . . with reference to its political implications in the late eighteenth century' (M.A. thesis, University of Manchester, 1958)
McMinn, J. R. B., 'The Rev. James Brown Armour and Liberal Politics in North Antrim, 1869-1914' (Ph.D. thesis, Queen's University of Belfast, 1979)
Makey, Walter, *The Church of the Covenant, 1637-1651*, Edinburgh (John Donald) 1979
Manning, Bernard Lord, *The Protestant Dissenting Deputies*, Cambridge (Cambridge University Press) 1952
Mastertown, Charles, *Christian Liberty Founded in Gospel Truth, or The Great Argument of Christian Liberty Explained in Its Necessary Connection with Sound Principles in Opposition to Some Dangerous Notions Relating to Both, in a Sermon upon John viii. 32*, Edinburgh 1727
Mather, Cotton, *The Great Works of Christ in America*, Edinburgh (Banner of Truth) 1979
Mathieson, William Law, *Politics and Religion: A Study in Scottish History from the Reformation to the Revolution*, 2 vols, Glasgow 1902
Miall, Charles S., *see* Skeats, Herbert S.
Miller, David, 'Presbyterianism and "Modernisation" in Ulster', *Past and Present*, 80 (Aug. 1978)
—— *Queen's Rebels: Ulster Loyalism in Historical Perspective*, Dublin/New York (Gill & Macmillan/Barnes & Noble) 1978
Millin, S. Shannon, *History of the Second Congregation*, Belfast 1900

Milton, John, *Complete Prose Works*, 8 vols, New Haven/London (Yale University Press) 1953-82
—— *Prose Writings*, London (Dent) 1958
Mitchel, John, *Jail Journal, with an introductory narrative of trans actions in Ireland*, London (Sphere) 1983
Mitchell, Austin, 'The Association Movement of 1792-3', *Historical Journal*, IV, 1 (1961)
Moody, T. W., and Beckett, J. C., *Queen's, Belfast, 1845-1949*, London (Faber & Faber) 1959
Moore, Tom, *A History of the First Presbyterian Church, Belfast 1644-1983*, Belfast (First Presbyterian Church) 1983
Morgan, Edmund, *Visible Saints: The History of a Puritan Idea*, New York (New York University Press) 1963
Morgan, James, *Recollections of My Life and Times*, Belfast 1874
Morley, John, *Walpole*, London 1903
Murry, John Middleton, *Jonathan Swift: A Critical Biography*, London (Cape) 1954
New, Chester W., *The Life of Henry Brougham to 1830*, Oxford (Oxford University Press) 1961
Newman, John Henry, *The Arians of the Fourth Century*, London (Longman, Green & Co.) 1908
—— *An Essay on the Development of Christian Doctrine*, Harmondsworth (Penguin) 1974
—— *Historical Sketches*, 3 vols, London (Longman, Green & Co.) 1891
—— *On the Scope and Nature of University Education*, London (Everyman) 1965
Norman, E. R., *Anti-Catholicism in Victorian England*, London (George Allen & Unwin) 1968
—— *The Catholic Church and Ireland in the Age of Rebellion, 1859-1873*, London (Longman, Green & Co.) 1965
Nuttall, Geoffrey, *Richard Baxter*, London (Nelson) 1965
O'Cahan, T. S., *Owen Roe O'Neill*, London (T. Joseph Keane) 1968
O'Connor, Charles, *Columbanus ad Hibernos No. 2, or, A Second Letter with Part 1 of an Historical Address on the Calamities occasioned by Foreign Influence, in the Nomination of Bishops to Irish Sees*, London 1810
Ó Cuív, Brian, *see* Wall, Maureen
O'Faolain, Seán, *The Great O'Neill*, Cork (Mercier Press) 1970
Owen, John, *Works*, 16 vols, Edinburgh (Banner of Truth) 1978
Paine, Thomas, *Common Sense*, Harmondsworth (Penguin) 1982
—— *Rights of Man*, Harmondsworth (Penguin) 1971
Parker, T. H. L., *John Calvin*, Berkhamsted (Lion Publishing) 1977
Parliamentary Papers, *Fourth Report of the Commissioners of the Irish Education Inquiry, 1826-7*, 1826-7, XIII
—— *Minutes of Evidence on the State of Ireland, brought from the Lords*, 1825, IX
—— *Minutes of Evidence taken before the Select Committee of the*

House of Lords Appointed to Inquire into the Progress and Oper-
ation of the New Plan of Education in Ireland, 1837, VIII
—— *Third Report from the Select Committee (Minutes of Evidence)*
on the State of Ireland, 1825, VIII
Patterson, Henry, *Class Conflict and Sectarianism: The Protestant*
Working Class and the Belfast Labour Movement, 1868-1920, Belfast
(Blackstaff) 1980
Paul, John, *Works*, ed. D. Bates, Belfast 1855
Pearson, A. F. Scott, *Church and State: Political Aspects of Sixteenth-*
Century Puritanism, Cambridge (Cambridge University Press) 1928
—— *Thomas Cartwright and Elizabethan Puritanism, 1535-1603*,
Cambridge (Cambridge University Press) 1925
Pelham MSS, Public Record Office of Northern Ireland, T755/2
Perceval-Maxwell, Michael, *The Scottish Migration to Ulster in the*
Reign of James I, London (Routledge & Kegan Paul) 1973
Philander, Theophilus [John Cameron], *The Catholic Christian, or*
The True Religion Sought and Found, Belfast 1769
Pole, J. R., *Foundations of American Independence, 1763-1815*,
London/Glasgow (Fontana) 1973
Porter, J. L., *The Life and Times of Henry Cooke, D.D., LL.D.*, Belfast
1875
Presbyterian Church in Ireland MSS, Public Record Office of Northern
Ireland, MIC IP
Presbyterian Synod of Ireland, *Report of the Missions of the Presby-*
terian Synod of Ireland, distinguished by the name Seceders, to the
South and West of that Kingdom, as it appeared in the Christian
Recorder for November 1821, Glasgow 1821
Presbytery of Antrim, *A Narrative of the Proceedings of Seven General*
Synods [1720-26], Belfast 1727
Purves, Jock, *Fair Sunshine: Character Studies of the Scottish Coven-*
anters, Edinburgh (Banner of Truth) 1968
Rainy, Robert, *The Ancient Catholic Church, from the Accession of*
Trojan to the Fourth General Council (A.D. 98-451), Edinburgh 1902
Reformed Presbyterian Synod, *see* Eastern Presbytery
Reformed Presbytery, *Act, Declaration and Testimony for the Whole*
of our Covenanted Reformation, Belfast 1832
Reformed Presbytery of Ireland, *Causes of Fasting, and Thanksgiving*,
n.p. 1792 [A manuscript note in Chancellor Collection, R. P.
Theological Hall, attributes it to James McKinney.]
Reid, James Seaton, and Killen, W. D., *History of the Presbyterian*
Church in Ireland, 3 vols, Belfast 1867 [Vol. III, p. 237 to end of
book written by W. D. Killen.]
The Repealer Repulsed: A Correct Narrative of the Rise and Progress
of the Repeal Invasion of Ulster, Dr Cooke's Challenge and Mr
O'Connell's Declimature, Tactics and Flight, Belfast 1841
Report of the Committee of the Lower House of Convocation appoint-
ed to draw up a Representation to be laid before the Archbishop and
Bishops of the Province of Canterbury concerning Several Dangerous

Propositions and Doctrines contained in the Bishop of Bangor's Preservative and his Sermon Preached March 31st 1717, Dublin 1717

Ritchie, John, *Reply to Rev. Dr Henry Cooke, including, at his request, a Critique of his Report of the Belfast Discussion, an Offer to Discuss with him, in Edinburgh or elsewhere, the Question of Questions, a Letter on the West-Kirk Meeting and a Letter on Dr Cooke's Cowardly Flight*, Edinburgh 1837

Robb, John H., *see* Fisher, Joseph R.

Rodgers, Robert James: 'James Carlile, 1784-1854' (Ph.D. thesis, Queen's University of Belfast, 1973)

—— 'Presbyterian Missionary Activity among Irish Roman Catholics in the Nineteenth Century' (M.A. thesis, Queen's University of Belfast, 1969)

Rousseau, Jean-Jacques, *The Social Contract and Discourses*, transl. G. D. H. Cole, London (Dent) 1955

Row, William, *see* Blair, Robert

Royal Belfast Academical Institution MSS, Public Record Office of Northern Ireland, SCH 524

Rutherford, Samuel, *Letters, with a sketch of his life and biographical notices of his correspondents by Andrew A. Bonar*, Edinburgh (Banner of Truth) 1984

Sandeen, Ernest R., *The Roots of Fundamentalism: British and American Millenarianism, 1800-1930*, Chicago 1970

Scott, Sir Walter, *Old Mortality*, Harmondsworth (Penguin) 1982

Second Book of Discipline, *see* Kirk, James

Shaw, William A., *A History of the English Church during the Civil Wars and under the Commonwealth, 1640-1660*, London (Longman, Green & Co.) 1900

Sherrard, John, *A Few Observations on the Nature and Tendency of the Changes Lately Proposed to be made in the Constitution of the Protestant Dissenting Church*, Belfast 1803

Short, H. L., *see* Bolam, C. G.

Simms, J. G., *Jacobite Ireland, 1685-91*, London (Routledge & Kegan Paul) 1969

Skeats, Herbert S., and Miall, Charles S., *History of the Free Churches of England, 1688-1891*, London [1891?]

Slater, G. J., 'Belfast Politics, 1798-1868' (D. Phil. thesis, New University of Ulster, 1982)

Sloane, W. M. (ed.), *The Life of James McCosh, a record chiefly autobiographical*, Edinburgh 1896

Smith, David Baird, 'François Hotman', *Scottish Historical Record*, XIII, 52 (July 1916)

Smyth, D. H., 'The Volunteer Movement in Ulster, 1745-85' (Ph.D. thesis, Queen's University of Belfast, 1974)

Southey, Robert, *The Life of John Wesley*, London 1904

Spottiswoode, John, *The History of the Church of Scotland*, 3 vols, Edinburgh (Spottiswoode Society) 1851-65

Stanley, Arthur P., *Lectures on the History of the Eastern Church*, London 1861

Steele, E. D., *Irish Land and British Politics: Tenant Right and National- ity, 1865-1870*, Cambridge (Cambridge University Press) 1974

Stevens, Abel, *The History of the Religious Movement of the Eighteenth Century called Methodism*, 3 vols, London (Wesleyan Conference) 1878

Stevenson, David, *Scottish Covenanters and Irish Confederates*, Belfast (Ulster Historical Foundation) 1981

Stewart, A. T. Q., *The Narrow Ground: Aspects of Ulster, 1609-1969*, London (Faber & Faber) 1977

—— 'The Transformation of Presbyterian Radicalism in the North of Ireland, 1792-1825' (M.A. thesis, Queen's University of Belfast, 1956)

Stewart, David, *The Seceders in Ireland, with Annals of their Con- gregations*, Belfast (Presbyterian Historical Society) 1950

—— *see also* McConnell, James and S. G.

Stewart MSS, Public Record Office of Northern Ireland, D1759

Story, Robert Herbert (ed.), *The Church of Scotland, Past and Present*, 5 vols, London n.d.

Struthers, Gavin, *History of the Rise of the Relief Church*, Edinburgh/ London 1848

Swift, Jonathan, *A Letter from a Member of the House of Commons in Ireland to a Member of the House of Commons in England con- cerning the Sacramental Test* (1709) in *Prose Works*, II, Oxford (Blackwell) 1939

Sykes, Norman, *The Church of England and Non-Episcopalian Churches in the Sixteenth and Seventeenth Centuries*, London (SPCK) 1949

Synod of Ulster, *Records of the General Synod of Ulster, 1691-1820*, 3 vols, Belfast 1890-98

—— *Records of the General Synod of Ulster*, published annually in pamphlet form, Belfast 1820-40

—— *see also* General Assembly

Tennent MSS, Public Record Office of Northern Ireland, D1748

Thomas, R., *see* Bolam, C. G.

Thompson, David, 'The Liberation Society, 1844-68' in Hollis, Patricia (ed.), *Pressure from Without in Early Victorian England*, London (Edward Arnold) 1974

Thompson, E. P., *The Making of the English Working Class*, Harmonds- worth (Penguin) 1978

Tierney, Brian, *Foundations of the Conciliar Theory*, Cambridge (Cambridge University Press) 1955

[Tisdall, William], *The Conduct of the Dissenters of Ireland with respect both to Church and State*, Dublin 1712

[——], *A Sample of True-Blue Presbyterian Loyalty in All Changes and Turns of Government*, Dublin 1709

Tone, Theobald Wolfe, *An Argument on Behalf of the Catholics of Ireland*, Belfast (Athol Books) 1983

Toon, Peter, *The Emergence of Hyper-Calvinism in English Nonconfor- mity, 1689-1765*, (Olive Tree) 1967

—— *Evangelical Theology, 1833-1856: A Response to Tractarianism*, London (Marshall, Morgan & Scott) 1979

—— *God's Statesman: The Life and Work of John Owen*, Exeter (Paternoster Press) 1971

Tracy, Joseph, *The Great Awakening: A History of the Revival of Religion in the Time of Edwards and Whitefield*, Edinburgh (Banner of Truth) 1976

Travers, Walter, *A Full and Plain Declaration of Ecclesiastical Discipline out of the Word of God*, n.p. [1704?]

Trevelyan, George Macaulay, *The Life of John Bright*, London 1913

Trevor-Roper, H. R., *Archbishop Laud, 1573-1645*, London (Macmillan) 1962

Tweedie, W. K. (ed.), *Select Biographies*, 2 vols, Edinburgh (Wodrow Society) 1845

The Voluntaries in Belfast: Report of the Discussion on Civil Establishments of Religion held in Belfast on the evenings of the 16th and 17th March 1836, Belfast 1837

Walker, Brian, 'The Land Question and Elections in Ulster, 1868-86' in Samuel Clark and James S. Donnelly, jr (ed.), *Irish Peasants: Violence and Political Unrest, 1780-1914*, Madison (University of Wisconsin) 1983

Walker, Graham, *The Politics of Frustration: Harry Midgley and the Failure of Labour in Northern Ireland*, Manchester (Manchester University Press) 1985

Wall, Maureen, 'The Decline of the Irish Language' in Brian Ó Cuív (ed.), *A View of the Irish Language*, Dublin 1969

Walsh, J. D., 'Élie Halévy and the Birth of Methodism', *Transactions of the Royal Historical Society*, 5th series, XXV (1975)

Wardlaw, Ralph, *National Church Establishments Examined: a course of lectures delivered in London during April and May 1839*, London 1839

Whelan, Irene, 'New Lights and Old Enemies: The Second Reformation and the Catholics of Ireland, 1800-1835' (M.A. thesis, University of Wisconsin, 1983)

Whitefield, George, *Journals*, Edinburgh (Banner of Truth) 1978

Willman, Robert, 'The Origins of "Whig" and "Tory" in English Political Language', *Historical Journal*, XVII, 2 (1974)

Witherow, Thomas, *Historical and Literary Memorials of Presbyterianism in Ireland*, 2 vols, London/Belfast 1879-80

—— *see also* Croskery, Thomas

Wright, Frank, *see* Bew, Paul

Index

I am most grateful to Esther Hewitt of the Public Record Office of Northern Ireland for preparing this Index.